HONG

OF

PLATE

*A Culinary Journey
with recipes from some of
the world's best restaurants*

Frances Bartlett and Ivan Lai

Roundhouse Publications (Asia) Ltd

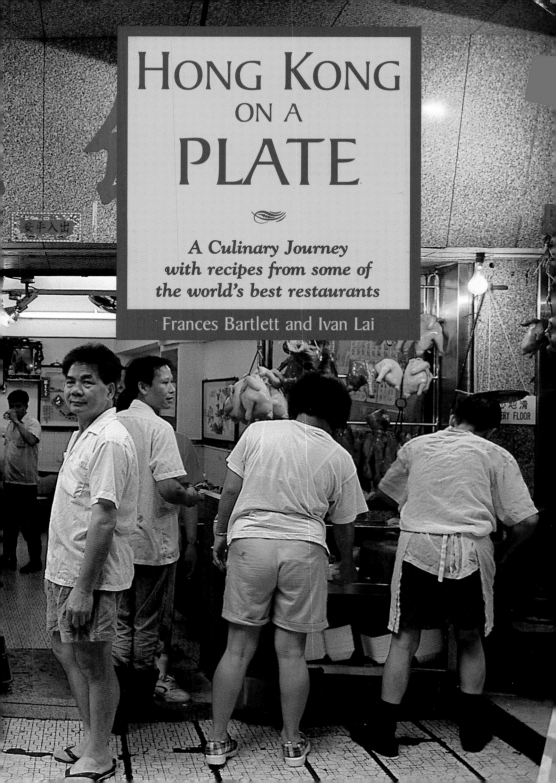

HONG KONG
ON A
PLATE

A Culinary Journey
with recipes from some of
the world's best restaurants

Frances Bartlett and Ivan Lai

Published in Hong Kong by:
Roundhouse Publications (Asia) Ltd
409 Yu Yuet Lai Building
43-55 Wyndham Street
Central, Hong Kong

© Copyright 1997 Roundhouse Publications (Asia) Ltd
ISBN: 962-7992-06-2

Editors	Robyn Flemming
	Debra Maynard
Recipe Editor	Debra Maynard
Layout	Polly Yu Production Ltd
Cover	Harris Asia
Photography	Tim Hall
Glossary	Cindy Chiu
Index	Don Brech

Colour separation by Output Square Ltd
Printed and bound in Hong Kong by Arting Press Ltd

Also available in the series: *Macau on Plate* (ISBN962-7992-01-1) and *Vietnam on a Plate* (ISBN 962-7992-02-X).

Visual materials courtesy of:
Conrad International Hong Kong *Pages ix, 41, 51, 55*
Dairy Farm Company Ltd *Page 18*
Hong Kong Museum of Art *Pages 4, 12 & 13*
Hong Kong Museum of History *Pages 133, 185*
Hong Kong and Shanghai Banking Corporation Limited *Pages 3, 8, 11, 53, 112, 130*
Lincoln Potter *Pages 170, 205*
Public Records Office *Pages 15, 160*
The Regal Hongkong hotel *Page 68*
The Regent Hong Kong *Page 72*
The Peninsula, Hong Kong *Page 197*
Wattis Fine Art *Page x*

*Pages ii–iii: A restaurant specialising in roast meats and rice; **pages vi–vii**: 'Hong Kong Still Life IV' by Richard Winkworth, courtesy of the owners, Mr and Mrs Christopher Lawrence.*

Acknowledgements

Throughout the lengthy process of researching and writing this book, the truth of its theme—that by exploring the cuisine of a place one reaches the heart of its people—was brought home to us time and again. Our thanks to the many chefs and restaurateurs who welcomed us into their kitchens and answered our questions with such overwhelming patience and good humour. We are indebted to Willy Mark, Stephen Wong and Johnny Yip for sharing their culinary views and passions. Thanks also to countless friends, strangers and acquaintances for sharing their secrets to dining well, and to Debra and David for neverending support. Last, but not least, our thanks to Debra Maynard for asking.

Frances Bartlett and Ivan Lai

The publishers would like to thank the Grand Hyatt Hong Kong, the Furama hotel, the Peninsula, Hong Kong, Amy Yeung, John Tsang, Helen Chung, Richard Winkworth and Lucy Simmonds for their contributions to and assistance in the production of this book. Special thanks to Cheng Sea-Ling, Mina Leung and all the restaurants and chefs who gave their recipes and time, and Tony Weiss and friends and colleagues who helped to make the recipes home-friendly.

Contents

Preface

It is revealing that so many people, upon learning that the third book in this series would focus on Hong Kong, said with varying degrees of astonishment, 'But Hong Kong has no cuisine of its own.' Despite its reputation as a Mecca for gourmands, and an astonishing proliferation of restaurants, Hong Kong, indeed, can claim no indigenous cuisine. Therein lay the challenges: to bring to light the distinctive nuances of the peculiarly Hong Kong flavour that has been nurtured in this roiling culinary stew, to assess their impact on an incredibly multi-faceted dining scene and to explore what they could tell us about the nature of this place, its people and, of course, its food.

We had first to wrestle with a culinary environment of tremendous depth and diversity, where Cantonese, Peking, Shanghainese, Sichuan and Chiu Chow cuisines flourish alongside the rather lesser-known ones of Yunnan, Yangzhou, Hangzhou and Shunde. Another significantly broad strata consists of other Asian cuisines: Malaysian, Thai, Japanese, Vietnamese, Korean, Nepalese and Indonesian, to name but several. Then there are the Western restaurants, which range from stolid remnants of Empire to French bistros to California-style open-kitchens. A comprehensive study of every culinary sector was deemed impossible and, more importantly, inappropriate. Instead, we chose to focus on those cuisines and aspects of eating which are most representative of Hong Kong: within the context of the population and its history, these distilled naturally to Chinese and Western.

The research process took two forms: academic and personal. Considering the breadth of Chinese culinary tradition, and the length of its history, there are surprisingly few in-depth explorations of it — in English, that is. Those that have achieved 'classic' status provided a solid understanding of the role of food in Chinese society; a variety of cookbooks communicated essential information about the development of crops and cooking methods (see bibliography). Exploring how the role of food was manifested in Hong Kong society required the personal approach — the lack of printed works on this topic may be redressed within the

next few years, but there is currently little written material available. Insights came from a wide range of people: those who work in the food industry, of course, but also many who simply love to eat (a description which accurately sums up the majority of the Hong Kong populace). Chefs, food critics, restaurant managers, journalists, graphic designers, students and secretaries all contributed invaluable nuggets of information.

From these formal writings and innumerable interviews and discussions it was possible to glean a picture of how Hong Kong people have, in a relatively short history, developed subtle and, for the most part, shared attitudes and approaches to food which are uniquely theirs. In view of Hong Kong's return to Chinese sovereignty, the search for a separate Hong Kong identity is certain to gain momentum and will, no doubt, be reflected in culinary attitudes.

Within a diverse culinary environment are subtle shadings unique to Hong Kong

1

A Collision
Of East And West

'Hong-Kong presents perhaps one of the oddest jumbles in the whole world. It is neither fish, flesh, fowl, nor good red-herring. The Government and principal people are English—the population are Chinese—the police are Indians—the language is bastard English mixed with Cantonese—the currency is the Mexican dollar, and the elements no more amalgamate than the oil and vinegar in a salad.' Across the distance of almost a century, British diplomat Lord Redesdale's shudder of dismay is still palpable. Most of the specifics of his description have changed—pidgin English is only a feature of old films and misinformed mini-series, the police force is predominantly Chinese, the Hong Kong dollar is accepted worldwide—and considerable time has passed since the 'principal people' were solely of English nationality. The details have changed, but the critical diplomat nevertheless nailed Hong Kong's essential nature on the head and his description has a certain validity even today. Less a melting pot in which judiciously selected bits of European and Oriental culture tastefully mingle, the character of this abrasively seductive city has been shaped by geography, politics and the utter incomprehension with which East and West viewed each other.

'Chow-Chow (Chinese Supper) at Hong Kong'; London Illustrated Daily News, *July 1857*

This progeny of two empires—one insular, the other rapacious, both arrogant in the extreme—was formed in a clash of arms and cultures. The pitched battles between Britain and China were fierce but brief; the cultural barriers never really came down. As if the duality which lent the place such dramatic range, and which made it such a clutter if one leans towards Lord Redesdale's view, wasn't sufficiently compelling, the provisions of Britain's annexation of the New Territories in 1898 gave Hong Kong a unique date with destiny. The handing back of a capitalist territory to a socialist government has no historical precedent and, not surprisingly, has guaranteed intense interest in this city-state of just 420 square miles and its 6.3 million inhabitants.

ADVENTURERS, TRADERS and opportunists—Hong Kong attracted them all, and in droves. 'A great influx of natives—all the ruffians from Canton [Guangzhou]—have erected huts and shanties, where are drinking booths and gambling booths and every kind of debauchery,' wrote naval surgeon Dr Edward Cree of his April 1841 visit to the newest British possession. In an effective counterpoint to the good doctor's disapproval, the behaviour of Cree's countrymen incurred the wrath of American Osmond Tiffany, who wrote just eight years later: 'Scapegoats and scoundrels from the purlieus of London, creatures that only missed Botany Bay by good fortune, were to be found in the town of Victoria, lording it over natives, many of whom were more respectable and respected than they had ever been or ever could be.'

Mutual suspicion and distrust characterised the early relationship between English and Chinese, a not surprising consequence of invasion and occupation. But there was more to it than that. As Jan Morris points out in *Hong Kong: Epilogue to an Empire*, Hong Kong 'was not like other colonies: the presence of that far larger Chinese community, itself a community of settlers, with its smells and its noises, its disregard for privacy and its unsettling air of indifference, made the infant Hong Kong feel less than utterly British.' That the Chinese had been brought up secure in the belief that they were superior in every possible way to any foreigner was a further affront.

The colonials retaliated in the way of colonials everywhere, making every effort to impose on their new colony a British lifestyle, however unsuitable. 'I am going this afternoon to see the thoughtless part of the garrison play cricket. I call them thoughtless because I conceive it to be perfect madness on the part of any man to play cricket under a vertical sun.' Lt Orlando Bridgeman's letters

from China and Hong Kong during 1842–43, published in the *Journal of the Royal Asiatic Society*, communicate the lethargy of body and mind which afflicted some expatriates. 'I get up at 6am and walk for two hours before breakfast,' wrote the gloomy subaltern. 'I remain in my room all day during the heat of the sun and walk again in the evening and go to bed early. I live on fish, fruit and curry and drink but little wine.'

The eminently more cheerful Dr Cree had a much jollier time of his visits to Hong Kong. A keen, good-natured observer, his journal is filled with gems of word and sketch; the results of his mining of a crusty social hierarchy that had formed with astonishing swiftness. Visiting Hong Kong again in 1845, he not only watched, but involved himself in some of the local tangles. 'I walked into the room with the Belle of Hong Kong on the day she had rejected a gallant officer of the 4th. ... There was a large party and some good music, champagne iced,

Hong Kong Harbour and Victoria Peak, by an unknown artist of the Chinese School, c 1862

Transplanted traditions soon took hold in early Hong Kong: the annual revelry of the St Andrew's Ball was captured by an artist for The Graphic, *in 1887*

and a capital supper, dancing and green-tea punch to finish.'

Also on Cree's social calendar was a regatta organised by the Navy. 'All the beauty and fashion of Hong Kong on board the *Agincourt*: about forty ladies and four times as many men. ... After the racing the prizes, consisting of purses of dollars, silver cups, &c., which were distributed by the ladies on the poop of the *Agincourt*. At 6 dinner, but only half, about 140, could sit down at one time, although the table extended the whole length of the main deck.' When not occupied with his medical duties, or writing and sketching in his journal (published as *Naval Surgeon—The Voyages of Dr Edward H. Cree, Royal Navy, 1837–1856*), Cree took part in lively picnics, joined expeditions to Green Island 'to practise shot and shell', danced at balls ('so much dissipation with the thermometer at 80° rather takes it out of one'), caroused at the mess ('champagne and devilled bones for supper') and delighted in the courting contortions in a place where single women were few and far between ('Ladies are so scarce and doctors so plentiful, that each lady has her own doctor exclusively').

SMALL SETTLEMENTS had dotted the archipelago many centuries before the chief superintendent of trade, Captain Charles Elliot R.N., commanded the Royal Navy to fire on Chinese war-junks and set in motion the events leading to Britain's cession of Hong Kong Island in 1841. Excavation of early habitation sites on Lantau and Lamma islands has uncovered Stone Age pottery and Bronze Age fish-hooks, adzes and pottery vessels. These, coupled with the absence of permanent structures, paint a picture of a nomadic, seafaring people who left only remnants of their existence. Chinese records refer to the establishment of a military garrison during the Tang dynasty (AD 618–906), in what is now Tuen Mun in the New Territories, charged with protecting the entrance to the Pearl River. A government gazette from the Song dynasty (AD 960–1279) described the inhabitants of Lantau Island: 'The inhabitants neither farm nor make silk, nor do they pay taxes or do labour service. They live by fishing and salt-making.' Around AD 1100, farmers from central China fleeing the Mongol incursion settled in the green valleys of what is now the New Territories. Also driven south was the child-emperor Duan Zong. Arriving in what is now Kowloon in 1277, the boy, his court and his army spent a year in the area before the putative leader of the Song dynasty died at the age of nine.

Hong Kong waters have supported generations of fisherfolk, most prominently the Tankas, whose lifestyle was entirely waterborne

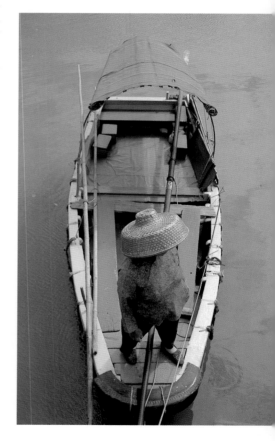

By the early 19th century, 'scattered communities existed throughout the islands, and in the fertile flatlands of the peninsula. There were rice-farmers, salt-producers, fishermen, quarrymen, incense-gatherers. There were not a few pirates, who found convenient retreats among the myriad islands at the mouth of the great estuary (hence the name Ladrones, which means "pirates" in Portuguese)...,' relates Jan Morris in *Hong Kong: Epilogue to an Empire*. The people represented four Chinese races: the Punti or Cantonese, the Hoklos, the Hakkas or 'guest people' and the Tankas. There was little mingling; the desire to retain distinct societies bounded by familial lines was personified by the Five Great Clans of the Cantonese (Tang, Hau, Pang, Liu and Man), who formed their own, usually walled, villages. The rest of the populace tended to live on boats. Despite the disparate origins and beliefs of its residents, Morris describes a community ordered by adherence to tradition and law, where rules of Chinese geomancy, known as *feng shui* (literally 'wind and water'), were followed and where books and theatre were an important part of everyday life. The territory's geographic position at the mouth of the Pearl River and surrounding a magnificent natural harbour ensured its constant association with waterborne travellers—not only Chinese, but also Indians, Arabs, Portuguese, and later British and Dutch. Through the deep, well-protected harbour sailed butterfly-winged sampans, cargo-junks, schooners, imperial vessels and, more surreptitiously, pirate ships.

The natural fertility of southern Guangdong province proved amenable to the cultivation of fruits and vegetables introduced by traders who plied the Silk Road of the Sea

'AMONG THE fruits and vegetables produced on the island, are the mango, lychee, longan, orange, pear, rice, sweet potatoes, and yams,' wrote A.R. Johnston in 1843. He went on to add: 'Since the occupation of the island by the English, the potato of Europe and fruits of Canton and Macau have been introduced; and lately a great many European seeds have been brought by the agent of the Horticultural Society of London, and distributed.'

Southern Guangdong province, which borders Hong Kong, is the most fertile region in China. Along with the indigenous bounty of local fields and waters, the position of Guangzhou as a prominent stop on what was known as the Silk Road of the Sea, trade routes linking China with Southeast Asia and Europe, meant that its people were familiar with the foods and eating styles of traders from Arabia, India, Persia, Japan and Korea. During the Tang dynasty, such items as spinach, lettuce, almonds, leeks, shallots, peaches, beets and figs were introduced to the mainland and absorbed into the cuisine. Europeans arrived in numbers during the Ming dynasty (1368–1644), bringing with them peanuts, sweet potatoes and corn. For some time, though, these were considered 'famine foods', and even when grown in abundance, as Ken Hom writes in *The Taste of China*, 'these "new" Western foods were consumed almost entirely by the poor, that is, the great majority of people.' The wealthy classes enjoyed a richly diverse diet; the cornerstone of Cantonese cuisine, which is renowned for its wide range of ingredients and cooking methods.

While Hong Kong's expatriate gardeners were planting the Horticultural Society's offerings, entrepreneurs attracted by the opening of this colonial door on to the mainland were sowing the seeds of enterprise. Before circumstances forced him on to the war campaign trail, Hong Kong's first governor, Henry Pottinger, had seen the potential of the place and encouraged growth by awarding land grants. His efforts were interrupted: the Convention of Chuen Pi had not settled affairs and fighting continued. The First Anglo-Chinese war did not end until 19 August 1842 with the Treaty of Nanking, which stipulated the transfer to Britain of Hong Kong in perpetuity, so that Britain could have 'a Port whereat they may careen and refit their Ships, when required, and keep Stores for that purpose. ...'

While Pottinger and the Royal Navy fought their way to Nanjing, and eventual Chinese capitulation, buildings began to line the waterfront and dot the lower reaches of the hills behind the nascent town of Victoria. Appropriately, given the well-known canniness of the contemporary Hong Kong developer, the first land sales were a bit of a bun fight, with local Chinese offering and selling parcels of territory with great disregard for whether or not they held title to them. The purchasers' speculative risks paid off when Hong Kong was officially declared a British Crown colony on 26 June 1843. By 1845, the population numbered 30,000.

DURING HONG KONG's first decade, merchant companies occupied hastily built premises along a mud-sodden Queen's Road and Praya. The hongs, or trading houses—Jardine, Matheson; Dent and Company; and Russell and Company—were soon held to be the real powers behind Hong Kong. Their surroundings may have been tropical, but in dress and in work ethic they followed

By the 1920s, rows of distinguished, colonnaded buildings had risen alongside the Praya of Hong Kong

a standard of high Englishness. The same was true when they were at table: an English chef prepared meals for Jardine management, though Dent's broke the mould: 'At 7:30 to dine with Mr. John Dent, whose French cooking sent up one of the best dinners I ever sat down to, in London or Paris,' recollected novelist, playwright and entertainer Albert Smith in 1858. 'A claret cup was also a thing to recollect,' he added.

Smith dined at a Chinese restaurant and was impressed with its 'panels carved *au jour*, and painted and gilded recesses, for private parties and opium smokers.' The practice was not widespread among the expatriate community, but in the late 19th century, Chinese official Ho Siu-Kei recorded: 'The red hair have been seen in Chinese restaurants.' Not all Westerners chose only the familiarity of their native cuisine. The 'red hair' were probably first served a Chinese meal, and doubtless more, in the tea houses, inns and brothels of Sai Ying Pun.

Established to serve the Chinese community of mainly labourers and small merchants who had moved there shortly after Hong Kong was wrested from China, these venues grew more elaborate as their patrons' businesses flourished. Restaurants were commonly located next to brothels, and as anthropology student Cheng Sea-Ling discovered while researching her dissertation on food in Hong Kong families, 'business transactions, merchant-official agreements were frequently found, accompanied by conspicuous consumption, in these establishments.' Hang Fa Lau Restaurant, which opened in 1845, facilitated deals for food and sex: diners would send a note to the brothel next door and the women of their choice would join their party. In modern Cantonese parlance, a 'late supper' still refers to the practice of paying a bar an agreed sum to escort one of its hostesses to dinner. Hang Fa Lau eventually became a community centre, and a plaque across the street from the former restaurant site on Staunton Street commemorates the fact that Dr Sun Yixian (Sun Yat-Sen) made campaign speeches there.

Morris noted that 'Victuals as varied as Dublin stout, English ham, tripes and tinned oatmeal were regularly shipped from Britain, alcohol seems to have been unlimited—they drank claret with their breakfasts, beer with their midday tiffin, and in the evenings great quantities of claret, champagne and port.' The popularity of supplies from home cannot be attributed simply to chauvinism, or an inability to adapt to local conditions. Matilda Sharp, namesake of the Matilda Hospital, who with her banker husband Granville arrived in Hong Kong in December 1858, wrote: 'It is far cheaper to send for your stores from England.' Though she thought their sugar 'very nice', '...what do you think it is? Sugar candy pounded...in a pestle and mortar for our daily consumption.'

The Western merchants' appetite for profit was as prodigious as their hunger for home-style food and drink. Business was held to be Hong Kong's sole *raison d'être*, and clashes between the interests of hong and government were frequent, with each side showing no small contempt for the other. For most of its residents, no matter what their nationality, Hong Kong was a way-station on the road to wealth, and the resulting transience did little to encourage civility or soul. Scholar and translator Wang Tao, who moved to Hong Kong from Shanghai in the 1860s, wrote: 'The people of Kwangtung [Guangdong] province have always had something of a monopoly on commerce, and thus Hong Kong has proved to be attractive to craftsmen from far and wide. Business flourishes here, and trade relations have been established with many places.' Scornful of the unhinged pursuit of riches, Wang added: 'Hong Kong's prosperity now exceeds that of Canton, and it is all the result of fate and chance.'

Dine-Dance

"GET THE HABIT"

of meeting at the

CAFE REGENT

(OPPOSITE HONG KONG HOTEL.)

EXCELLENT CUISINE   EVERY ATTENTION
QUICK SERVICE   PLEASING MUSIC
COMFORTABLE SOCIAL RENDEZVOUS.
OPEN FROM 8 A.M. TO MIDNIGHT.

TEL. C. 3056.   PEDDER BUILDING.

Hotels and restaurants, clustered mainly in the Central district, made attempts to enliven the leisurely lifestyle

There are 26 hotels and taverns listed in *The China Directory* for 1862 (among them the charmingly named Land We Live In and Old House at Home), but only two Western restaurants, both on Lyndhurst Terrace and both apparently lacking names, since only the proprietors' details are given. Lawlessness prevailed ('I have learned to load Matilda's revolver,' wrote Lucilla, sister-in-law of Matilda Sharp) and disease whittled away at the populace. The Taiping Rebellion in China (1851–65) brought more and more refugees, and criminal activity flourished. 'The fearfullest hole in the world, for I might say it is inhabited by a den of thieves' was how a member of the King's Dragoon Guards described Victoria. Even so, some newcomers noted with pleasure the lively blend of cultures that thrived in Hong Kong's streets. Dr W.M. Wood, of the United States East India Squadron, sketched a picture of the colourful street life: 'The pork-butcher is dealing out his slender cutlets, the fruiterer his pines, bananas, oranges, and huge pomellons. Next to this golden-coloured merchandise, are masses of green salad, cabbages, peas, beans, with radishes and tomatoes. There are dried fish and fresh, with bunches of dried ducks, split open, pressed flat, as if rolled between heavy rollers, and dried with transparent thinness.'

Perhaps year-round residence was to blame for the malaise which seems to have affected so many expatriates. The climate was difficult to bear for most of the year, typhoons wreaked devastation, and malaria struck with fatal result. Laurence Oliphant, Lord Elgin's private secretary, complained in 1862 that the only social options were a game of billiards or a choice of two walks, which might result in a nasty case of fever. 'It was not difficult to account for a certain depression of spirits and tone of general irritability, which seemed to pervade the community. A large bachelor's dinner was the extreme limit of gaiety. It was provoking that a place possessing so many scenic attractions should have been so entirely devoid of charms. Like a beautiful woman with a bad temper, Hong-Kong claimed our admiration while it repelled our advances.'

DESPITE THE bright future forecast by Henry Pottinger, Hong Kong was of moderate consequence until late 1856, when Sir John Bowring, governor of Hong Kong, seized upon the *Arrow* incident, involving a Chinese arrest of the crew of a British-registered lorcha (a junk-rigged schooner), as a reason for bombarding Guangzhou. The hostilities developed into the Second Opium War, also known as the Arrow War. Foreign factories in Guangzhou came under attack, forcing British traders to regroup in the young colony.

An 1846 painting of a bustling Victoria Harbour bears out Henry Pottinger's optimistic forecasts

The conflict surfaced in quite a different manner in Hong Kong on 15 January 1857, when baker Cheung

Alum, who held the contract to supply Her Majesty's forces and European residents, tried to poison the expatriates with loaves leavened with arsenic in his Pottinger Street bakery. Fortunately, the bread was so heavily poisoned that anyone eating it suffered immediate vomiting, and though the colony's doctors were run off their feet that day, there were no immediate deaths.

The Convention of Peking, which concluded the Arrow War, provided for cession of the Kowloon Peninsula and Stonecutters Island to Britain. Another sizeable chunk of land was added in 1898, when China was forced to lease the British another 350 square miles of territory (including 233 islands) for 99 years beginning 1 July 1898. The move was designed as much to prevent the French and other European countries from moving in as it was to increase Britain's holdings. The rather unusual terms of the agreement sealed the colony's fate, for as it became evident that Hong Kong could not exist without the New Territories, as the area north of the Kowloon Peninsula was called, it became equally obvious that the countdown to 1997 applied to the whole of Hong Kong. But it would be many decades before that issue was first publicly mooted.

A little over four decades after the British took possession of the island of Hong Kong, commercial buildings lined the waterfront from Western to Shau Kei Wan, while graceful residential villas dotted the middle reaches of Victoria Peak

As the colony rounded the cusp of the 19th century, gracefully colonnaded buildings lined the Praya of Hong Kong Island and elegant villas and bungalows sheltered the wealthier set from Kennedy Town to Happy Valley. The area along the Western Praya, however, was a social and environmental disaster, with more than 150,000 Chinese residents living in mean shanties which lacked the basics of running water and drainage. When the bubonic plague struck Hong Kong in the last decade of the century, the majority of the 2,500 who died did so in appalling conditions.

The Peak Tramway, a marvel of technology, was built in 1888. Expatriates could forgo an uncomfortable hour or so on horseback or in a sedan-chair in favour of being whisked up Victoria Peak to their spacious colonial villas. Less elegantly, a carefully worded Peak Government Ordinance put into effect the year before reserved the Peak exclusively for European residents and their servants. (The ordinance remained on the books until the late 1940s.) Lofty cathedral spires drew the eye upward to hills which bore the fruits of dedicated tree-planting, hotels fairly burst at the seams, and clubs around town provided evenings of stately entertainment and stolid Western meals. The Chinese community by this time included wealthy and increasingly prominent entrepreneurs and business owners. Four Chinese newspapers were printed every day, social organisations were ministering to the needy, and there were Chinese Justices of the Peace.

IN CHINA, the 20th century began with the Boxer Rebellion in 1900 and Dr Sun Yixian's launching of a movement in 1905 to topple the Ching dynasty. In 1911, Dr Sun and his followers succeeded and the Republic of China was declared. Hong Kong continued to absorb successive waves of immigration from the mainland, as people sought temporary respite from political upheaval. Some were simply attracted by the opportunities afforded by the colony's *laissez-faire* approach. In an atmosphere of minimal government interference, inventiveness and flexibility thrived and hard work paid off.

Tram lines were laid in 1904, connecting the eastern and western coastlines of Hong Kong Island. One of the effects of this venture was a gradual confluence of Chinese and foreign residents, as Chinese homes, shops and restaurants moved beyond Western district to Sheung Wan, Central and Wan Chai. As the Chinese society expanded to include a burgeoning middle class and a select, very wealthy upper class, so too did the gastronomy of that society. The Hong Kong Club may have been off-bounds to non-Europeans, but the well-off Chinese merchant could partake of roast beef dinners at Chinese-owned Western-style restaurants like the Wellington and enjoy lavish Chinese meals at the Ying King Grand Restaurant in Wan Chai. A lively dim sum (*dím sàm*) culture evolved: the famous Luk Yu Tea House was opened by Guangzhou owners in 1922. A full-page advertisement in the *Hong Kong Dollar Directory* for that year carries the promise of 'Kitchen Under European Supervision' for the King Edward hotel on Des Voeux Road. 'Doctor Brand' lager, guinness, sparkling muscatel, creme de menthe and 30-year-old whiskey could be obtained from The Colonial Commercial Co. Ltd in the Post Office buildings. Should a customer wish to carry home his purchases, hire of a sedan-chair in Victoria, with two bearers, would cost 25 cents for one hour, according to the legalised tariff of fares.

World War I did little to disturb Hong Kong's established lifestyle ('During the European War, the Company uninterruptedly supplied the Colony with all its accustomed foods and continued to furnish as well the regular delicacies,' recorded The Dairy Farm Co. Ltd), save for a mild economic dip. More serious disaffection struck after the war. The post-revolution chaos which wracked China—in 1921, Beijing was controlled by warlords while Dr Sun Yixian was president of the Republic in Guangzhou—coincided with a growing sense among the Chinese of Hong Kong of their potential political power. A seamen's strike in 1922 and a general strike in 1925–26, which paralysed the city for some four months, were unprecedented displays of strength by local people protesting labour and living conditions which kept them mired in poverty. The small European community was suddenly reminded of its minority status (4,500 versus 750,000 Chinese). In a city where the exclusion of Chinese from residing on Victoria Peak, and even along Peak Road on Cheung Chau Island, was considered right and proper, the shock must have been considerable.

Periodic chaos north of the border continued to bring influxes of refugees, swelling Hong Kong's population from 625,000 in 1921 to 1.6 million in 1941. During the same period, revenue almost trebled. As Nigel Cameron wrote in *Hong Kong: The Cultured Pearl*, 'The resilience of its traders, Chinese and foreigners alike, the prodigious feats of its workers (all Chinese, and most grossly underpaid), the continual stream of new labour fleeing from the uncertainties, the civil strife, the armed Japanese aggressions in China itself; and the unique conditions for trade and commerce in Hong Kong—all these factors kept it bustling, growing, lively and firmly in British colonial hands.'

The manufacture of ice cream — and ice — were early enterprises, and ones destined for success, given the sultry heat and extreme humidity of the Hong Kong summer

NEVER WAS a ball so inappropriately named. The Fancy Dress Victory Ball at the Peninsula hotel, sponsored by the Hong Kong Chinese Women's Club, had 800 high-society guests dancing away the night of 7 December 1941—the eve of the Japanese invasion of the territory. The event won a second identification, as the last dance of the British Empire. 'A brilliant function,' said the *South China Morning Post* the following day, in papers printed just hours before Japanese planes swooped on Hong Kong, destroying the small RAF fleet stationed at Kai Tak.

Having seized Manchuria in 1933 and installing a puppet government, Japan took control of Beijing in 1937 and its troops began to move south. Despite the threat inherent in these actions, Hong Kong put on a convincing show of blithely ignoring the fractious state of affairs across the border. Tourism slowed to a trickle, and hotel rooms, and often hotel ballrooms and other public areas, were occupied by as many of the multitude of refugees as could be accommodated. But scattered alongside the newspaper notices of blackout drills and rationing were notices of races, recitals, tea dances and, of course, balls.

On 18 December, Japanese troops landed on Hong Kong Island. For the next week, General Maltby's forces struggled against dire odds. The hoped-for assistance from Jiang Jieshi's (Chiang Kai-Shek's) army did not materialise and the sinking of the Royal Navy's *Repulse* and *Prince of Wales* scuppered any chance of help from that quarter. The defenders of Hong Kong were mostly inexperienced, hampered by bad communications and a strategy based on disastrous underestimation of the enemy. Many instances of bravery were recorded, by both enlisted men and civilians. The Hong Kong Volunteers proved their talent for raising more than a glass: Scottish, Portuguese and Chinese companies fought alongside the regular troops; and the Hughesiliers, all older than 55, held the North Point power station against repeated attacks, surrendering only when their ammunition was exhausted.

When World War II ended, the original owners of Jimmy's Kitchen bought back their restaurant and by 1946 it was opened for business in the China Building

On Christmas Day, General Maltby informed the governor that resistance was no longer possible: 15 minutes later, the order to surrender was conveyed and the white flag went up on Government House. That evening, General Maltby and Sir Mark Young were escorted across the harbour, now a melancholy stretch of burned-out and half-sunk hulls, and strode into the Peninsula hotel, where they formally surrendered to Lieutenant-General Sakai.

The people of Hong Kong suffered terrible privation during the war years. Allied soldiers and nationals were herded into prison camps in Sham Shui Po and Stanley, and vast numbers of Chinese residents were forced into China in anticipation of looming food shortages. Indeed, the Japanese invasion had already blighted the region's capacity for diverse crop production. Researchers E.N. Anderson Jr and Marja L. Anderson later reported, 'Our informants in Hong Kong remembered the period as one of living on sweet potato vines, wild herbs, and worse; virtually every family had lost members due to starvation.'

The territory was systematically plundered—cars, statues, even books were shipped to Japan—and its infrastructure destroyed. However, a semblance of a social life was restored mere months after the invasion when the Peninsula opened under Japanese management as the Toa (East Asia) hotel. Meanwhile, the snack bar of the Hong Kong hotel became a tempura grill and Jimmy's Kitchen was dubbed the Sai Mun Café. Government House grew a Japanese-style tower and gardens, and one room was fitted with tatami mats for His Excellency Lieutenant-General Rensuke Isogai, a practitioner of the elaborate Japanese tea ceremony.

When the Japanese surrendered on 14 August 1945, Hong Kong's future as a Crown colony hung in the balance. Allied powers had agreed that liberated territories would be surrendered to the liberator, but no one had actually liberated Hong Kong. Franklin Gimson, the senior official internee in Stanley Prison Camp, forestalled any discussion about Hong Kong being handed to Jiang Jieshi— by dint of his being supreme commander of the war zone in which Hong Kong was situated—by appointing himself acting governor and immediately setting up administrative offices in the territory. As a result, Hong Kong remained a British possession, but the colonial superiority which had characterised its first 100 years had been broken. As the military and residents set about swiftly repairing damage inflicted during the occupation, the burgeoning strength of the Chinese business people and entrepreneurs made it clear that a new status quo was being shaped.

POST-WAR HONG KONG was a city on permanent boil. Mao Zedong's

Pre-World War I Dairy Farm delivery trucks make their rounds. The company first supplied the colony with milk from a herd of 80 imported cows in 1887

declaration of the People's Republic of China in 1949 sent more floods of immigrants southward, among them wealthy Shanghainese textile manufacturers. Drawing on the cheap labour that ballooned at the opposite end of the migrant scale, they energised Hong Kong's transformation from an entrepôt to a thriving manufacturing centre. Some of the more salubrious names in the food industry trace their roots to this period. Mr Chan, a noodle-maker, sold his wares from two baskets hung on a pole which he carried over his shoulder. In 1948, he opened a factory in Yuen Long. Almost 50 years later, his descendants are at the helm of Ho To Tai, busily encouraging younger patrons to try spinach, vegetarian and carrot noodle, along with the old-style hen and duck egg pastas.

Another food legend was formed in the late 1940s. K.S. Lo's dream of making a soya milk which would have the nutritional quality of cow's milk and be readily accepted by the lactose-intolerant Chinese digestive system had been interrupted by the hostilities. But by

1950, the Hong Kong Soya Bean Products Co. Ltd had built a new factory in Aberdeen to fill wide-mouth glass bottles with Vitasoy. At first, bottles of the soya milk were delivered on bicycles to home consumers every morning before 8am. Noting the leap in popularity of soft drinks, Lo began promoting Vitasoy as a thirst-quenching drink, rather than a milk substitute, and sales took off.

Thanks to its residents' singleminded industriousness, the territory weathered the United Nations' boycott of Chinese goods during the Korean War, the greatest effect of which was to solidify Hong Kong's position as a manufacturing centre. Another, not inconsequential, effect of that war was to promote Hong Kong's suitability as the 'rest and recreation' choice for US forces.

In these years, Hong Kong's amorphous identity began to take on greater definition. Here, Chinese found themselves living and working with compatriots who shared their ethnic origins but spoke different dialects, ate different food and practised different customs. The diversification of the restaurant scene in the early 1950s reflected an increasingly complex population. Chefs had migrated, too, and everything from small cafés to formal dining rooms opened to satisfy the cravings of a largely transient, homesick populace. The choice included Peking, authentic Sichuan and Hunan, Shanghai and, of course, Cantonese cuisines. With the development of a white-collar middle class, the rural population decreased. By the end of the 1950s, less than seven per cent of the working population were engaged in farming, forestry and fishing.

The fall-out from social unrest and China's Cultural Revolution stalled Hong Kong's powerful economic machine, but not for long. Tourism was bruised by riots in 1966, over a price rise in the Star Ferry fare. Anti-colonial sentiment was whipped to fever pitch the following year, with demonstrations and bombings in Hong Kong and the unsettling appearance of brigades of Red Guards marching through the colony's streets. But by the end of the year, calm had returned and eventually, after a concerted public relations exercise, so did the tourists.

Richard Nixon's fence-building visit to Beijing in 1972 and the establishment of China's open-door policy in 1978 set the stage for Hong Kong's next metamorphosis. Promoting itself as the gateway to the mainland, the territory capitalised on its sophisticated infrastructure and business people capable of linking foreign investment to Chinese ventures. Hong Kong became the regional centre of choice for multinational companies and, by the early 1980s, had gained a reputation as a dynamic, affluent city that lived and breathed business. This image was rocked in October 1987 when the management of Hong Kong's stock market took the unprecedented step of closing the exchange for four days after

Hong Kong has thrived in the latter half of the 20th century, emerging from its position as a low-cost manufacturing centre to a nexus of finance and commerce

Black Monday. It took a government rescue package of HK$4 billion and changes to the running of the exchange to restore confidence.

Two years of Sino-British talks on the future of Hong Kong resulted in the Joint Declaration, announced on 26 September 1984. Britain agreed to relinquish sovereignty at midnight on 30 June 1997, and China agreed to make no major changes to the economic or social status quo of the new Special Administrative Region for at least 50 years. Hammering out the terms was an often acrimonious process, and differences in interpretation periodically strained Britain and China's relationship. Checking the colony's confidence level became a daily exercise for journalists here and overseas, and was usually measured in terms of the 'brain drain' caused by immigration. This barometer jumped after June 1989, when the pro-democracy movement which had gripped Beijing ended in tragedy with the People's Liberation Army's massacre of students in Tiananmen

Square. Hong Kong's populace responded at a grassroots level, with massive, peaceful demonstrations.

Confidence in the future alternately wavered and strengthened in the run-up to the handover. The ambiguities of the 'one country two systems' philosophy espoused by Deng Xiaoping have been endlessly defined and debated. As the generations of Chinese born in Hong Kong make their mark in academia, politics, business and technology, the definition of the essential Hong Kong identity has gained impetus. Despite the uncertainties, the prospect of finally being 'masters of our own house' is deeply compelling on emotional and intellectual levels. No doubt there will remain some vestiges of the disparate, unamalgamated elements which so offended Lord Redesdale a century ago, for Hong Kong has established itself as a nexus of international commerce. But weathering instability and emerging from difficult times with new strength is not only a tradition in Hong Kong, it is a talent.

YÜ, THE REGENT HONG KONG
Steamed Fish With Soy Sauce

Eastern star garoupa, whole*	1 kg
Chinese parsley (coriander), roughly chopped	3 large stalks
Spring onion, finely chopped	8 stalks
Peanut oil	2 tbsp
Sauce:	
Light soy sauce	150 ml
Sugar	1 tbsp
Chicken stock**	3 tbsp

Scale, gut and clean the fish, leaving the head and tail intact. In a large steamer, bring the water to the boil, then steam the fish for 10 minutes. Remove from the heat, sprinkle with the chopped spring onion and parsley and keep warm. Working quickly, heat a wok on medium heat and add the soy sauce and chicken stock until it is heated through, remove and keep warm. Turn the heat to high, re-heat the wok and add the peanut oil. Cook the oil until it is boiling then pour over the fish. To finish, pour the soy sauce and stock mixture over the fish. Serve immediately.

* If you cannot buy eastern star garoupa (*dung sing bahn*), mandarin fish is suitable; it is recommended for inexperienced cooks as it holds its texture better if the fish is inadvertently over-cooked.
** Freshly-made chicken stock will produce a more delicate, less salty flavour.

JIMMY'S KITCHEN
Steak and Kidney Pie

Rump steak, trimmed and cubed	750 g
Lamb kidneys, skinned, cored, chopped	450 g
Flour, all-purpose	75 g
Lard	100 g
Brown onion, large	1
Mushrooms, fresh	4 large pieces
Red wine, dry	50 ml
Worcestershire sauce	25 ml
Parsley, fresh, chopped	2 tsp
Thyme	1 tsp
Flaky pastry	225 g
Egg yolk	1
Cream	25 ml
Salt and milled black pepper (for seasoning)	

Place the meat in a bowl and season with salt and pepper, add the flour and mix. Heat 3/4 of the lard in a pan, add the beef and kidney and brown. Remove from the pan, drain off excess fat and place in a deep oven-proof casserole dish.

Chop the onion and slice the mushrooms. Heat the remaining lard and sauté the vegetables for 3–4 minutes, then add to the casserole. Pour 300 ml of cold water into the pan and bring to the boil. Add the red wine, Worcestershire sauce, parsley and thyme and season with extra salt and pepper. Simmer for 2 minutes, then pour into the casserole and mix well.

Roll the pastry out to a thickness of 5 mm and slightly larger than the diameter of the dish. Wet the edges of the dish with cold water and place the dough on top. Cut off the overhanging dough and press down the edges. Beat the egg and cream together and brush over the dough. Place in a pre-heated oven (225°C) and bake for 40–50 minutes, until the meat is cooked and the pastry is golden brown. (Serves 6.)

2

Home Of
The Everyday Epicure

I t is almost 8pm and the narrow streets of the market are quiet. Two hours ago, the slender passages were thick with shoppers selecting, bargaining for and carrying home their dinner ingredients. Stalls have been battened down with tight wrappings of the ubiquitous red, white and blue plastic sheeting; overturned wicker baskets lean in wobbly stacks; and the uneven pavement is slick from the water that has slopped out of basins holding live prawns, garoupa, pomfret, eels and other sea creatures brought in to tempt the early evening crowd. Strung along several narrow intersecting lanes, bisected by a street that in daytime is a roar of belching mini-buses, the market is practically deserted.

Except for one corner. Where Graham and Wellington streets cross, before the former drops down to meet Stanley Street, a lone stall is illuminated amongst a row of darkened ones. Hovering around the glow of its low light is a clutch of people. They wait patiently and silently, their eyes fixed on a bare-chested man working at a makeshift table that is little more than a battered sheet of plywood placed across cartons. Before him is a round, much-used chopping block, a cleaver, two white plastic bags and neat rows of empty soup bowls. Into each white and blue bowl he drops a quantity of chopped spring onions and whole peanuts.

Hong Kongers nourish a passion for food from a young age

Reaching behind him, he tears a strip off the lengths of raw fish that hang there on a hook, places it on the block and slices it thinly with the cleaver. From one plastic bag he takes a handful of minced beef mixed with rice vermicelli and dribbles a small amount into the bowls. Then are added several slices of fish. Turning, he dips a ladle into a tall steaming pot sitting on a blackened gas ring beside him, and pours hot congee into as many bowls as there are customers. Grabbing a bunch of fresh coriander from the second plastic bag he drops on a leafy topping, sticks a spoon into each bowl and with a graceless, but hospitable, wave of his arm, gestures for the waiting diners to come forward for a dish of 'sampan congee' (*yú pin jùk*), so-called because it used to be served from sampans in the harbour to folk on other vessels. Then there is only the sound of soup being slurped, of porcelain spoon clinking on porcelain bowl. It's delicious, but no one says so; no one says a word.

Sampan congee is also known as 'raw fish congee'; its success depends on the rice gruel, which must be piping hot, so that the fish is instantly and tenderly broiled. Cantonese use the phrase 'raw fish congee' to describe, for instance, scraping by on an exam, or just managing to meet a deadline. There's a mono-sodium glutamate saltiness to the soup, but the strong-flavoured coriander competes handily. Minutes later, sated diners hand their empty dishes to a second man, who deposits them in a water-filled styrofoam container and pockets their money. A few cats prowl nearby, licking up the dregs which the dishwasher flings on to the ground. The crowd melts away and another one forms. Probably most of those disappearing down the dark lanes are going home to dinner.

Scenes like this one are played out all over Hong Kong, at practically all hours, day and night. The Chinese share an exuberant and enduring passion for food. Here, where space and leisure time are limited and many daily rituals are of necessity thrust on to the streets, it is a passion any observer can encounter. It sometimes seems impossible to walk for more than five minutes without tripping over, dodging, smelling or nearly being run down by food in some shape or form: sidewalks covered with neat rows of orange peel and lotus root laid out to dry; staff in a noodle shop, who are surrounded by bins of dumpling filling and stacks of wrappers, scoop-wrap-pinch the 2,000 won ton for tomorrow; the murmur of hot pots can be heard before the night-time alley restaurant is seen; and mobile woks outside cinemas sizzle with sausage, green pepper and squid that has been marinated to a frightening day-glo orange.

The nature of Hong Kong as a microcosm of Chinese ethnicity lends extraordinary vigour to its food culture. Having absorbed waves of immigrants

from virtually every corner of the mainland, Hong Kong's mainly Cantonese population includes significant numbers of Shanghai, Chiu Chow, Sichuan, Hakka, Fukien and Beijing people, each of which has contributed another delicious layer to the multi-textured restaurant scene. These refugees who had fled famine or political strife north of the border longed for home always. If they couldn't see it or touch it, they could taste it in the regional *dai pai dong* (street stalls) and restaurants that catered to their hunger. Sharpened by reminiscence and homesickness, their expatriate palates demanded the distillation of home, the perfection of culinary creation that would, at least for the length of a mealtime, satisfy their craving.

A fond, if diminished, institution, the dai pai dong—*literally 'cooked food stall'—is gradually dying out under the weight of stringent government regulations and re-development schemes*

'Surely no culture on earth, even the French, is so concerned with gastronomy as the Chinese.'
—E.N. Anderson Jr and Marja L. Anderson,
Food in Chinese Culture

27

THE MERITS of one cuisine over another can be debated endlessly, but few argue with the accepted wisdom that the Chinese are the most food-oriented culture in the world. Nowhere is Hong Kong's innate Chineseness more apparent than in its devotion to all levels of the dining experience and to just about all regional varieties of Chinese cuisine. The famously futuristic skyline is deceptive; it is at street level that the chimera of Westernisation dissolves most quickly. The alleys and side streets jutting at steep, twisting angles off Central's skyscraper-shaded financial district are chock-a-block with shops, stalls and restaurants that revolve to the everyday needs of the local palate. Steam from bubbling vats of rice porridge and broth obscures the windows of the tiny open kitchens at the front of copious congee and noodle shops; panting men and women push trolleys weighed down with containers of plastic-wrapped Chinese cabbage (*choi sum*), red peppers and tiny cobs of corn; bicycle deliverymen blithely pedal their Flying Pigeons across the paths of buses bearing down on pedestrian-clogged intersections, the vehicle's basket quivering with plucked ducks or rumps of beef receiving a dubious open-air seasoning; the crackle of bubbling cooking oil from a hawker's mobile wok stand hits one's ears just seconds before the unmistakable stench of fermented tofu assaults the nostrils; the proprietor of a hole-in-the-wall shop pulls back the metal grate protecting his narrow patch of retail space and dusts the jars of chilli, plain or soy sauce tofu lining the shelves. The terrifying lunch-hour charge begins and phalanxes of office workers—more effective blockers than a row of linebackers—seethe towards restaurants serving dim sum (*dím sàm*), or

Food is graphically present in the city's quotidian life

vegetarian Chinese dishes, or won ton noodles (*wàhn tàn mihn*), or Chinese-style Western set meals.

In Hong Kong, *dai pai dong*, congee and noodle shops, and fast food restaurants seem always to be dishing up food to new arrivals. Main meals are enjoyed at midday and in the evening, but a typical day will also include the consumption of up to three smaller ones, known as *siu sihk* (snacks). 'I'm writing a series about a perfect day's eating in Macau,' says a professional man who feeds his food obsession by writing a lively culinary column in an upmarket weekly newspaper. A keen observer of culinary habits and mores, both Western and Asian, he sees nothing unusual in the fact that this assignment will be in five parts: for his readers, the ideal dining experience comprises breakfast, lunch, afternoon tea, dinner and a late-night snack.

———··———

THE DEVOTION to food begins at a young age. When Michael Bond, professor of psychology at the Chinese University of Hong Kong, explored the foundations of caretaking in his book *Beyond the Chinese Face*, he described a tendency towards 'early indulgence, especially with food', and quoted Warner Meunsterberger: 'Few children are fed and treated with so much permissiveness. As far as we can ascertain, oral deprivation does not occur during this early period. Experience with hunger is avoided by feeding the child upon hearing him cry.' According to Dr Bond, this early pampering 'establishes a lifelong preoccupation which lays the foundation for what psychoanalysts have labelled "oral-receptive mastery"'— the root of the Chinese obsession with food.

The difficulty with labels like 'passion' and 'obsession' is the limits they impose on an explanation of this wholehearted awareness of food, suggesting simply an unhealthy fixation. China's is one of the oldest documented cuisines in the world, and writings from very early periods suggest the depth to which attitudes towards food are intertwined with attitudes towards health and ritual. In attempting to trace Tang dynasty cooks' use of pungent and spicy ingredients, Dr Edward H. Schafer notes in *Food in Chinese Culture*: 'It is not always easy to discover the evidence for the degree of their exploitation in T'ang cookery, since the arts of pharmacology and perfumery were not sharply distinguished from the kitchen arts.'

During the Chou dynasty (1122–256 BC), points out Dr K.C. Chang in *Food in Chinese Culture*, 2,271 (almost 60 per cent) of the staff who ministered to the king's residence handled food and wine. There were 162 master dietitians,

335 grain, vegetable and fruit specialists, 28 meat dryers, 340 wine servers, 62 pickle and sauce specialists, and 62 salt men, to name just some of the servant categories. This does not signal mere indulgence, though great power and the privileges and obligations associated with it are, of course, important factors. This inordinate concentration of staff also underlines the extreme importance placed on food preparation, serving and eating. There was more at stake than pleasing the monarch's palate; mindbogglingly complex standards of ceremony, quality and paying of tribute had to be upheld and advanced. *Li Chi*, the Chinese *Book of Rites* which was compiled in the 1st century AD, gives scrupulously detailed instructions on serving food to suit the occasion, on the complexities of placing specific dishes on the table, and the multitude of factors to consider when devising the correct seating plan.

The ultimate convenience food is immortalised in the neon spectacle that illuminates the Hong Kong skyline

> 'For the people, food is heaven.'
> —Chinese proverb

'HOW PEOPLE eat in Hong Kong is very complicated,' says Stephen Yau, executive assistant manager, food and beverage, at the New World hotel. It's not that the food scene is so convoluted—it's more that identifying the various levels of dining is akin to peeling an onion. Convenience food, such as won ton noodles, 'fills up space'; the contemporary tea house or café (*chàh châan têng*) offers an incredible range of *dai pai dong* and other dishes in indoor surroundings and at low prices; restaurants serving what is sometimes called 'Chinglish' food serve up pseudo-Western dishes with enough Chinese trappings (such as rice and lashings of soy sauce) to be recognisable to diners not entirely comfortable with a totally foreign meal; so-called retro restaurants fulfil a hunger for the food of one's youth; neighbourhood Cantonese restaurants provide tasty encounters for informal gatherings of family and friends; and upmarket Cantonese, regional Chinese and Western restaurants are ideal for impressing dates or business partners.

Notwithstanding the millennia of food traditions that they absorb, to all intents and purposes unquestioningly, Hong Kong Chinese also have a more prosaic reason for dining out so often. The bulk of the population lives in cramped conditions, with postage stamp-sized kitchens which simply don't allow for easygoing home entertaining. With many families of four or more occupying a home of sometimes just 300 or 400 square feet, it is difficult enough to feed one's relatives, let alone host a business meal. Rather than risk serious loss of face by welcoming people to less than comfortable surroundings, restaurants are the preferred venue for family and business encounters.

Commercial, retail and residential premises are stacked on top of each other in cramped Hong Kong

'Many people here have two, or even three jobs,' says Yau. His take on the near-constant tide that flows through restaurant doors is typically pragmatic: 'Chinese people find great enjoyment in dining; we make our meals social occasions because this saves time—if we eat with our friends, we don't have to find other time to be sociable.' Killing two birds with one edible stone carries even more weight in a place where recreational opportunities are fairly limited. In Hong Kong, eating wrestles with shopping for the number one ranking on the list of favourite pastimes—and wins. Anyone who has ventured into the maelstrom that is Sogo or Wing-On or any of the massive shopping malls on a Saturday afternoon will agree that's a feat not to be sniffed at.

———•••———

FINANCIAL JOURNALIST turned chef, food critic, writer of cookbooks and roving culinary ambassador for the Hong Kong Tourist Association, Willy Mark, loves to tell a story about the time he was invited to the chateau owned by the Hennessy Cognac family. 'When I arrived, I met several Chinese journalists who were just leaving. "It was terrible," they told me. "We had no rice for four days!" I said, "But what about the lovely foie gras and other French foods you've eaten?"' Shaking his head at the memory, he adds: 'That didn't matter to them. Chinese really miss their food—especially rice.'

Fluffy, steamed rice is the cornerstone of the Chinese meal, except in the north of the mainland, where noodles and steamed bread dominate

Fluffy white long-grain rice, perfectly boiled so that the grains easily fall apart, is the simplest, most effective and certainly most essential ingredient of the Chinese meal. Less stodgy than noodles, and more delicate in texture, steamed rice (*baahk faahn*)is the cornerstone of a meal, absorbing and enhancing the flavours of meat, fish, sauces, and pickled and stir-fried vegetables. Chinese meals comprise a balance of two elements: *faahn*, or 'cooked rice', referring to the grains and other starches (such as noodles and steamed bread) served; while the accompanying meat and vegetable dishes are grouped together as *sung* (side dishes). Thus, *faahn* is most important, and in lean times, bowls of rice with a few shreds of pickled vegetables would suffice as a meal.

Rice produces more calories per acre than any vegetable crop with the exception of potatoes, and when not polished, it has a substantial amount of protein and B vitamins, as well as other nutrients. The

cereal has been grown in China since the 4th millennium BC, and there are several thousand varieties. The *Chinese Cookbook* likens rice appreciation to wine tasting and rice to grapes, since 'every crop differs from every other: paddy field by paddy field, region by region and season by season'. The secrets to cooking the perfect bowl of rice over a wood or gas fire have largely disappeared now that the Japanese rice cooker has become an accepted necessity in just about every Hong Kong kitchen. The device produces good steamed rice; and in a place where most cooks have a two-burner cooker, the electric appliance is a bonus.

Dr Chang in *Food in Chinese Culture* contends that Chinese cuisine is set apart and at least partially defined by the relationship between *faahn* and *sung*. The preparation of every meal revolves around providing the necessary balance of these elements. So as not to overwhelm the rice, side dishes are generally composed

Different varieties of rice fill the barrels of an old-style shop, where it is bought by the catty—a Chinese measurement equivalent to just over a pound

of the mixing of flavours by combining many ingredients, which are chopped before cooking. In Chou dynasty books, the word for culinary art translates as 'to cut and cook'. Send a Chinese cook into an American kitchen, says Dr Chang, and whether given Asian or Western ingredients, he or she will '(a) prepare an adequate amount of *faahn*, (b) cut up the ingredients and mix them in various combinations, and (c) cook the ingredients into several dishes and, perhaps, a soup.' No matter what the origin of the ingredients, the resulting spread will be inherently Chinese.

> 'A counsel in England pressing a witness as to how long he saw
> a person, would be surprised to receive such an answer as
> "the time it would take to drink a cup of tea", or again,
> "the time it would take to eat a bowl of rice".
> These are replies I have often heard in court.'
> —Sir William Meigh Goodman, 1907, Hong Kong

A VISITING American chef taken to a trendy Chinese restaurant looks closely at the walls and ceiling and announces his surprise at the lack of noise-absorbing tiles. His companions burst out laughing. 'When I choose a restaurant to go to with Chinese friends, I want it to be somewhere we can laugh and talk and make a lot of noise. If I'm going with Western friends, I have to think about whether the atmosphere is right.' There is a hint of exasperation in the voice of the thirty-something graphic designer. Born and bred in Hong Kong, she has inherited the imperviousness to noise which most foreigners, whose ears simply can't filter out the sounds of incessant traffic, construction and the dreaded home karaoke unit, find astounding and come to envy.

A television blaring from the cashier's counter is not uncommon in mid-range restaurants, and some supposedly classier venues have sets hanging from the ceiling. Not even the plush carpet, crystal chandeliers and muted decor of upmarket Chinese restaurants can hush the Cantonese, especially when at dim sum. That exuberance permeates discussions about food. The autumn arrival of Shanghai hairy crab causes excitement on a par with the Superbowl or the Premier League final. 'If you've never tried it, wait for a few weeks,' says a teacher, with a wink. 'That's when the female crab are harvested; they have more roe and they're supposed to be, uh, better for men.' Seasonal specialities, like summertime's cooling winter melon soup and cool-weather hot pot, are enjoyed with enthusiasm.

'*Dauh mìuh!*' chants a table of eight, in total agreement that the dish of tender pea shoots, stir-fried with a little oil, garlic and crab meat, is the most appealing of the winter vegetables suggested by the waiter.

Deeply superstitious, Hong Kong Chinese gain as much satisfaction from consuming dishes whose names equate to good fortune and prosperity, as from a meal which simply tastes good. *Pán choi* is a case in point. This Hakka dish, known as 'treasures in a wooden bowl', was traditionally consumed at festivals. Teams of eight diners would gather around a wooden baby bathtub and plunge their chopsticks into the eight layers of food that had been cooked and placed inside. Recently, Super Star Seafood Restaurant, among others, has revived and upgraded the ritual with ingredients like superior quality abalone and fish maw. But the gusto with which *pán choi* is consumed has little to do with the flavour of what is basically a hodgepodge of expensive foods: the original intention of the *pán choi* gathering was to encourage prosperity. 'You eat *pán choi* and you feel rich!' explains Alice Kok, manager of Super Star's Wan Chai branch, shrugging off the possibility that the terrine might not be a pleasing taste sensation. The promise of feeling wealthy can be just as appetising as inhaling the fragrance of a truly savoury dish.

Bird's nest is tasteless, yet the secretions of the swift's large saliva glands (which hold together their flimsy constructions of leaves, moss and feathers) are highly prized, and just as highly priced. Lynn Pan, in *Sons of the Yellow Emperor*, describes its legions of Chinese fans as hypochondriacs who can 'only think of all the good that it is doing them, and all the afflictions that it is

The word for fish in Cantonese (yú) also means plentiful—at table a whole steamed fish takes pride of place

keeping at bay—the digestive troubles it is preventing, the phlegm it is dissolving, the ageing process it is retarding, the loss of vigor its tonic qualities are remedying'. As with *pán choi* the perception of benefits accorded a food or dish, whether to health or pocketbook, is profoundly important. Faith either adds flavour or makes its absence palatable.

Food infuses the language, as well. 'Have you eaten yet?' is the most common Cantonese greeting. On the mainland, the 'iron rice bowl' refers to the job-for-life scenario that prevailed until market reforms were introduced by Deng Xiaoping. A colloquial Cantonese phrase for celibacy translates as 'going vegetarian'—a lifestyle choice that finds little sympathy or understanding; why refuse to eat perfectly good meat? Many foods are eaten for their symbolic benefits. Vermicelli is a symbol of longevity, and so has an important place on birthday and wedding tables. Foods and dishes whose names sound like 'prosperity', 'wealth' and 'abundance' are eaten more in the belief that they will live up to their name, than for the taste. *Fat choi*, for example, which is a homonym for black sea moss, has cachet at meal times because it also means to become wealthy. While the name for the ever-present fish on dinner tables, *yú*, means plentiful or abundance.

The extremes of noise and the acceptability of littering the table with bones and other meal-time detritus can blind foreigners to the myriad delicacies of behaviour that are ingrained within Chinese culture. Everyone, it seems, has childhood memories of being rapped on the knuckles for pointing with their chopsticks and not finishing their rice. Some habits are veiled in concerns about face. 'Soup is extremely important to Cantonese, but my friends and I don't often order it in restaurants,' says Cecilia Lui, public relations manager of the Excelsior hotel. It takes her a moment to pin down the reason: she disapproves of MSG and rather than question the waiters on the subject, thereby putting them in a position where they might lose face by admitting the flavour enhancer is added to the restaurant's soup, she prefers not to order it at all.

> '*No food is really enjoyed unless it is keenly anticipated,*
> *discussed, eaten and then commented upon…*'
> —Lin Yutang, 1935

AN ABSOLUTE lack of food taboos speaks volumes about a culture. The Chinese predilection for eating anything on four legs, except a table, and anything that flies, except a kite, is attributed to having scraped through times of famine and crop failure by applying a dedicated ingenuity to finding nourishment. Although conditions were frequently difficult, it is generally accepted that the Chinese were not so terribly deprived by the land. As Dr K.C. Chang asserts in *Food in Chinese Culture*, 'Poverty and the consequent exhaustive search for resources provide only a favorable environment for culinary inventiveness and cannot be said to be its cause.' His explanation of the Chinese renowned creativity with food is 'the simple reason that food and eating are among things central to the Chinese way of life and part of the Chinese ethos'. The inventiveness of culinary attitude, then, is linked to a more positive approach than a diet of frequent starvation would suggest, which seeks gratification by exploration.

Centuries of keeping an open mind to food sources has shaped an approach to cuisine which is adventurous

A trip to the market, for fresh vegetables, meat or seafood, is still part of many cooks' daily itinerary

and questing. The approach reaches its apex in Hong Kong where, in a dish as simple and audacious as ostrich lightly stir-fried with spring onions and a speckling of sesame seeds, one tastes the fruit of 40 years of rising prosperity and availability of foodstuffs from around the world. Fook Yuen Seafood Restaurant in Causeway Bay first put ostrich on its list of specials, but moved them across to the main menu after just a couple of months when it was clear that its well-off clientele's taste for the bird had gone beyond the experimental; they were partial to the flavour. Palates needing little coaxing to sample new ingredients, pockets lined with the cash to pay for exotic, expensive or simply faddish cuisine, chefs reaching the upper stratosphere of quality and invention to tempt a fickle population spoiled for choice—these are the ingredients of an invigorating food scene.

Some market stalls offer a rich medley of dried mushrooms, pickled vegetables and various spices and seeds

'Cantonese don't eat black rice!' exclaims Mina, shocked at the suggestion that she might order eight treasure sweet pudding, a speciality of Shanghainese vegetarian restaurant Kung Tak Lam. She concedes there is a remote possibility that she might find the dessert palatable, but obviously considers it extremely unlikely. This from a young woman who delights in sharing information about marvellous *dai pai dong* dishes, who in winter goes out for bowls of snake soup when she is feeling a little delicate, and who knows about the claimed health-giving attributes of ingredients such as frog's bladder and dried gecko in the packaged soups sold by Chinese herbal medicine shops. There are limits to the famed adventurousness of the Cantonese palate. The spectrum of food enjoyed by Hong Kong people is doubtless broader than anywhere else on the planet, but, says Karen Joffe of California Entertainment Group, 'Cantonese eat everything, although they tend to eat certain foods always the same way.' Pork lung is only used in soup, for instance. And while some of Joffe's dishes at the group's latest venture, The Noodle Bar, seem Asian to Westerners, they are in fact non-traditional: putting mushrooms, slices of chicken and a green vegetable with udon noodles is not how it's usually done. The traditional Cantonese intolerance of chilli has singlehandedly created a sub-text of Thai and Sichuan cuisines somewhat deficient in authentic potency. Perhaps the vastness of the Cantonese food culture is partially responsible for its tenets and prejudices being taken as gospel. Distilling and teaching how to prepare a vast multitude of grains, vegetables, cereals, herbs, meats, seafood and legumes, and the incredible variety of cooking methods involved, may well have required a dictatorial approach, the legacy of which lingers in accepted, unquestioned eating habits.

———

MORE THAN the lack of taboos (in what is eaten, if not how it's prepared), what makes the Chinese attitude to food unique is its singular integration of food and drink with health, within the context of an ancient philosophy which categorises food as warm or cold (and wet or dry, though these categories are referred to less frequently). Maintaining a state of good health is reliant upon achieving a balance between these qualities, which relate to the fundamental elements of yin and yang. According to *The Hongkong and China Gas Chinese Cookbook*, hailed as one of the most comprehensive compendiums of Chinese cuisine since at least the Chou dynasty, 'The *Yin* has represented the female, negative, dark, cold, wet facets of the world and everything in it; and the *Yang* has represented the contrasting male, positive, bright, hot, dry qualities.'

Customers pause for a quick cup of cool medicinal tea

The Chinese people were among the first to trace the links between good health and food. In the 14th century, dietitians on the mainland were aware of vitamins and their importance in preventing certain diseases. Hu Ssu-hui, imperial dietitian from 1315 to 1330, is thought to be one of the first to express the view that diet alone could, in fact, cure diseases such as beri-beri. *The Imperial Cookery Book of the Mongol Dynasty* counselled: 'Apart from foods which are poisonous in themselves, there are many which should not be eaten together as they do not harmonize and are apt to cause great discomfort and inconvenience.' Chinese believe that illness represents an imbalance in the body. In order to treat disease, a countervailing force must be provided, and that force is often to be found in food, depending on what it represents to the system. Cooling foods are those which are bland, thin and low in calories; heating foods are rich and oily. Cooking methods can intensify, or even change, the category of a food. The coolest form of cooking is cold-water infusion; the hottest is deep-frying. Boiling, however, is regarded as cooling, while stir-frying is medium-heating.

The origins of this folk medicine are obscure, and it has no scientific basis, though it is generally regarded as Hippocratic. ('One must have faith to embark on a course of Chinese preventive or curative treatment,' writes T.C. Lai in *At the Chinese Table*.) Nor is it unique to the Chinese people; according to *The Sociology of Food*, 'versions are widespread today in South and Southeast Asia, China, Africa and in rural/peasant societies of Latin America'. In Hong Kong, one of its more prominent practitioners has been chef Dai Hon-Lung, former executive chef at Conrad International's Golden Leaf Restaurant. He spent much of the 1970s and all of the 1980s away from Hong Kong, working first in Jakarta, then in Singapore and Kuala Lumpur. As he cooked in foreign kitchens, he began a study of Chinese herbal medicine and started incorporating herbs traditionally used for healing into his dishes. He began infusing the Golden Leaf menu with his deeply-felt philosophy in 1992 for which he earned a devoted following. Chef Dai's youthful frame and skin are probably the best possible testimonials to his beliefs, and he was frequently asked by regulars to create personal menus they could follow at home to stay in good health.

Some customers' requests would quash any speculation that the significance of food for good health might be diminishing in the onslaught of modernity. On one occasion, chef Dai prepared a special dinner for a group of seven customers who had asked him to prepare turtle. 'Chinese people believe that turtle can flush toxins, even cancer, from the body,' he explained. The live animal was flown to Hong Kong from a breeding farm in China and from it he prepared soup and two other dishes. The bill for the turtle portion of the meal was HK$20,000.

The ingredients of the Golden Leaf's steamed crab with wine and ginger are combined to enhance blood circulation

'When we're growing up, our parents talk to us about food all the time,' says Mary Wong, eldest of six and a nurse for 16 years before she traded shift work for the more sociable hours of an insurance agent. At the dinner table, Chinese children absorb an almost encyclopaedic body of knowledge on the subject of food and can rattle off, at the drop of a hat, a lecture on the warming/cooling qualities of ingredients and dishes, or suggest a cooling snack to counterbalance the warming effect of, say, a heavily carnivorous session over the barbecue. Not many people, though, consciously choose their dinner based solely on a desire for internal balance.

The enduring importance of the warm/cool food categorisation can be attributed partly to the fact that, as the *Chinese Cookbook* states, 'Every aspect of life in China is governed by the balance between the complementary elements of *Yin* and *Yang*.' There are doubtless other, less spiritual reasons that explain people's adherence to a philosophy that relies on belief, rather than proven scientific fact. 'If pressed, I bet people would say, "I believe, just in case"—it's good insurance,' says Michael Bond, author of *Beyond The Chinese Face*. 'And then there's the fact that "how do you know?" is not a question that's asked often in a hierarchical society.'

The attitude of modern young Chinese women to the multitude of food and behaviour restrictions placed upon them when they become pregnant exemplifies both these attitudes. 'During the first months of my pregnancy, my mother advised me to eat bird's nest so the child will have good skin,' said one mother of two young children. 'I don't know how true it is, but I wanted my baby to look good.' She ate the bird's nest. Papaya will make the baby's skin yellow; watermelon is too cold and shouldn't be eaten by pregnant women; drinking chocolate and coffee will darken the child's skin; eating shellfish will give the baby eczema— these are just some of the food-related restrictions. A pregnant woman's actions are similarly restrained: moving house is inadvisable, as is using a hammer or having a major appliance installed. Should some of these activities be absolutely necessary, the pragmatic Chinese have rituals which will offset the negative effects. 'My colleagues and I used to say that we wouldn't pay attention to such things,' said one woman who works for an international hotel chain. 'But when I was pregnant, I didn't want to take the risk.'

CHINESE TASTE buds are trained at an early age to discern the five categories of taste: sweet, sour, hot, bitter and salty. In *At the Chinese Table*, T.C. Lai explains: 'According to the Chinese, each foodstuff is accompanied by a certain taste which, upon reaching the stomach, directs itself to its designated organ: sweetness enters the spleen, sourness the liver, hotness the lungs, bitterness the heart, and saltiness the kidneys.' Thus neatly explaining the predilection for deer's penis and other supposedly aphrodisiacal elements, despite conservationists' concerns and a decided lack of scientific study to back up the claims.

The appreciation of texture for texture's sake is not easily understood by Westerners, who wonder at the alacrity with which Shanghainese devour cold

jellyfish. The thick strands of this gelatinous, multi-tentacled ocean fish are frequently referred to, not always fondly, as 'rubber bands' by non-Chinese. Asked why the dish is one of his favourites, a Hong Kong-born man of Shanghainese parentage (and culinary preference) looks up, startled. After a long pause, the best explanation he can come up with is that he ate jelly fish as a child. Prodding gently at the tangled mass with his chopsticks, he adds, 'But these should be a little crunchier,' and looks relieved at having at last identified the attraction.

Temple Street restaurateurs attract diners first with a feast for the eyes

---

IN THEIR contribution to *Food in Chinese Culture*, Anderson and Anderson wrote of Hong Kong: 'Everyone from the lowest beggar (looking for scraps) to the highest official knows where to find the best.' The passion play that is the Hong Kong food scene has its roots in the centuries-old culinary traditions that are central to life at and beyond the Chinese table. But the geographic insularity and frenetic pace of the place have added a unique flavour. Mention an unusual dessert consumed in Temple Street Market, or a hole-in-the-wall noodle stall in Aberdeen serving gigantic won ton, or a decrepit bakery-cum-coffee shop renowned for its pineapple buns and most every local resident will not only know exactly what you're talking about, they'll break in and correct your imperfect description of the shop's origins and/or menu. It's no wonder most Chinese restaurateurs rely solely on word of mouth to build their business—people here love to talk about food, sharing tasty morsels of information and storing away choice nuggets for the next time a craving strikes.

GOLDEN LEAF,
CONRAD INTERNATIONAL HONG KONG
Steamed Crab Claws With Wine and Ginger

Fresh crab claws (medium–large)*	12
Water	4 litres
Iced water	2 litres
Marinade:	
Cornflour	2 tsp
Egg whites	4
Sauce:	
Minced ginger	80 g
Shaoxing rice wine	4 tbsp
Salt	1/3 tsp
Chicken stock powder	1 tsp
Cooking oil	2 tbsp
Sugar	1/4 tsp
Water	6 tbsp

Bring water to the boil and blanch the crab claws for 5 minutes. Drain and place the crab claws in the iced water for 5 minutes. (If using frozen crab claws, thaw at room temperature before blanching.) Remove the claws from the shells by lightly tapping them with the flat side of a chopper and set aside. Combine the cornstarch and egg whites, put the crab claws into the mixture and marinate for 5 minutes. Mix the sauce ingredients together and set aside. Remove the claws from the marinade and arrange them on a plate, pour the sauce over them and steam for 8 to 10 minutes. Serve immediately.

* The restaurant uses fresh male green crabs; it is acceptable, and more economical at home, to use frozen crab claws. This recipe is also suitable for lobster tail.

THE NOODLE BAR
Lobster Dumpling Soup

Lobster meat	*250 g*
Coriander, chopped	*1/2 tsp*
Chinese mushrooms, chopped	*3 tbsp*
*Won ton wrappers (5-inch square)**	*12*
Soy sauce	*2 dashes*
Salt	*1/4 tsp*
White pepper	*1/4 tsp*
Chicken broth (stock)	*4 cups*
Chinese egg noodles	*3 servings*

Chop lobster meat and mushroom and mix together with coriander, soy sauce, salt and pepper. Place 1-1/2 teaspoons of the mixture in the centre of a won ton wrapper, raise all sides of the wrapper at the same time, folding the wrapper around the mixture then twist and gently press together the gathered top edge of the won ton to close. Repeat with the remaining wrappers and set aside. Cook the egg noodles in boiling water for 3 to 4 minutes, or until tender, remove, strain and divide amongst 3 soup bowls. Re-boil the water and add the won ton and cook for 4 minutes or until they float. Remove, drain and place on top of the egg noodles. Bring the chicken stock to the boil and add the stock to the bowls of egg noodles and won ton. (Serves 3.)

* Won ton wrappers can be bought fresh from Hong Kong noodle stores or frozen from supermarkets or Chinese delicatessens. If using frozen wrappers, thaw out to room temperature before beginning dumpling preparation.

GOLDEN LEAF,
CONRAD INTERNATIONAL HONG KONG
Braised Diced Vegetable in Soup

Dried black fungus, soaked and finely chopped	40 g
Bamboo shoots (tinned), finely chopped	40 g
Dried straw mushrooms, soaked and chopped	40 g
Dried black mushrooms, soaked and chopped	40 g
Baby sweet corn, fresh (left whole)	40 g
Heart of Shanghai cabbage, cubed	10 pieces
Chicken broth (stock)	3 cups
Corn starch	1 tsp

Poach the fungus, bamboo, straw mushrooms (which have been soaked for 10 to 15 minutes until tender) and black mushrooms in salted boiling water quickly. Remove from the water and set aside. Bring the chicken broth to the boil in a wok or pot, then place the cabbage in the broth and simmer on low heat for 5 to 10 minutes or until the cabbage is almost tender. Add the corn starch, stirring thoroughly and cook until the stock becomes slightly thick. Remove from the heat. In another wok, heat a little vegetable oil and add all the remaining vegetables and stir-fry over medium heat until tender but still slightly crisp. Add the cabbage and stock mixture to the wok and stir thoroughly. Season with salt and pepper to taste.

3

Southern Comfort

'Western dress; Chinese heart,' murmurs a Hong Kong Chinese television producer. He is talking about a colleague, but in that concise, precise description he captures the essence of his birthplace. With its continually re-laid carpet of cloud-clawing buildings and clutter of international designer brands and fast food outlets, Hong Kong confounds the visitor whose expectations have been moulded by its pop culture portrait as a lair of oriental exotica. Yet, the internationalism that on first impression seems to dominate Hong Kong is a thin veneer. Scratch at the surface and you see, hear and, most importantly, taste a Chinese city.

Then again, tagging Hong Kong with a catch-all 'Chinese' label is also overly simplistic. The battle of signs bristling for attention along just about any single block of Wan Chai's Lockhart Road or Kowloon's Nathan Road (a.k.a 'The Golden Mile') are neon signposts to the variegated strands of a diverse society and complex culinary environment there for the tasting. Cantonese, Peking, Shanghai, Chiu Chow, Sichuan and Hunan restaurants are thriving members of a food scene that has a reputation almost as widespread as the logos emblazoned on a *tai-tai*'s handbag. In Hong Kong, the 'ladies who lunch' are spoiled for choice. Conspicuous consumption, hushed discretion, scruffy earthiness, cold minimalism and overblown retro—there is a Chinese restaurant to suit every occasion.

A shopkeeper is sandwiched between cured, flattened geese and clusters of Chinese sausage

Look back 40 or so years and the seeming cohesiveness of Hong Kong's Cantonese bloc crumbles like a fortune cookie. Today's so-called melting-pot generation was not born of one monolithic Chinese population, but rather fragments of many different ethnic groups, each representing a different slice of China. The post-World War II babyboomers and Chuppies (Chinese yuppies) are so well integrated into the local Cantonese culture that schoolchildren visiting a friend's family are often startled to find that the *lingua franca* of the other's home is an incomprehensible Chiu Chow or Hokkien or Fukien dialect.

The Chinese who settled in Hong Kong hailed from all parts of the mainland, from large urban centres as well as remote rural villages. Despite recent strides towards greater cultural unity, much of which can be attributed to powerful advances in mass communication, China remains, by and large, a country of countless regional dialects and unique native customs. In this environment, the concept of a 'melting pot' is unimaginable.

Hong Kong, though, was anything but a typical Chinese town and the definition of 'tradition' was as varied as the ethnic variety of the place. Over time, the colony became home to an amalgamated Chinese population. Newly arrived Chiu Chowese would naturally gravitate towards the community their compatriots had established in Western district. Likewise, the Shanghainese who poured in after 1949 tended to settle in North Point and Castle Peak. But business dealings couldn't be restricted similarly, and neither could relationships. Successive waves of immigration fashioned a bold city, and an even bolder food scene, which has been shaped by the influences of just about every region of China. Not so much melting pot as smorgasbord, the road to diner's heaven is paved with Chiu Chow, Peking, Shanghai and Sichuan restaurants. Eclipsing this profusion of more distant regional tastes is Cantonese—the premiere cuisine of Hong Kong and, for gourmands of many nationalities, one of the world's most rarefied.

> 'Nowhere else are the culinary arts and sciences, empirical and theoretical, and the mundane and the spiritual aspects of food so consciously and conscientiously joined.'
> —Ken Hom, *The Taste of China*

'CANTONESE CUISINE *is* bland—that's its shortcoming and that's the beauty of it.' With this wonderfully ambiguous comment, chef and cookbook writer Willy Mark puts into words the subtlety which sends the cuisine's devotees into

rapture and drives new explorers to distraction. A true understanding requires, he says, an appreciation of the difference between bland and flat. It is rather like being able to discriminate between mineral and distilled water; detecting the soft sweetness in the former and the vaguely metallic weight of the latter. Savouring the distinction is all-important.

This delicacy of interpretation infuses the cuisine. Cantonese chefs seek to enhance, not alter or mask, the taste and fragrance of their ingredients. Freshness is of paramount importance and timing crucial. Cooks speak of being able to 'see' the steam in the food, of 'hearing' in the crackle of the oil or the hiss of the steam when a dish is ready to be whisked from the flame. When tossing the wok, deftly throwing, say, thinly sliced beef in controlled arcs, chefs must sense the precise moment at which to divert the food from fire to plate.

Vegetables in taro nest, prepared by chefs of Golden Leaf Restaurant

Passers-by are invited to sample XO, oyster and other sauces from a stall perfectly situated amongst the seafood restaurants of Lei Yue Mun

Books about Cantonese cuisine invariably quote a popular adage which advises one to be born in Suzhou, which is renowned for its beautiful women; to eat in Guangzhou, because of its fine cooking; to dress in Hangzhou, because of the quality of its silk; and to die in Liuzhou, home of the best coffin wood. Of all the reputations enshrined in this ancient saying, pundits generally consider that of Guangzhou still to be secure. Since some food historians believe that Cantonese cuisine has been famous since the time of the First Emperor of Ch'in (221–206 BC), this is one enduring reputation. And, since Cantonese food actually originated not in Guangzhou, but in Shunde, a town in Guangdong province west of Guangzhou, it is also slightly askew. Shunde was a wealthy place, where the main business was lending money to the farmers. The 19th century, when trade and agriculture flourished, was a particularly well-fed time for a rich populace with a passion for culinary invention. The best of the chefs took their skills to the capital, Guangzhou, and made a lasting impression on the city's flourishing restaurant scene.

Restaurateur Patrick Au has resurrected many of Shunde's superior dishes for his Classic Passion restaurants, which have become the darlings of Hong Kong's prosperous professionals. An excellent wine list comprising French and Chinese selections adds to the appeal, which is built on a menu of astonishing range. Pigeon boiled in soy sauce for an intense smokiness, lightly fried sea perch and salted superior chicken draped with pickled mustard greens are offered alongside Eurasian dishes like oysters in parmesan and spare ribs with strawberry sauce. The menu defies categorisation, instead revelling in the profusion of influences which lent Shunde/Cantonese cuisine such diversity.

Cantonese cuisine owes as much to the incredible fertility of the region as it does to Shunde's deep pockets. 'South China may well cultivate more crops, at least on a commercial scale, than any other comparable region,' wrote E.N. Anderson Jr and Marja Anderson in *Food in Chinese Culture*. Favourable conditions in Guangdong province allow three rice harvests a year; and where water is too deep for rice, but too shallow for fish, crops like taro, lotus root and water chestnut flourish. The 2,000-kilometre-long coastline lends itself to a prosperous fishing industry, while the mainly subtropical climate brings fruitful cultivation of sugar cane, bananas, oranges, lychees and longans.

Guangdong's legendary cuisine is also defined by the adventurousness of its peoples' palates. Living in one of

Chinese food stall by George Chinnery

China's most accessible ports, they were privy to culinary influences, both from other parts of their own country and from foreigners come to trade. Special techniques employed by cooks in Beijing, Suzhou, Yangzhou and Sichuan province were adopted and became an integral part of Cantonese cooking, while the West contributed the art of baking. The result was, and is, a cuisine of incredible, seemingly infinite variety—a trait noted by Royal Navy surgeon Dr Edward Cree, who in 1845 wrote in his journal: 'Keying [Qiying; a friend and relative of Emperor Daoguang] gives a dinner to all the bigwigs, heads of departments, at Hong Kong, at which about 500 different Chinese dishes were produced.' Sadly, Dr Cree neglected to describe even one of the delicacies prepared by Keying's chefs.

'Cantonese is the most sophisticated, most adventurous and most refined of Chinese cuisines.' Puffing on his pipe, Willy Mark smiles mischievously; he's well aware that these are fighting words to passionate fans of Shanghai or Hunan food. There exists the belief that the refinement of their cuisine reflects very nicely on the Hong Kong Cantonese, thank you. A saying in the restaurant trade sums it up: on Kowloon, south of Austin Road, you cook with less salt; north of Austin Road, you use more salt. Austin Road is the symbolic demarcation between Kowloon and the New Territories: between Cantonese and immigrant, in other words.

There is no argument about the breathtaking diversity of Cantonese cuisine. Most restaurant menus are pages and pages long—too long, sniff critics who ask how it is possible to maintain quality when a kitchen is preparing upwards of 200 dishes. There are communication problems, too. Expatriates seeing a luscious dish presented to the next table are often unable to find anything matching its description on the menu because it is listed on the tent card of specials written only in Chinese. Cantonese is a continually evolving cuisine, but the twists and turns of creative trends are often lost on non-Chinese. Unless Westerners speak Cantonese, frequent hotels where bilingual menus are standard or come across a sympathetic waiter, they are doomed to fairly repetitive meals. (Of course, there's no harm in looking and pointing; generally, other diners don't object to being politely asked what they are eating and what they might recommend.) Chefs here face the dual challenges of cut-throat competition and prosperous, demanding diners. It's not enough to serve classics like shark's fin soup, stewed black chicken, roast suckling pig, stewed goose web and snake soup. They must continually create new dishes.

'Hong Kong's beat is faster,' says Robert Y.L. Tam, comparing his hometown experience with the years he spent cooking in Singapore. Keeping up the pace takes stamina: now master chef at the Excelsior hotel, Tam introduces 22 new dishes every three months to the menu at the elegant Yee Tung Heen Cantonese Restaurant. 'We can cook with foods from all over the world because Hong Kong is so energetic and aggressive at importing supplies and using them,' he adds. For inspiration, he consults news clippings, suppliers' information, even the Internet. Whether combing the virtual supermarket or testing a wholesaler's newest product, his defining theme is always healthy food. After a brief flirtation with Chinese nouvelle cuisine in the mid-1980s, diners and chefs settled on the wave of the future: healthier cooking—without sacrificing taste. Customers' awareness of cholesterol, fat and MSG is factored into Tam's menu. Tenderloin beef Chinese-style, for example, used to be slathered with a sauce made from ketchup and water. Chef Tam prepares instead a sauce of celery, tomato and carrot simmered together and he uses his cleaver, instead of MSG, to tenderise the beef. Another dish, fried vermicelli, is tossed in the barest amount of light peanut oil and studded with generous amounts of Japanese enoki mushrooms, chilli and duck. Fresh and preserved vegetables figure heavily in much of Tam's cooking, as in stir-fried garoupa with finely chopped, deep-fried preserved vegetables and a hint of chilli. Healthily cooked dishes, such as steamed scallops, prawns and bean curd in black bean sauce, and steamed chicken, are plentiful.

'I don't like to marinate chicken, because that takes away the natural, essential flavour,' explained chef Dai Hon-Lung, formerly in charge of Conrad International's Golden Leaf Restaurant. Instead, before and during

Hong Kong's hotels are famed for laying on a delectable selection of creative gastronomy in rarefied surroundings

poaching, the bird is soaked in chicken essence. The result is tender and flavourful meat. Fresh crab claw is succulent but cooling, an effect which Dai minimises by steaming the meat with minced ginger and rice wine. Fried, and especially deep-fried, dishes will never be healthy, but no Cantonese restaurateur would dream of leaving them off the menu. However, Dai points out, making sure that cooking oil is the right temperature prevents noodles, for example, from absorbing too much grease. His signature dessert, deep-fried crispy turtle oil with herbs, is coated in a feathery batter and plunged into boiling, top-quality oil. The coating provides a crispy contrast to the black jelly, with no hint of oiliness.

In the expanding quest to cook with health and nutrition always in mind, Hong Kong is little different from the West and many of its Asian neighbours. But there is another trend afoot and it speaks eloquently about a new introspection. A renaissance in art deco-style restaurants, impeccably decked out in etched glass, fringed lamps and dark wood panelling, have been catering to a heightened nostalgia and

Chef Dai applies his in-depth knowledge about the medicinal properties of foods and herbs to the preparation of healthful Cantonese cuisine

subsequent yearning for flavours past. Some attribute this trend to people having sought to re-explore what makes up a unique Hong Kong identity in the run-up to the handover to Chinese sovereignty. On the other hand, there is considerable weight to the argument that the babyboomers are simply, predictably, now of an age and prosperity level to indulge in sensory explorations of their past. Combine these explanations with the rising prominence worldwide of Asians as an economic force and a compelling reason for introspection emerges.

The Dynasty restaurants at the New World Harbour View and New World hotels, one on each side of the harbour, are upmarket retro venues which reel in legions of happy punters with consistently fine home-style Cantonese cooking. Explorations of the past go well beyond the new old-style venues, filtering through to menus otherwise unselfconsciously modern. Seasonal pomelo skin with shrimp sauce appears on the menu at Fook Yuen Seafood Restaurant in Causeway Bay, an evocative reminder of childhood for Mary Wong. 'We were six kids and our parents in a one-room flat, probably measuring about 100 square feet. We didn't have much money; this dish was cheap and my mother made it often.' Its preparation took a week: the skin of the pomelo must be burned, to remove the waxy exterior, then soaked and squeezed and soaked again, so that the bitterness leeches away, then it is stewed for a very long time. Fook Yuen's version has the consistency of mashed taro or potato, mounds of it swimming in a rich shrimp sauce. The taste is unusual, difficult to place and delicious.

———••———

'I WANTED to write my Master's thesis on soup,' says Cheng Sea-Ling, 'but then the first two families I stayed with didn't make it—not once! I was so shocked!' The Hong Kong University anthropology student spent a week with each of six families of varying economic and social levels, observing their eating patterns. She found that the 'prevalence of soup is somewhat mythical today, despite its avowed importance'. 'We may not have it every day,' she concluded, 'but we believe in it.' Faced with the soup delinquency, she changed her dissertation subject to the broader 'Diversity of Food in Hong Kong Culture'.

Chinese cuisine lays claim to literally hundreds of soup recipes and a correspondingly rich variety of cooking methods. 'There are two ways of using heat in Chinese cooking: direct fire and hidden heat,' explains Robert Tam. Stir-frying, the most obvious example of the former, makes food extremely hot, though yin/yang specialists caution that this is not necessarily good for the health. 'Hidden heat takes time,' Tam continues. 'The heat finally reaches to the heart of the food to release the essence, and the essence is the most important thing.' Double-boiling, also called indirect steaming, is the Chinese cook's prime means of coaxing ingredients to relinquish their essence. As in its closest Western approximation, the *bain-marie* or double-boiler, food is not in direct contact with the heat source. Instead, it is placed in a closed container which in turn sits inside another tightly closed container of boiling water. Double-boiling doesn't necessarily take any longer than regular boiling. It is most prominently used in soups. Tam prepares a richly flavourful double-boiled soup with Chinese ham, cabbage and fish maw. The cooking method introduces a robustness which is not a quality he wants for the clear broth of his bean curd soup with fresh crab meat and conpoy.

Cheng's experience notwithstanding, soup is extremely prominent in the Cantonese diet. 'Every day, a Cantonese must have soup,' says one food critic, who links the tradition to centuries past when well-bred eating habits centred on eating very small amounts of meat, fish and vegetables. Soup was thus an important source of nutrition and liquid. 'The higher the class,' Cheng relates, 'the less the people eat the contents of the soup. The very wealthy drink only the broth.'

'My grandmother, who was a Western-trained doctor, insisted on soup at both lunch and dinner,' recalls journalist Patricia Chew. 'She made it from scratch, with bones, root vegetables and Chinese herbs.' Medicinal and

Hemmed in by tall commercial towers and facing increasing competition from modern supermarkets, street markets still attract legions of customers who prefer buying meat, seafood and produce open-air, rather than vacuum-packed

herbal ingredients have always been integral to recipes, and soups are regarded as keepers of one's vitality and health. Shark's fin soup, made from the dried cartilage of, most popularly, the fins of hammerhead and tiger sharks, is credited with being an excellent tonic for the skin. (The plight of the sharks, which are usually tossed back into the sea only to suffer a slow, agonising death once the all-important fin has been lopped off, does not make much of an impact on the soup's popularity.)

For most Hong Kong people, a home-cooked meal still begins with soup. Restaurant-goers, however, are tending to shun not only soup (except for expensive shark's fin and bird's nest), but often rice as well. 'It's a status thing,' says Chew exasperatedly, though she grants that one particular shifting social pattern may be more responsible for soup's diminishing importance than Hong Kong's tendency towards conspicuous consumption. 'All Chinese amahs knew how to make hundreds of soups,' she points out. 'They knew the seasonal soups, which were best for certain health conditions. When you interviewed them, you always asked them about soups. Now that so many people have Filipino maids, there isn't the same emphasis on traditional Chinese cooking.'

THE WAITER places the platter on the table, conversation pauses, and the customers draw breath for a collective 'waaahh' of appreciation. Each dish served is given the once-over, but the strongest response at Fook Yuen Seafood Restaurant is heard when the fish arrives. The red garoupa has been cooked in typical Cantonese fashion; plucked live from a tank in the kitchen to be killed, cleaned and rubbed with salt, its skin slashed twice on each side, then steamed whole with shavings of ginger, poured over with spoonfuls of boiling chicken stock and scattered with sprigs of spring onion. The flesh is tender and yielding, and falls off the skeleton without falling apart. It is the quintessential expression of the clearness, freshness and blandness of Cantonese cuisine.

'Steaming is a difficult skill; you can only learn from experience.' As the chef overseeing the kitchen of Yü, a restaurant named for the lofty fish (yú means 'fish' in Cantonese), Ivan Man has clocked up enough hours over steamer and wok to gauge exactly how long a Maori or red garoupa should be cooked. Not that he's complacent, mind. A one-kilogram fish usually requires ten minutes of steaming, but its shape must be taken into account. Shave two minutes off that time for a thin fish; add a little for a chubby one. Even with these guidelines, this is a dish to be hovered over: seconds make a difference.

Something most of the customers at the seafood-inspired restaurant in the Regent hotel know intimately.

Cooks at Yü pan-fry, grill, steam or poach, on command. They use Chinese or Western spices and technique, as preferred, on the array of whole fish. They will net the customer's choice of spiny lobster, green crab, baby abalone or jumping shrimp and cook the catch in the 70-litre cauldron of simmering bouillon that's made fresh every day for the open kitchen. Still, with all this expertise on hand, a customer will occasionally dismiss the usual options and request that a fish be deep-fried or laced with conflicting spices. 'We suggest they try it our way,' says restaurant manager Louis Chan, 'but if they insist, we'll do it.' Waiters are well versed in the qualities of the fish and shellfish available on the night and make informed recommendations, but sometimes they must bow to customers willing to pay between HK$760 and $2,000 a kilogram.

The exceptional steps, not to mention expense, taken to ensure the absolute cleanliness and freshness of the seafood at Yü might have been dismissed as just another sample of conspicuous innovation had it not been for an outbreak of cholera that struck Hong Kong around the time the restaurant opened. Health inspectors traced the bacteria to restaurants which filled their tanks of live seafood with water taken directly from the treacherously polluted 'Fragrant Harbour'. New regulations of storage were hastily imposed, but Hong Kong's obsession with seafood was seriously jolted. In the midst of this health scare, Yü's US$1 million, 10-tonne curved bubble-wall fish tanks and high-tech water purification system—and especially the timely fact that none of the imported fish or shellfish ever touch local water—received more than the usual fanfare of publicity accorded a bright new star in Hong Kong's restaurant constellation.

———

'THERE USED to be over 10,000 fishing families here,' says resident, Mr Lai. 'Now there are 400, at the most.' The piers of Aberdeen are bubbling with morning activity. The commercial fleets are unloading the night's catch, and vans from seafood wholesalers and major restaurant chains are lining up to load. Garoupa, snapper, monkfish of all colours and sizes thrash about in holding tanks. Busy hands scoop them out and weigh them on Chinese scales, then they're passed into huge barrels aboard the vans, amid shouts and curses from the vendors.

'My eldest daughter is 17,' says Mrs Lai. 'She doesn't like to tell her friends she lives on a boat. She spends all her money on fashion magazines.' When the teenager and her siblings were younger, their day began before dawn when their father cast anchor and directed their motorised junk out into the South China Sea. Fishing is a tough business and most of the old-style junks have hung up their nets in the face of impossible competition from large commercial fleets armed with state-of-the-art radar. Now, when many of their fellow Tanka families have abandoned their nomadic, seafaring lifestyle, the Lais have managed to make their boat pay by renting it out to film and television companies. They will have brunch today, do some shopping on shore (the selection is so much better than on the sampan shops that cruise by daily), then pick up their children from school for a few hours' 'fishing' under the watchful lens of an Australian camera crew.

Seafood is such a passion for Cantonese that their expression for a refined palate literally means 'to have pointy teeth and a sharp mouth'. To a Hong Kong seafood buff, the concept of frozen fish is as unthinkable as canned corn beef would be to an Argentinian rancher. The Cantonese word for seafood is *hoi sin*, or 'fresh offerings from the sea', which is why fish tanks feature prominently at any self-respecting seafood restaurant. Urban street markets feed the passion, with buckets of live fish, shrimp and crabs. When the capture of a record 250-kilogram garoupa made newspaper headlines, a fierce debate arose between gourmands and conservationists about the future of the denizen of the deep. The restaurant that shelled out HK$120,000 for the prize won the battle, but before the fish became guest of honour at a banquet, Buddhist monks conducted prayers and burned incense to bless its journey to the next world.

A seafood lunch or dinner on Lamma Island is practically a ritual for a largely (though not entirely)

Fishermen at Aberdeen, 1946

Simple yet subtle: steamed fish is the quintessential Cantonese dish

expatriate crowd, especially those working in the financial sector, who commandeer their company junk whenever a visiting executive provides the excuse. Gripping plastic bags filled with beer, wine, potato chips and pretzels, crowds of hearty Lamma-goers board their boats at Queen's Pier every Saturday and Sunday and set a course for Sok Kwu Wan, a tiny village tucked into a small bay lively with fishing boats and fish-farm rafts. Beyond the row of restaurants built out over the waterfront is an atmospheric temple to Tin Hau (the fisherman's patron goddess) and an easygoing trail across the hills to the small town of Yung Shue Wan. Few visitors come for the hiking. Seafood officionados also seek out the one busy restaurant on Po Toi, which is an hour south of Hong Kong Island by public ferry.

Hong Kong's love affair with seafood has been affected by the short-lived cholera episode and ongoing qualms about growing pollution in its waters and beyond. Not that you'd know it on a spring evening at Lei Yue Mun in East Kowloon or Sai Kung in the New Territories, or Sunday lunchtime at Sok Kwu Wan village anytime in the year. Walking along the waterfront at Lei Yue Mun or Sai Kung whets the appetite, with vendors crying out the price per catty of lobster, jellyfish, shrimp, elephant clams, conch, squid, eel, octopus, mussels, baby oysters, garoupa and crab in the tanks at their feet. Your purchase is scooped up in a net, bagged and ready to be cooked by one of the ready and willing cooks in the seafood restaurants across the narrow street. It is a good idea to have some knowledge of local prices and to compare one store from another before settling down to savour your catch, as prices are sometimes reported to be inflated, particularly at Lei Yue Mun.

Groups disembarking a company junk at Sok Kwu Wan on a slow day are ambushed by restaurateurs trying to lure them from their reserved tables with offers like 'We'll cook you a garoupa for half their price!' No matter where they end up, nine times out of ten the diners will soon be plucking with their chopsticks at platefuls of deep-fried squid, parboiled or salt and pepper shrimp, stir-fried Chinese cabbage, steamed garoupa, fried mussels, chicken in lemon sauce and fried rice. The only surprise is the seasonal vegetable. Which suits this crowd just fine: they're after an inexpensive, well-cooked meal and reasonably priced beer or Portuguese wine in bucolic surroundings and that's what they get on the waterfront, complete with fed-up villagers who shriek vitriol if a camera lens is pointed their way as they row out to the fish farms. The competition for customers has leeched into the area of restaurant names: there are two Lamma

Sampans bobbing in the harbour are reminiscent of Hong Kong's early existence as a primarily fishing community

Hilton restaurants. Legend has it that years ago one of the venues (there is a real dispute among locals as to which one) mistakenly charged HK$5 for a bowl of rice instead of the customary 50 cents. The recipient examined the bill and cried, 'Hey, this is more expensive than the Hilton hotel!' The name stuck (twice, apparently), and the Lamma Hilton now competes with the Lamma Mandarin, Lamma Conrad et al.

Back in Aberdeen, Mr and Mrs Lai are met at the pier by their children. The youngest boy busies himself with the box of dim sum his parents have brought back from the tea house. His father pulls out his mobile phone and confirms arrangements with the film crew. Replacing the phone in his pocket he has a brief conversation with his wife. She nods and heads over to the market. 'We have to buy a few fish,' explains Mr Lai. 'They want us to cook fish on board, but the current is not right and we may come up empty-handed.' The boy nods and chews loudly on a pork bun. His father smiles broadly. 'When they pay you to go out there, you can't disappoint them.'

A cook in the Peninsula hotel's Chinese kitchen lowers a skewered bird into the barrel-shaped roasting oven

THE SKILLS of the Cantonese chef must encompass steaming, stir- and pan-frying, boiling, baking, roasting, grilling and deep-frying. In the old days, to learn those techniques budding apprentices had to convince a series of established chefs that they were worthy. Even then, says Ho Pui-Yuen, executive chef at the Peninsula hotel, 'Some of the old masters wouldn't teach everything. You had to learn by watching and experimenting.' By most accounts, these older chefs were an irascible bunch. The Excelsior's Tam took raps on the head from one ladle-wielding chef; and, along with fetching and chopping, his duties included washing his master's underwear. Tam hasn't taken a utensil to any of the several apprentices who have studied under him for more than a decade, and they certainly are not responsible for doing his laundry. 'Even so,' he says, 'it's still very difficult for juniors. Tempers flare in the kitchen and if anything goes wrong, they get the blame.'

French cuisine has the Cordon Bleu Cooking School in Paris; in New York there's the New York Restaurant School. Chinese chefs learn on the job. Hong Kong's Haking Wong Technical Institute has offered courses in Western food preparation since 1977, but a Chinese cooking course wasn't introduced until 1991—and then in the face of great resistance. The first year, students worked in a Jockey Club kitchen in Sha Tin; by the next year, the school had its own Chinese kitchen. 'I was told it would fail, simply because of how the Chinese kitchen is run,' recalls Mrs Varney, head of the Department of Hotel-keeping and Tourism Studies, which sees some 330 food course students graduate every year. They still join the apprentice system, but they're able to progress up the rungs faster.

The traditional Chinese kitchen is a law unto itself. Joining one is like joining a family, with all the hierarchical strictness and demands on loyalty that that implies. The roles of the kitchen staff are rigidly compartmentalised, so there are more grades of employee than in the Western kitchen: chopper, wok cook, steamer cook, abalone cook, for instance. Young apprentices can spend years cleaning and chopping vegetables, before they're allowed to stir-fry a dish. In this environment, the chef is all-powerful. If he becomes dissatisfied and leaves his job, his entire team will go with him. Some restaurants cannot recover from this disaster—everyone in the industry knows at least one business that had its back broken by the departure, not only of the kitchen team, but the entire wait staff, who also usually operate as a single unit. But in the mid-1980s, the system began to bend, ever so slightly, as the international hotels began operating their own Chinese restaurants, as opposed to simply renting the space. By employing their customary Western approaches to hiring and training, by arranging for chefs to work overseas and by encouraging a little personal celebrity, the hotels gradually introduced some flexibility to a famously rigid system.

When he was 17 years old, chef Ho spent half a year at the side of his noodle master. It's an experience he recalls with a wince. 'We used a manual system,' he explains. 'I would put the flour in a large basin for sifting, then sit and bounce on a long bamboo chute, half of which was pressing down on the sieve. I was a thin boy—my bottom was sore for six months!' He apprenticed with a

Wok ranges, with knee-level levers to control the intensity of the flames, are ideal for the rapid cooking styles favoured in Cantonese cuisine

baker, too, then learned roasting and barbecue techniques in his grandfather's restaurant, helping to prepare a daily batch of 50 to 60 ducks and up to 50 suckling pigs if the day's bookings included a wedding banquet. But having to get up at 2am, day in and day out, to learn the art of dim sum (dím sàm) making made him miserable, and despite his grandfather's anger, he dropped that pursuit and applied himself in the main kitchen. Remembering the drawbacks of the apprentice system, which is still very much in practice today, he sighs: 'It's a Chinese characteristic, to be very secretive. Sometimes, if I had to ask my master a question, he would hit me.' Long a master of his own, high-profile Spring Moon kitchen, chef Ho prefers explanation to smacking; he takes his young apprentices through the cooking processes step by step, so that they understand the theory as well as the action.

CHONG FAT Restaurant in Kowloon City may not look the part, but it is Hong Kong's version of the Polo Lounge. Late most nights, stars big and small of the Hong Kong film and television industry descend on its humble rooms to sit on hard-backed chairs and plant their elbows on tiny wooden tables. They rest their heels on a floor that could use a more thorough mopping and order dishes of cold crab and fish, oyster omelette and dishes of preserved vegetable to spoon into bowls of thin congee. Too much traffic, customers and waiters alike, treads from the dining room to the small open kitchen by the entrance to the dozens of small tanks outside where various shellfish are kept in salt water. The menu is Chiu Chow and it is the latest craze.

Think of Guangdong as a Chinese Switzerland: within its boundaries exist dozens of townships and prefectures, many of which possess distinctive dialects and cuisines. Within the Cantonese subgroups, Chiu Chow (also known as Chaozhou) is by far the best known and the most noticeable. Chiu Chowese originated in the eastern port of Shantou, on the Han River delta. Descendants of immigrants from the Central Plains, their cuisine has been shaped as much by their Han Chinese roots and the habits of the Fukienese (who emphasise food's natural flavour) to the north as by the cooking of Guangdong. Chiu Chow immigrants came to Hong Kong as day labourers on the wharfs. In the hospitable economic environment of a booming seaport, many of these industrious people prospered and amongst today's wealthy echelon are many families of Chiu Chow extraction.

'Hearty' is the word most often used to describe Chiu Chow cuisine—but this should not imply a lack of subtlety. Chiu Chow chefs rival Cantonese in producing elegant shark's fin and bird's nest dishes. In comparison to Cantonese, Chiu Chow flavours are more concentrated and forceful; preserved and salted foods feature prominently. 'Chiu Chow food uses flavourful ingredients such as Chinese celery and green garlic buds,' says Fung Hoi-Chun, executive chef of the Regal Chiuchow Restaurant. 'Dishes are often simmered for a long time, so that intense flavours are released and absorbed.' According to Fung, the four major characteristics which add up to 'Chiu Chow style' are seafood skills (steamed, cold lobster and crab are specialities), a prominence of vegetable dishes (though not vegetarian, since ribs and other bones are simmered with the ingredients and removed just before serving), sauces, and an unusual emphasis on desserts.

Time was when a big spoonful of pure lard added the desired richness to Chiu Chow shark's fin soup. Both the fat and the seafood are the subject of bad press, but only the former has fallen victim to shifting tastes. Chefs cater to health

Regal Chiuchow Restaurant specialities include cold crab, 'golden guava' egg-white wrapped chicken dumplings (top left) and bird's nest dumplings

concerns by banishing lard from their kitchens and reducing the soup base, made from chicken, Yunnan ham, spare ribs and chicken oil, with longer boiling to achieve the desired thickness.

'Chiu Chow cuisine has the widest variety of desserts of any regional cuisine,' says chef Fung. The ingredients, too, go well beyond the typical red and green beans that are the base of so many Chinese desserts. Root vegetables like taro and pumpkin are used, and the methods of preparation include mashing, mincing, frying and braising. The results range from sweet soups to puddings and dumplings. One popular dessert is made by slowly cooking ginko nuts with sugar until it melts, creating a soft, chewy peanut brittle; another involves mincing taro, then frying it with sugar and ginko nuts until a thin pudding forms. The breadth of desserts is due entirely to the traditions surrounding the Chiu Chow wedding banquet. 'They always start with a sweet dish, to bring luck,' explains chef Fung. 'Usually, two sweet courses are interspersed with the savoury, and there is, of course, dessert to finish.' This concentration of festive sweets is not carried on outside the region, but on chef Fung's menu there is a choice of 13 desserts.

Some traditional dishes are time-consuming to prepare. To make deep-fried chive dumplings, for example, one must pound the chives until a juice is formed; the liquid goes into the wrapping. For this reason, and because lard is an essential ingredient, the dumplings are not on the Regal menu (though they can be ordered in advance). Fortunately, Chiu Chow spring rolls, with taro in the filling, and steamed Chiu Chow dumplings are still a dim sum staple. The latter are made with fragrant ingredients like peanuts, Chinese celery and dried shrimps, and are especially potent compared to the Cantonese version.

Sauces are the most visible distinction of the cuisine. Cold sliced spicy goose is served with a small dish of chopped garlic in clear vinegar. Swirl the entire slice of meat in the liquid and the vinegar will overwhelm its tender smokiness—dip only the strip of goose edged by skin and the slight oiliness is pleasantly cut by the sauce. One of the most sublime marriages of sauce and seafood can be experienced at Harbour City Chiuchow Restaurant in Causeway Bay. In an open kitchen, surrounded by hanging goose, lobster and crab and presiding over vats of gravy and other sauces, a chef steams a thick steak of silver cod to perfection and serves it cold alongside a dish of natural fermented bean sauce. Dipping moist, tender pieces of fish into the sauce gives

Chilled crab hanging in a restaurant window are silent clues that the venue specialises in Chiu Chow cuisine

it a gorgeously piquant saltiness. Fried and deep-fried dishes come with a sweet sauce made with sugar and malt syrup, while 'lucky oil', made from kumquat, sugar and spices, is designed for dipping squid. The influences of Thai and Vietnamese cuisine are tasted in the prevalence of fish sauce in Chiu Chow cooking.

'This is very authentic Chiu Chow food,' says Willy Mark, of what looks like a codfish ball on the Harbour City Chiuchow menu, but is called deep-fried sea moss. The black strands visible in the dish are described as 'hair vegetable', actually known as dried hairweed, which is grown in the semi-desert land of Inner Mongolia but is botanically an algae similar to seaweed. Covered in a light batter and deep-fried, it is dunked in a sweet, cloying black sauce.

Until recently, Chiu Chow restaurants occupied a very narrow spectrum in Hong Kong's food scene. Public relations executive Amy Yeung, whose father was

Chiu Chowese and her mother Cantonese, remembers eating her first Chiu Chow meal when she was eight. 'Then, there were a lot of home-cooking restaurants on the upper floors of buildings in Sheung Wan. My uncle took around 10 of us to a family's home. They'd laid out two tables and we ate dishes that had been pre-ordered.' She smiles broadly, recalling the harsh fluorescent lighting of the sitting room and vague impressions of food. In the 1980s, her family frequented the long-gone Parliament Restaurant in Causeway Bay, and the Far East Chiu Chow Restaurant, still going strong in Central. 'Usually, we'd order goose, jellied blood, kale, thick sliced beef in sauce, pork tripe soup and oyster cakes,' she says.

There has been a softening of the Chiu Chow heartiness in the past two decades. The cuisine has gone upmarket, and smoothing out its robust tastes makes it more palatable to a wider audience. But there's more behind the transition than marketing. 'The characteristics of the traditional cuisine were shaped by the livelihood of the people,' explains chef Fung. 'The people used to be very poor; they could have maybe just two dishes with their rice. So those dishes needed to be very flavourful, to be satisfying. It's tied to economics—as the people become wealthier, the cuisine changes.' A chef with a deep, quiet enthusiasm for his native cuisine, Fung views the trend positively.

Some Western observers have dubbed the Chiu Chowese the Sicilians of China, because of their fondness for late-night dining. The truth of this claim can be seen in a leisurely nocturnal stroll along the back streets of Causeway Bay or the alleys of Sheung Wan. But not for long—redevelopment in Sheung Wan is forcing the tiny clutch of ancient Chiu Chow *dai pai dong* to move or close. There was a sense of history vanishing when, with the bulldozers and pile drivers closing in, Tau Kee Restaurant closed in February 1997 after some 70 years in business. Until its final hour, woks in the tiny, low-ceilinged basement venue, totally lacking in atmosphere but as comfortable as a well-worn shoe, were kept busy preparing platter after platter of famous Chiu Chow chicken (marinated boneless chicken bordered by deep-fried *jàn jyù yihp*, or pearl leaves), fried tofu, sliced beef slathered with rich, peppery gravy and Chiu Chow fried rice. If there is any consolation to be found in the ending of this era, it is in the fact that Tau Kee's legions of fans will not be spoiled for choice when next they seek Chiu Chow food.

———

'GOOD HAKKA food is only found in the home nowadays,' laments one local newspaper food critic. As Chiu Chow restaurants rise in popularity, Hakka cuisine is experiencing a notable decline. The Hakka roots in Hong Kong predate many of the Chiu Chow immigrants, but their origins lie not in Guangzhou but in the North Central Plains of China. 'Hakka' literally means 'a guest who has made his home here'. The Hakka people are nomadic clans who migrated to the east and southeast of China and their communities are now found along the southern coast and onward to the Southeast Asian peninsula and Indonesia.

Many of the early Chinese immigrants who settled in those countries were of Hakka origin, a fact not lost in the local version of Chinese food. Over the years, Hakka cuisine picked up certain Cantonese aspects while maintaining its northern roots. It is most famous for its rich, salted-down flavours. Baked salt chicken, pork with preserved cabbage and a variety of offal dishes are typical. Hakka bean curd, which is steamed with minced shrimp paste stuffing, is renowned. Often called the ultimate comfort food, this dish is one of the most popular. Years ago, there were quite a few Hakka restaurants in Hong Kong. Their numbers have dwindled, and there remain only scattered venues, though some Cantonese restaurants, like Chau's Restaurant in Kowloon and any of the four Classic Passion outlets, serve Hakka selections. Ke Du Seafood Restaurant in Times Square has gained a small following, but devotees generally travel to the New Territories, to Yuen Long and the Dai Foon Hay Restaurant, where the enduring Hakka presence in the nearby villages and new towns ensures a tasty degree of authenticity.

'WITH THIS restaurant, we created something that hadn't existed in Cantonese restaurants before.' Patrick Leung managed the Regent hotel's award-winning Lai Ching Heen when it opened ten years ago; in 1989 he emigrated to Florida ('Portion size really counts there—people eat so much!'), but in mid-1995 he returned to Hong Kong and stepped back into his old job. He immediately noted that his customers were drinking more wine and that they were as interested in food presentation and restaurant ambience as they were in the food quality— heaven help the waiter who neglected to offer a regular diner all five choices of chilli sauce!

Other regional Chinese cuisines will always experience the ebb and flow of fickle popularity, but Cantonese cuisine reigns in Hong Kong. The spectrum of venues has expanded dramatically; those commanding high prices must complement the talents of their chefs with tasteful surroundings. That Cantonese cuisine is now subject to the tastes and whims of a discriminating public adds depth to an already vibrant dining scene.

Lai Ching Heen blends the subtleties of Cantonese tastes with the artistry of Western presentation

The understated elegance of Lai Ching Heen is measured with a knowing eye, and the achievements of chef Cheung Kam-chuen are known in detail. However, if standards are high, it is a little amusing to find that the customer does not always respond in kind. Jade table settings are a much-publicised feature of Lai Ching Heen, and it sometimes happens that the jade napkin ring, carved fish chopstick stand, or ivory and silver chopsticks somehow go missing during the course of a meal—which is why one staffer is charged with 'jade patrol' each meal time. In the ensuing discreet conversation between staff and diner, the latter always denies responsibility, the former gently and unaccusingly advises the customer that the waiter must shoulder the financial burden of the loss and, a few minutes later, the jade pieces are back where they belong and nothing more is said.

CHEF FUNG HOI CHUN,
REGAL CHIUCHOW RESTAURANT
Chicken With *Chin Jiu* Sauce

Chicken, boned*	1/2
Pearl leaves**	100 g
Sichuan peppercorns, crushed	2-1/2 tsp
Sesame oil	a few drops
Vegetable oil	1 cup
Chicken stock	2 tbsp
Fish sauce, bottled	1/2 tsp
Cornstarch, mixed with water	1 tsp
Dark soy sauce	2 tsp
Shaoxing rice wine	1 tsp

Cut the chicken into bite-sized pieces, place in a bowl and mix in 1 teaspoon of the soy sauce and set aside. In another bowl mix together the crushed peppercorns, remaining soy sauce, rice wine, sesame oil, fish sauce and cornstarch and set aside. Heat a cup of oil in a wok until very hot, add the chin jiu leaves and stir-fry for about 30 seconds until crisp, then remove from the oil with a wire skimmer. Arrange the leaves around a serving plate, leaving the centre free for the chicken.

Drain off about half of the hot oil from the wok, re-heat if necessary and add the chicken, stir-frying over high heat until tender (about 2 minutes). Drain the chicken into a wire skimmer placed over a pot to catch the oil. Return the chicken to the wok, add the chicken stock and peppercorn mixture and stir fry over medium to high heat until well combined (about 1 minute). Spoon the chicken into the centre of the serving plate and serve immediately.

*   Executive chef Fung recommends using fresh chicken purchased from the market and boned at home for a superior flavour.
**   Pearl leaves (*jàn jyù yihp*) are a popular Chiu Chow vegetable resembling basil leaves in appearance, but not flavour.

YÜ, THE REGENT HONG KONG
Deep-fried Squid With Lemon Pepper

Squid (prepared rings)	400 g
Lemon pepper, bottled	2 tsp
Batter:	
Cornflour	250 g
Plain flour	125 g
Beer (small bottle)	1-1/2 bottles
Baking powder	2 tsp
Vegetable oil	1/3 cup
Lemon pepper, extra	to taste

Prepare the batter 24 hours ahead. Mix all the ingredients together (except the lemon pepper) in a bowl, cover and refrigerate. To prepare the squid, cut away the innards and legs, leaving only the main body of the squid, and wash thoroughly. Cut the squid into 1 cm-wide strips, cutting across the body to produce rings (as in the usual preparation for calamari). Remove the batter mixture from the refrigerator and add enough water to thin out the mixture to the approximate consistency of pancake batter. Add the lemon pepper and stir thoroughly. Add the prepared squid to the batter and mix well to cover all the squid. Heat the oil in a wok until smoking and add the squid, draining the excess batter from the squid rings before lowering into the oil. Deep-fry the squid until golden brown. Remove with a slotted spoon and drain on absorbent paper. Place on a serving dish and sprinkle with the extra lemon pepper, to taste.

SPRING MOON RESTAURANT, THE PENINSULA, HONG KONG
Fillet of Pork With Cabbage and Soya Bean

Pork fillet	300 g
Head cabbage (Western-style), chopped	1 cup
Yellow soya bean paste (bottled)	1 tbsp
Bouillon (chicken)	3 tbsp
Garlic, finely diced	1 tbsp
Cornflour	1/2 tsp
Water, to mix with cornflour	2 tbsp
Salt	1/2 tsp
Sugar	1 tsp
Chicken stock powder	1/2 tsp
Rice wine	1 tbsp
Oyster sauce (bottled)	1 tsp
Peanut oil	2-1/2 tbsp
Meat tenderiser	dash

Slice the pork fillet finely (into strips about 5cm x 1cm) and place in a small mixing bowl. Add a few dashes of cornflour and water and powdered meat tenderiser and let stand for about half an hour. Trim and wash the cabbage, cut into fine strips and set aside. Heat the peanut oil over high heat in a wok and stir-fry the pork over medium heat for about 45 seconds, then remove with a slotted spoon and set aside. Add the garlic to the hot wok with a little extra oil, if necessary, and stir-fry briefly. Add the cabbage and stir-fry for about 40 seconds, remove with a slotted spoon and set aside. Now add to the wok the bouillon, soya bean paste, salt, sugar, oyster sauce, rice wine, pork and cabbage. Mix together, cover the wok with a lid, lower the heat to medium and cook for about 45 seconds. Add the cornflour, which first must be mixed with the 2 tablespoons of water, and cook the mixture for a little longer until the sauce thickens slightly. Serve immediately.

會總夜城天

獎酒 京菜 京

PEKING RESTAURANT

行金寶珠

英雄難與命爭俠

四老應雙堂相命

化神

PALMISTRY

新京城 卡拉OK 娛樂城

4

Elsewhere On the Culinary Compass

'The biggest change in Hong Kong's Shanghainese food occurred a few years after the 1967 riots.' Charles Y.K. Sun's contention gives one pause. Local gourmands are well aware that the food culture grew exponentially after 1949, when Mao Zedong's victory over the Nationalists sent thousands hurtling southward to apolitical Hong Kong. Northern manufacturers, industrialists and labourers brought their money, their skills and their culinary customs. The restaurant scene rapidly reflected the regional diversification, although it would be a few years before the newcomers found much of a following among the Cantonese, many of whom felt frankly threatened by this northern influx and were disinclined to patronise restaurants where their dialect was often neither spoken nor understood.

The culinary significance of the 1967 troubles (a status quo-threatening spillover of the Cultural Revolution then under way on the mainland) is not nearly as dramatic as the epicurean eruption of the 1950s. But its effects are still felt today and, as in that earlier period, the Shanghainese are credited with being the instruments of change. Many members of that community left Hong Kong after the riots and lived in Europe and North America for several years before returning to settle, yet again, in the territory. They brought with them a

After Cantonese, northern cuisine is one of the most popular in Hong Kong

taste for healthier food; a preference which they communicated effectively to restaurateurs. 'Actually, the riots helped improve Shanghainese food in Hong Kong— that was when we stopped using lard and switched to vegetable oil,' says Sun, managing director of Lao Ching Hing, a popular Shanghainese restaurant which is also one of Hong Kong's oldest.

'It was a shocking step at the time,' confers Pierre Tang, Maxim's senior manager of sales and public relations, who remembers the restaurant group making the same change, a move partly prompted by tourists, whose curiosity about the oil used in Hong Kong's kitchens was so persistent that restaurateurs must have wondered whether travellers to the region were being issued with a lard warning.

The kaleidoscope of Hong Kong's dining environment took on new colour and texture during that all-important post-war period. Shanghai and Peking venues began to make their mark; likewise, though to a lesser extent, Sichuan and Hunan. In the ensuing years, acceptance of

Peking duck, its crisp skin defly removed with a cleaver, is a showpiece at Peking Garden

the first two cuisines has matured to the point where they may be savoured in all manner of surroundings, from earthy to ritzy. Either of the 369 Shanghai restaurants fit the down-to-earth bill, with their dreary interiors and wonderful chicken in wine sauce, fiery mama's bean curd and plump dumplings. Whereas, finer ambience can be had in Shanghai Shanghai in the Ritz-Carlton hotel, with its carefully crafted art-deco tone, or Peking Garden, where white-gloved waiters relieve Peking ducks of their crispy skin and a showy noodlemaster performs dough-to-spaghetti magic every night. Lovers of Sichuan food, however, are a disappointed lot for lack of a range of venues, and there exists only a few Hunan restaurants. Hong Kong's image as the sublime evocation of all things right and delicious in Chinese cuisine is missing a few pieces.

——·——

APRIL IN Paris turns a young man's fancy to love; September in Hong Kong does the same, although the object of desire—for all sexes—is the Shanghai freshwater hairy crab. Around the time of the Mid-Autumn Festival, live crabs, trussed in green straw, are displayed outside restaurants which compete fiercely to serve up the first batch, much in the way wine stores jockey to sell the first bottles of Beaujolais Nouveau. Full-page advertisements herald the news, and some restaurants drape their entrances with flaming red banners to signal to the world that hairy crab, steamed in rice wine, is theirs to enjoy in return for crossing the restaurateur's palm with hundreds of Hong Kong dollars.

It is often argued that there is no such thing as Shanghainese cuisine. Even experts' explanations can be confusing and convoluted. In the Lao Ching Hing menu, Charles Sun writes: 'Shanghai cuisine is popularly known as "Hu" cuisine, which is a collection of a variety of Jiang-Zhe [Jiangsu] food.' In conversation, he describes an interweaving of Yangzhou, Shaoxing and Suzhou cooking styles. Places like Hong Kong Old Restaurant in North Point further muddy the waters by offering Yangzhou, Shanghainese and Sichuan dishes. The pairing of the first two is understandable, since many Yangzhou people moved to nearby Shanghai, but about all they have in common with Sichuan is latitude. The similarity in Shanghai and Peking menus also begs the question of culinary definition. Great Shanghai in Kowloon, for instance, covers northern and eastern bases by offering Peking duck and beggar's chicken, while Peking restaurant Long Xin Lou lists fortune chicken (a euphemism for beggar's chicken) on its menu.

China's eastern provinces (Fujian, Jiangxi, Anhui, Jiangsu and Zhejiang) benefited from exceptionally conducive crop-growing conditions and steady

After transforming mounds of dough into long, perfectly even strands of noodle, this chef will take them to the kitchen of Three Thousand Bowl to be cooked

prosperity, thanks to their location as a hub of important domestic and international trade routes. The region is known as the country's rice heartland, and in addition to the southern paddies, fields in the north produce quality crops of wheat and barley. Fertility and affluence fostered the development of distinctive cuisines, and also their fame and exportation. As *The Chinese Cookbook* points out, many of the culinary features for which certain eastern centres became renowned are an integral part of what tends to be grouped under the umbrella of Shanghainese cuisine. Nanjing was famous for its pressed duck; Yangzhou developed sizzling rice dishes and wheat-flour noodles used in soups; Shaoxing made the superb-quality wine (actually a rice spirit) that is essential for 'drunken' dishes; and Amoy soy sauce was considered the finest in the land, as was Suzhou's dim sum and Hangzhou's freshwater fish.

Sugar is used liberally in eastern cooking—up to one tablespoon for five ounces of meat, added to dark soy sauce, according to Margaret Leeming and May Huang Man-Hui in *Chinese Regional Cookery*. The authors describe a tendency to pour oil with a heavy hand: 'It is normal to have almost double the amount of oil used in the south; either it falls to the bottom of the plate and is not eaten, or, more typically, it is left in the pan to be used for cooking another vegetable dish.'

Pragmatism lies at the heart of the reason why a rather disparate and scattered collection of cooking styles came to be known as Shanghainese. Some 1,000 years ago, Hangzhou was the capital of China. Court life naturally involved the refined preparation and enjoyment of good food, and even after the imperial seat moved north in the 15th century, there remained enough of a wealthy class to support elegant culinary traditions. In the first half of the 20th century, the reputation of Shanghai, a Treaty Port and China's largest, most cosmopolitan city, eclipsed that of all other Chinese centres. As neighbouring Hangzhou had done centuries before, it attracted ambitious chefs from the surrounding area, and when numbers of them joined the 1949 exodus, it was natural that they would name their restaurants, and cuisine, for the most famous city in China.

A sign advertising Yangzhou dishes simply would not have the impact of one which read 'Shanghai'. Cognoscenti know that Shanghai Village in Causeway Bay specialises in Hangzhou cuisine, but the blurred boundaries of Shanghai cuisine are such that the presence of drunken chicken, bean curd in spicy sauce, and braised eel on the menu more than suffices for those who aren't up on the many sectors of cuisine embraced by the term 'Shanghai'.

Tightly-wrapped bundles of noodles: southern noodles tend to be lighter in texture, while the northern variety are chewy and take longer to cook

Stir-fried freshwater shrimp is a Shanghainese staple; much ordered at Lao Ching Hing

SHANGHAINESE IN Hong Kong enjoy testing Westerners who profess to be fans of their cuisine by asking them where they eat. Frustratingly, the one restaurant that this fractious group agrees is the best and most authentic is run by a Shanghainese association and is off-limits to non-members. Astute *gweilos* can score points by casually rattling off names like the Ning Po Residents Association (which is open to the public) on D'Aguilar Street, Hong Kong Old Restaurant in North Point, the petite Andy's Kitchen in Causeway Bay and the 369 Shanghai restaurants. Old-timers claim to prefer Snow Garden's North Point location over the glossy Causeway Bay branch; and ever since Lao Ching Hing moved from cramped but reeking-in-atmosphere quarters in Causeway Bay to acres of chilly space in the Century hotel basement, it has lost the cachet value so prized by people in the know.

Hong Kong Old Restaurant, located in the basement of the Newton hotel, has a look as awkward as its name. The lights are too bright, the airconditioning too forceful, and on the back wall a curious relief mural of Shanghai's Bund is framed with scalloped red velvet curtains, giving the effect of a puppet theatre. But the friendly welcome is genuine, and being surrounded by people relishing what's on their plates pushes away stray critical thoughts about interior decoration.

From the cold appetiser section, jelly fish and smoked fish that has been deep-fried and topped with a sweet and sour sauce are on practically every table. So is thinly sliced pork served on rice noodles with an accompanying dish of chilli garlic sauce. Dumplings are essential. John Tsang, a Hong Kong-born businessman who has never been to Shanghai, yet who nevertheless considers himself Shanghainese by virtue of his parentage and an upbringing spent almost entirely among their tightly-knit community, is a self-confessed dumpling fanatic. While studying in northern England, he and several friends from Shandong province would appease their hunger for home-style food with a day in the kitchen. When they were done, every available surface was covered in dumplings. They wouldn't last long; each of the cooks could eat 20 to 30 dumplings in a sitting. The Old Restaurant's 'fried fresh meat buns', crispy on the bottom and filled with a fragrant mix of minced pork and chive shoots, more than pass muster.

'Let's order the freshwater shrimp—they're delicious here,' enthuses Tsang. The tiny shrimps are lightly stir-fried, then drizzled with a tangy vinegar for a roller coaster of taste, the jolt of the vinegar following hard on the heels of the initial sweetness. Another Shanghainese favourite, fried shredded eel, belies its unappetisingly brown and soupy appearance; sprigs of coriander, bean sprouts and shallots add a delicious complexity to the dish. The Sichuan angle is covered by dishes like cold boiled sliced pork with minced garlic sauce and diced chicken with red pepper—close attention to the English translation is necessary; the pepper referred to is a red-hot chilli, not capsicum.

Shanghainese cold appetisers of duck webs and sliced meats are arranged around a mound of jellyfish

'People say, "He's so lucky". There's no luck in this business.' Sipping a tall glass of *lung ching* tea, Charles Y.K. Sun traces the progress of Lao Ching Hing. His father opened the first venue in the early 1950s. It was a small establishment of ten or so tables in Ma Ta Wai, serving mainly Shanghainese textile manufacturers. The elder Sun took premises in Causeway Bay in 1955; almost 40 years later, his son doubled the restaurant's size with a move to the Century hotel in Wan Chai. 'The food quality is much higher,' he says, 'because the kitchen and storage spaces are larger.' Some ingredients, like rice wine sauce, have to be kept for years before they are used. Sun has some 2,000 Chinese hams in the storeroom, all tagged with the date of purchase so he knows when they have sat for the required year.

Lao Ching Hing has gained a stellar reputation and wealthy clientele thanks to its chefs' expertise both with home-style tradition and expensive showpiece dishes. Freshwater 'alcoholic' crab, which are taken live, drowned in rice wine and eaten raw, fall into the latter category, as well as the 'definitely an acquired taste' class. More familiar dishes, like braised eel and Zhejiang cold pork, are excellent, as is the braised duck with spring onion.

Sun won't describe himself as a chef, but he knows exactly how every one of the over 300 dishes on the menu should be prepared, and can tell at a glance whether the kitchen is following his explicit instructions. 'Shanghai restaurants in Hong Kong have evolved from what might be served in Shanghai,' he says. 'Cuisine there is not really a restaurant food; people used to have cooks, they ate at home. Shops serving food were small; they had snacks and street food, and only in the fall and winter because the people running them worked on the land in summer.' Restaurant food thus tended to be heavy and oily, cooked for warmth, not subtlety. Today, many restaurants in Shanghai have no menu; people choose from a small selection of daily dishes.

'In the old days in Shanghai, chefs had to have 15 years of experience before they could cook, and restaurants wouldn't accept anyone over 15 years old for training. Apprentices would spend two to three years cleaning food and they wouldn't cook until their tenth year in the kitchen!' Cooks move up the hierarchy with a little more speed these days, but Sun says the most difficult aspect of the restaurant business is managing the chefs. 'It's very difficult to tell them what to do,' he says. 'You can't treat them like you would office workers.' Joining a kitchen at such a young age leaves little room for education; the hours and pressures of work leave little time for expanding one's horizons beyond the chopping block and the wok range. Sun shrugs when asked about the exceptional competition in the restaurant business. 'Three years ago, I didn't have to come here every day—now I'm here daily.' The drive to maintain consistency and profit has nothing to do with luck.

THE GAUDY red banners and brilliantine golden dragons that used to be the unifying theme of Chinese restaurant decor have disappeared for the most part. The 1940s' retro style has spread so far so fast that it has rapidly achieved cliché status; the other popular look aims for subtlety, with muted patterns of brown, pink, grey or green, in silent hopes, perhaps, that the surroundings will infiltrate a silent 'shhh' on the typically boisterous enjoyment of food. Bistro Gold is giant strides away from either fashion—by a distance of some eight dynasties, to be precise.

'The Japanese do linear design, but they don't own it 100 per cent.' If he's explained his inspiration once, he must have explained it a thousand times, but Philip Kwok's tone is only slightly weary when he says the philosophy that inspired his restaurant's sleek simplicity was prevalent in China during the Tang dynasty. Glancing around the room, kitted out in wood the colour of rich milk chocolate, with a single panache leaf arcing across each wall recess and gently lit with parchment-shaded Spanish lamps, he allows that, yes, people thought it was a Japanese restaurant at first. Lunch specials served in bento boxes strengthens that impression, but the choice of tableware is based on Kwok's firm, if admittedly speculative, belief that the sectioned lacquer boxes originated in China. His own background as a graphic designer and visual director for Esprit during the 1980s is responsible for the thoroughness of style: he designed the uniforms, the menus, and the chopstick covers made from a linen–cotton weave.

Bistro Gold's warm, tranquil decor was inspired by the Tang dynasty

The minimalist serenity of Bistro Gold is the first clue that this is not your ordinary Shanghainese restaurant. Kwok and his chefs heaved out the quantities of dark soy sauce, oil and cane sugar that typically define Shanghai food in their quest for a lighter, healthier (theirs is an MSG-free kitchen) interpretation of the cuisine. 'Shanghai gets a lot of wintry days, and in olden times people kept warm with thick clothes and heavy food,' says Kwok. 'There are a lot of good classical Shanghainese

restaurants in Hong Kong, but I see them as more for festive occasions.' He believed that by applying restraint in the oil and seasoning departments and getting more creative with stocks and vegetables, he could serve food that was intrinsically Shanghainese, yet light enough to be enjoyed daily.

For a recent charity fund-raising recipe book, Kwok concocted a new dish: a salad of lotus root, mushrooms, sugar snap peas, black fungus and water chestnuts bathed in a dressing of lychee vinaigrette and sesame oil. The restaurant menu doesn't betray quite the same no-holds-barred approach, but the attention to vegetables is a constant theme, as evidenced by a crisp celery salad and pork spareribs served on a bed of crunchy green beans—a pleasant alternative to the usual puddle of oil. Egg tofu with baby Shanghainese spinach (bò choi) is the essence of simplicity; the almost custard-like bean curd provides the perfect foil for the vegetable cooked to al dente pertness and a flavourful soup stock made with Chinese ham and chicken.

A neon sign illuminates Hong Kong's adoption of this originally northern Chinese staple

One of the reasons Kwok is able to take on this rather dramatic 'makeover' of Shanghainese food has to be that his own origins are Cantonese. As an informed outsider, he can approach the cuisine more dispassionately and mess with traditions in ways that might seem heretical to someone steeped in the heritage. The eastern cuisine has always fascinated him; he doesn't know why. 'Maybe it's because the people are very adventurous,' he muses. 'Shanghai people go dancing; Peking people do calligraphy.'

—••—

'CHINA IS so big, there are many climates and many types of soil, so there are almost 1,000 varieties of mushroom. I can tell the difference between mushrooms from Beijing, Guangzhou and Shanghai—it's like tasting wine.' Lau Wo Ching brings out a bag of northern Chinese dried mushrooms. The tight, hard caps look like large dried seeds. 'These are good steamed,' says Lau. By contrast, the Fujian mushrooms feature long stems and wide caps, tinged with a slight pink. Placing one of these in a glass, he pours boiling water over the top of it and a pink 'tea' forms. It smells musty and unappetising, but the light taste is pleasant.

His business card identifies Lau Wo Ching as the chairman of the Shanghai Vegetarian Cuisine Ltd, the founding president of the Vegetarian Society of Hong Kong and consultant for the Hong Kong Adventist Hospital's vegetarian restaurant, as well as the founder of two branches of Shanghainese vegetarian restaurant, Kung Tak Lam. But his celebrity predates his culinary activities: for over 40 years, he was a film director at Shanghai Film Studio and he is married to a woman he met on set—the famous Hong Kong-born actress, Wang Dan Fung. The couple settled in Hong Kong in 1989, and in 1991 Lau opened the first Kung Tak Lam 'to communicate the philosophy of vegetarianism'. Asked whether running a restaurant is more taxing than making a movie, he laughs and gives an emphatic 'Yes!' Much of Kung Tak Lam's produce and sauces come from Shanghai, and it can be difficult to maintain a steady supply.

A gentle man, with dignified, almost courtly manners, Lau is greatly respected, if not revered, by his staff. 'Most of the dishes come from his head,' says the manager, with a hint of awe. Sweet and sour vegetarian pork (the mock pork is made from mushrooms) and deep-fried mushrooms coated in seaweed are his inventions. Shanghai cold noodles are usually served with two sauces; at Lau's suggestion, a selection of seven sauces (including soy, peanut, chilli oil, vinegar and hoi sin) turns a simple dish into an individual smorgasbord. Pan-fried wild mushroom and bean curd, cooked in a light broth, sends diners into raptures. 'I think about dishes, about what combinations might work well,' says the filmmaker-turned-restaurateur. 'Sometimes I adapt typical Shanghainese meat dishes. The chef and I experiment.'

'The difference between Shanghainese and Cantonese vegetarian food is that Shanghai dishes use more fresh vegetables, while many Cantonese recipes are made with wheat gluten,' explains Lau. His cooks use absolutely no MSG and as little oil as possible. The proof is in the pudding: the dessert of sweet pea paste cakes is deep-fried, but the flaky pastry surrounding the bright green filling is impossibly light and leaves not a hint of grease on fingers or plate.

Vegetarianism is not a widely sympathised lifestyle choice in Hong Kong—dissenters claim that a meatless meal doesn't adequately fill the stomach and that non-meat eaters test the patience of friends and family—but by taking the food to a higher level, Kung Tak Lam is quietly broadening its appeal. The grey robes and shaven heads of Buddhist nuns are often seen amongst the lunchtime crowd; so are business suits and pearls.

Cracking open the thick layer of clay encasing beggar's chicken releases a fragrant, smoky aroma

ON THE MENU, the English name is beggar's chicken, but the Chinese characters read 'fortune chicken'. It is not an error of syntax or translation; the name change is directly related to the Chinese superstition about names of foods and dishes. Local Peking restaurants changed the Chinese name 'so that people would feel better about ordering it, for example, for their grandmother's birthday,' says Pierre Tang. In contrast to the formal origins of most Peking dishes, beggar's chicken has humble beginnings. Legend has it that, centuries ago, beggars who helped themselves to dinner by stealing chickens would cook the birds over roadside fires. To disguise their illicit spoils, the thieves wrapped the bird in lotus leaves and sealed it in clay before burying it inside the fire. When the embers died, hours later, the chicken was done. Peking restaurants enter into the spirit, stuffing a whole chicken with mushrooms, cabbage, herbs and onions, wrapping it in fragrant lotus leaves and encasing it with clay (which comes from fish ponds and is used first to seal jars of Shaoxing wine) to be slow-baked. The ceremony usually associated with a court-influenced cuisine comes back into play when the dish is presented, along with a mallet with which the customer breaks open the clay. A gorgeously pungent smoky aroma is released, but the chicken can sometimes be disappointingly dry. Perhaps it was fitting that stolen meat should stick in the thieves' throats.

Peking cuisine shares an opaqueness of identity with Shanghainese food. It also shares more than a few culinary distinctions with its southern neighbour—beggar's (a.k.a. fortune or emperor's) chicken is claimed by both as a speciality, and Peking duck is served at some Shanghainese restaurants. Even defining the boundaries of northern cuisine is a subject of debate, though experts generally agree to classify the culinary style south of the Yangtze river as eastern cuisine and that of the provinces north of it, Hubei and Shandong, as northern.

Whatever regional identity Peking cuisine may have nurtured early in its existence has been subsumed by the influences of conquerors and cooks who besieged the wealthy capital. The Mongols' traditions filtered south long before Genghis Khan and his army broached the Great Wall, while the nomadic lifestyle of northern Chinese tribes was responsible for the infiltration of mutton and goat's meat into the culinary patterns of the region. Pork is notably less important than in other regional cuisines, as the invaders were mainly Moslem.

Just as the harsh climate dictates a limited supply of vegetables and fruits, along with a dependence on wheat-based bread and dumplings instead of rice, the cold winters have instilled habits of preparation that are geared towards helping to preserve the body's warmth. *The Chinese Cookbook* describes the measures taken by cooks: 'Sesame oil and other oils are used rather lavishly, to help combat the rigour of the climate. ... Vinegar and extra salt dominate flavouring, cutting the oil; and garlic and scallions are used to absorb some of the oily excess.' Full-flavoured vegetables and roots like ginger, garlic, leeks and peppers are prominent in northern dishes.

Staff of the no-frills Pine & Bamboo in Causeway Bay have a disconcerting habit of immediately shepherding foreigners to the upper level of the two-storey

A trader of ducks and geese displays another prime shipment from northern China

restaurant, and thence to one of the furthest corners of the large, chilly room. Having safely stowed their customers, one waiter quickly distributes menus and pours tea while another slaps down small plates of spicy pickled cabbage and damp, boiled peanuts. Amid the bubble and toil of the busy restaurant, the black and white-clad waiters smile readily and are clearly happy to recommend dishes. Pine & Bamboo is one of the stalwarts of the restaurant scene, and the confidence of its staff and chefs translates to a pleasantly easygoing eating experience. The *màh po dauh fuh* (grandmother's tofu), one of the barometers by which many diners gauge a Peking (or Shanghainese, such is the 'sharing' of dishes) restaurant, is made with silky-textured bean curd, braised to the point of perfection in meaty shrimp sauce. Another typical Peking dish, beef with chilli in sesame pockets (also called 'spectacle cases' because of their rectangular shape), which one stuffs with the stir-fried meat and vegetable mixture, is dangerously filling.

Northern China hot pot (also known as Chinese fondue) is Pine & Bamboo's wintertime *raison d'être*, and connoisseurs enthuse that the mutton version tops the fish, chicken, beef and prawn alternatives. This particular speciality, which has diners spearing a choice bit of raw meat or seafood and dipping it into a large brass pot of richly flavoured bubbling stock to be cooked, was introduced to the northern Chinese by the Mongols. Year-round, however, another Mongolian-attributed dish, Peking duck, is the big draw. These ducks are bred to have a generous layer of fat beneath thin skin, for extra moistness. They are air-dried, a process which helps the skin to separate, then 'blown' (to eliminate wrinkles), glazed and dried before being hung in a large barrel-shaped oven to roast. In imperial days, the dark, crisp skin was reserved for the aristocracy. Today, waiters in upmarket Peking restaurants should enquire whether the customer would like skin only, or skin with some meat attached, to wrap in the soft, chewy pancakes. Choosing the latter means having to forgo a second dish from the bird; stir-fried duck meat with rice and vegetables. Diners should also be asked whether they would like the bones made into soup, for the end of the meal, or wrapped up to be taken home (too often, and especially when serving a table of foreigners, wait staff simply carve away at the bird, making no mention of either the stir-fry or soup). 'Oh, wrapped up, please!' says the lone Chinese among a group of Westerners. 'Duck congee, mmmm…'

There is precious little ceremony attached to the serving of this imperial dish at Pine & Bamboo—no presentation of the whole, amber-coloured bird, no deft carving of the crispy skin by a waiter wielding a razor-sharp cleaver. Instead, platters of thin meat slices, bounded by a too-thin edge of wilted skin, are served alongside a stack of white doughy pancakes and individual saucers of sweet plum sauce, sliced scallion and cucumber. This restaurant doesn't require ordering in advance, which is a boon for those with a sudden craving. The downside is that when timing is left to chance, the duck is occasionally a little overdone.

Maxim's chain of Peking Garden restaurants presents Peking duck with all due pomp and circumstance. An average of 300 birds, which are imported from duck farms outside Beijing and Tianjin, are consumed every night. The group opened its first Peking Garden, in Causeway Bay, in the mid-1970s, at a time when the few restaurants serving the cuisine were small and down-to-earth venues, catering to northern migrants. Now, Maxim's serves a plethora of Peking duck and puts noodlemasters on display nightly, transforming mounds of flour-and-water dough into skipping rope-long lengths of spaghetti-thin noodles, in 11 locations around Hong Kong. They may be something of a 'tourist trap', as one food critic charges: busloads of visiting Japanese, German, English and other foreigners dine in the Tsim Sha Tsui outlet most nights. But if that, and the fact that dishes more frequently allied with Shanghai are among the menu offerings, are the most serious charges against the chain, they are outweighed by superior standards of service and food quality. Amongst the regular customers are plenty of local residents who don't mind paying above the odds for white-glove service.

'One distinctive Peking cooking method is what we call "explosive-fried",' explains Chiang Shing-Kung, executive chef of Long Xing Lou in Wan Chai.

Sizzling prawns are braised in a chilli-garlic sauce, then poured on a fiery hot platter, raising a thick cloud of spice-laced steam

'The food is cooked at such high heat that it crackles; this helps it to retain its natural flavour.' Fried salted sliced pig's stomach tips and kidney is cooked 'explosively', as is quick-fried shredded beef with chilli sauce. Chef Chiang was born in Shandong province and came to Hong Kong when a young boy. At 16, he started his career at the curiously-named American Restaurant, an old-timer among Hong Kong's Peking restaurants. Long Xing Lou is a new entrant, only a year old, and the restaurant aims to serve authentic, unpretentious Peking cuisine in pleasantly upmarket surroundings. 'One of our most popular dishes is braised prawns with shell,' says the chef. The thick, juicy prawns are braised in a delicious chilli-garlic sauce and served piping hot. Pulling the meat from the shells necessitates much finger licking—part of the earthy charm of the northern cuisine.

The cold starters which launch a Peking meal are especially delightful at Long Xing Lou. Sea blubber comes from the gelatinous jellyfish (the appetiser is also called jellyfish on Shanghai and Peking menus), which is soaked for several hours to dissipate its fishy smell, and is usually served in long, thick, pale yellow strands. Chef Chiang instead serves the more appetising-looking male jellyfish—the large dark brown portions look like cloud-ear fungus and have the perfect sensual crunchiness the dish requires. Mock goose consists of slightly smoky-tasting bean curd wrapped around a lively mixture of chopped fresh and pickled vegetables. Shredded chicken with bean vermicelli is topped with sprigs of coriander and drizzled with an addictive peanut sauce. Surrounded by this bounty of hors d'oeuvres, a knowledgeable fan holds forth on the beauty of authentic Peking cuisine. The best of the cuisine, he says, displays a determinedly 'provincial passion', with its own combination of earthiness and subtlety. Chopsticks poised over a salad of sliced pig's ear tossed with cucumber and sesame seeds, ever so lightly laced with vinegar, he directs his companions to savour how the tangy seasoning—faint, yet distinct and personable—enhances flavour and texture.

'THE ROAD to Sichuan is more difficult than the road to heaven.' The 8th-century poet was referring to the province's former inaccessibility, but his words effectively sum up Hong Kong's lacklustre showing when it comes to enjoyment of China's western cuisine. Art critic Lau Kin Wai is a serious fan of Sichuan food. On a visit to Sichuan province a few years ago, he spent three days in a hotel kitchen, absorbing everything he could about the chefs' recipes and techniques. He occasionally puts some of those lessons to work in his own home, but when struck by a mood to visit a Sichuan restaurant, he boards the Mass Transit Railway and travels to Lo Wu where he crosses the border into Shenzhen, the Special Administrative Region that has burgeoned into a massive manufacturing and business satellite of Hong Kong. There, he indulges in a true Sichuan meal, the like of which is impossible to find in his home town.

The most obvious reason for this sorry state of affairs is that the predominant ingredient is the chilli, the fiery taste of which is anathema to most Cantonese. *Chinese Regional Cookery* explains the reasons for the copious amounts of chilli employed in the western provinces: 'One is that the fire will stimulate the palate to distinguish the flavour beneath; another is that the heat induces perspiration and so helps people to keep cool; and another, from the cynics, is that chilli hides the taste of putrid meat.' Hunan's most famous native son,

Mao Zedong, came up with still another motive when he said, 'The more chillies you eat, the more revolutionary you are.'

Purveyors of the chilli-laden cuisines have had to bank their fires in order to win over the Cantonese palate, schooled as it is in mellifluous tastes and textures. Consequently, hot and sour soup tends to be watered-down, eggplant with chilli sometimes barely raises an eyebrow, let alone one's temperature, and sizzling prawns with chilli sauce usually needs an extra spoonful of the red stuff. Still, Sze Chuan Lau and Yin King Lau (with its Peking/Sichuan menu) in Wan Chai do a rousing business. Assuring the waiter that one adores spicy food can make for a reasonable chilli quotient. Red Pepper in Causeway Bay is perhaps a victim of its own popularity, with the amount of chilli in inverse proportion to the numbers of Western tourists flocking through the door. Surprisingly, one of the few Hunan venues, the elegant Hunan Garden in Exchange Square, turns up the heat with fiery dishes like fried chicken with chilli.

People aching for more spark in their *dân dân mihn* (a traditional Sichuan noodle dish that should be brimming with chilli) see a faint glimmer of hope in the successful introduction of Thai cuisine to Hong Kong. 'I don't know how that happened,' says one restaurateur. 'Cantonese don't like chilli!' Still, Thai and spicy Malaysian restaurants have boomed in the past several years. It's cold comfort for lovers of fiery Sichuan and Hunan cuisines, but hope springs eternal.

MAXIM'S
Wò Tip—Fried Dumplings

Dumpling wrappers*	48
Minced pork	300 g
Green vegetables (spinach is most suitable)	300 g
Minced ginger	1/2 tbsp
Spring onion, chopped finely	1 tbsp
Rice wine	1 tbsp
Sugar	1 tbsp
Soy sauce	1 tbsp
Cornflour	1 tbsp
Sesame oil	1 tbsp
Salt	1/2 tbsp
White pepper	1/4 tbsp

Place the minced pork in a bowl and add the wine, sugar, soy sauce, cornflour, sesame oil, salt and pepper, then mix thoroughly and allow to marinate for 30 minutes. Blanch the green vegetables in boiling water, then refresh under cold water and lightly squeeze out the excess water. Chop the vegetable finely and mix together with the minced pork mixture, ginger and spring onion. Place in the refrigerator for 1 hour. Place a teaspoon of the pork mixture slightly to one side of the centre of a wrapper and fold over and pinch the edges together to seal in the filling in a crescent shape. Put on a lightly oiled plate and repeat with remaining mixture and wrappers.

Heat a little oil in a large pan, add the dumplings and fry for 3 minutes. Add 1/2 cup of water, cover and simmer over low heat for 5 minutes until the liquid has dried up. Uncover, add 1/2 tablespoon of sesame oil and cook for a further 2 minutes until the dumplings are golden. Serve with a side dish of red wine vinegar and shredded ginger. (Makes 48 dumplings.)

* Use round wheat-flour wrappers which can be bought from a noodle store or look for them in a Chinese delicatessen. They are whiter in colour than won ton wrappers.

WILLY MARK
Eggplant and Pork Sichuan-style

Eggplant, cut into finger-sized strips	800 g
Minced pork	350 g
Peanut oil	1/4 cup
Ginger, finely chopped	1 tbsp
Garlic, finely chopped	1 tbsp
Spring onion, chopped	1 tbsp
Hot fava (broad) bean paste, mashed	1 tbsp
Sugar	1 tbsp
Cider or aromatic vinegar	1 tbsp
Sichuan peppercorns, ground	2 tsp
Sesame oil	1 tsp
Chilli oil	2 tsp
Dark soy sauce	1 tbsp
Chicken broth (stock)	1-1/2 cups
Cornflour, diluted in 1 tbsp water	2 tsp
Chinese rice wine	1 tbsp

Heat 2 tablespoons of the oil in a wok or pan and sauté the eggplant until soft. Remove and set aside. In a bowl, combine the hot fava bean paste, sugar, vinegar, peppercorns, sesame oil, chilli oil and soy sauce. Heat the remaining oil in the wok and add the ginger, garlic and spring onion and stir-fry for 30 seconds. Add the combined hot fava bean paste mixture and stir-fry over low heat for another 30 seconds. Now stir in the broth and return the eggplant. Cook, stirring over high heat for 15 seconds. Reduce the heat to medium-low, cover and simmer for 5 minutes. Stir in the cornflour paste and cook for 1 minute, add the wine and serve immediately.

PEKING GARDEN RESTAURANT
Pan-fried Sliced Beef With Spring Onion

Beef sirloin, sliced	*150 g*
Soy sauce, light	*1/2 tbsp*
White sugar	*1/2 tbsp*
Cornstarch	*1/2 tbsp*
Peanut oil	*1 cup*
Garlic, diced	*1/2 tbsp*
Rice wine	*1 tbsp*
Spring onion	*2 stalks*

Cut the beef into slender bite-sized pieces and place in a bowl. Add to the beef the soy sauce, sugar, cornstarch and oil and marinate overnight. Heat 1 tablespoon of the oil in a wok and stir-fry the garlic over high heat for 1–2 minutes, then remove with a slotted spoon. Add the remaining oil to the wok and heat until very hot. Add the marinated beef and deep-fry for 2–3 minutes, stirring constantly, then remove from the wok with a slotted spoon and set aside. Pour all but 1–2 tablespoons of the oil from the wok and stir-fry the spring onion in the hot oil for 1–2 minutes, then return the beef and garlic to the wok and add the rice wine. Toss together, then remove from the wok with a slotted spoon to a serving plate.

5

Sound and Fury

Travelling the short distance between the small bakeshop entrance on Stanley Street, with its neon-bright wedding cakes and slabs of gooey rice cake, and up the staircase to the dining hall is like riding a tsunami of sound that reaches an uproarious peak in seconds. The walls of the cavernous white room are decorated with framed calligraphy scrolls and paintings of a Hong Kong that ceased to exist maybe a century ago. Beneath the chrome fans and fluorescent lights, the glass-topped tables are thick with people reading newspapers, talking, drinking tea, eating. Many are construction workers; there are some groups, but many diners are solo. Lin Heung doesn't take reservations, and there is no *maître d'* ushering customers to a table. Newcomers prowl for an empty seat, or at least a space into which they can squeeze a spare stool. Women navigate unwieldy trolleys loaded with stacks of bamboo baskets, crying out '*sìu máai* (steamed dumplings filled with pork and shrimp) or '*fuhng jáau* (chicken's feet). An elderly man with frizzled grey hair totters in their wake with a tray of *hà chéung fán* (long rice-noodle rolls filled with shrimp) on a strap around his neck, a little unsteady on his pins, but smiling whenever he is hailed by a customer. There's an eruption of swearing at a distant table and loud laughter from a man grinning a silver smile. Waiters thread between the tables, taking orders for bowls of rice noodles with beef, Chinese sausage with rice, or steamed chicken, plucking big heavy kettles of boiling water from hot plates planted around the room at the foot of

Hong Kong's appetite for dim sum is such that many diners judge a restaurant by its 'pieces from the heart'

Maxim's City Hall restaurant packs them in for yàm cháh *every day of the week*

pillars and splashing long streams of the liquid into lidded cups. One can't reach the far side of a table, so he tosses a filthy cloth to a customer and tells him to wipe the glass. The old habit of rinsing one's tableware and chopsticks with hot tea has never seemed so sensible.

Dim sum (*dím sàm*) without the sensory overload that continually ebbs and rises at Lin Heung, Double Happiness and hundreds of other restaurants like them just wouldn't be the same. Much is made of the delicacy of dim sum dishes, and deservedly so, but basically this is a melee of a meal—anyone who doesn't wade in and compete with other diners to get dishes on the table will leave hungry. The choice of table can mean the difference between a steady flow of food and a lunch-hour spent waving your arms and entreating the trolley ladies to aim directly for your table. In recent years, most venues have increased efficiency, but spoiled the fun, by providing a small card on which one ticks off the desired dishes. For many dim sum lovers, the presence of trolleys or, even rarer, trays hung around the waiter's neck, adds an extra soupçon of pleasure. The dim sum at Lin Heung is, for the most part, of indifferent quality, but the sensation of stepping back 20 or 30 years more than compensates.

———••———

THE CONFUSION created by the seeming interchangeability of *yám chàh* and dim sum is akin to the pitfalls of pronunciation that inspired the songwriters to pen, 'You say tomato, I say tom-ah-to.' In Cantonese, *yám chàh* literally means 'to drink tea'. The translation of dim sum has many variations: 'to stimulate the heart'; 'heart's delight'; 'light touches from the heart' and 'dot hearts' amongst them. A simple phrase, *heui yám chàh*, 'going to drink tea', refers to a custom which embraces the leisurely drinking of tea and socialising with friends or family over anything from a traditional breakfast to

The old-style atmosphere that Double Happiness once offered its clientele is sadly waning as this and other old-timers close their doors

an elaborate brunch in the middle of the day and, thanks to Hong Kong's trend-setting hunger, even a midnight snack. Dim sum, on the other hand, is the term for the array of delicate bite-sized morsels of meat, seafood and vegetables wrapped in thin skins of wheat dough or near-transparent wrappers made from a gluten-free wheat starch, either steamed, braised, deep-fried or boiled, that is eaten while drinking tea. The meal also incorporates a variety of non-dumpling dishes, such as beef balls (they often contain pork, too) flecked with coriander (*ngàuh yukh kàuh*) and steamed pork spare ribs (*jìng pàaih gwàt*). Platters of cold sliced roast duck (*sìu ngaap*) or steamed chicken (*baahk chit gài*) are popular dim sum items, as are chicken's feet (sucked of their flavour, then spat out).

Before the trolley came the tray; and before the tray, the paper bag. In 1968, prior to a tour of Chinese tea houses, a member of the Royal Asiatic Society translated a section of a Chinese book which described how turn-of-the-century tea houses in Hong Kong packed dim sum in a large paper bag: 'This cost 10 cents and the number of dim sum was 18 pieces, usually sufficient for 8–9 persons.' The author of the original article dwelt at length on the fact that the sizes of dim sum pieces had decreased significantly and admonished: 'The difference in price in the old days and now is too great: people have said that it may be compared to the difference between the legs of mosquitoes and cows.' If he were comparing the paper bag era with today's gentrified dim sum, the disillusioned gentleman would no doubt replace 'cows' with 'elephants'.

It is doubtful that the paper bag will come back into fashion, but chefs like Po Kee, Super Star Seafood restaurants' dim sum supremo, are digging into history and reviving once popular recipes. One of chef Po's biggest successes is pan-fried

Delicate pastry filled with sweet red bean paste from Shanghainese eatery, Lao Ching Hing

glutinous rice with egg (*jin bohk beng*). 'We steam the sticky rice in lotus leaf, as usual,' he explains. 'Then we pan-fry it, pouring egg over it so that it becomes a kind of cake.'

Weekdays, dim sum at Super Star is a straightforward experience: customers simply order from the menu. Weekends, bells and whistles blow full blast: diners crowded into the din of the basement Central location can order dishes from a menu lavishly illustrated with photos, browse a buffet where a cook is frying dumplings and turnip cakes (*lòh baahk gòu*), or hail a trolley. The showiness of the buffet is partly to entertain guests and partly to emphasise the total freshness. In just eight years, Super Star has edged out a lot of the competition and obtained a high degree of popularity. Managing director Stanley Ho is quick to give the lion's share of the credit to his chef. 'He introduces 10 to 15 new dishes every month; he experiments all the time,' exclaims Ho.

Chef Po spent months working on his latest pride and joy: an eight-dumpling menu that is tasteful in every sense of the word. One creation is a scrumptious morsel of minced abalone and shrimp with crab roe filling the tiny pockets formed when the wrapping is pinched shut. Chopped snow fungus, chilli and cabbage, and sliced egg fill the vegetarian dumpling, topped with tiny cubes of red, green or yellow pepper. The stone fish dumpling is beautifully artistic, the small mound of filling surrounded by flattened, textured edges which have been lightly tinged with green vegetable colouring. Topped with a thick layer of crab roe, the fish dumpling has the shape and look of sushi. In the best dramatic tradition, chef Po has left the best to last with his whimsical marshmallow rabbit. 'I was trying different possibilities with marshmallow,' he explains. 'At first, I'd just make a pan of it, using fresh cream and egg. Then I tried putting the mixture in a decorating cone and I made the rabbit shape.' This he lightly dusts with coconut before dotting the 'head' with eyes made of duck egg yolk. Rich and smooth, the marshmallow rabbit is a fitting finale to a magical dumpling menu. 'This was worked out for the Hong Kong Food Festival,' says Ho. 'But afterwards, we put the most popular dumplings on the regular menu.'

———

WOULD-BE dim sum chefs must apprentice for three years, after which they are promoted to the level of cook. There they stay, for a further four to six years, before attaining the title of dim sum chef. The hours are unsociable; the work repetitive, meticulous and demanding. Of the 260 Maxim's (no relation to the French restaurant group of the same name; Maxim's is the English translation of the company's Chinese name, Mei Sam) restaurants in Hong Kong, 50 serve dim sum. The company's Tsing Yi Island facility seats 1,500, serving around 6,000 people on Sundays. A team of 40 prepares every piece of dim sum by hand.

'We've tried ceramic, stainless steel, plastic: bamboo is best. It holds the steam and is easily cleaned.' Impeccable in his charcoal-grey suit, Pierre C.H. Tang, senior manager of sales and public relations for Maxim's, points to four large steamers on which up to 70 bamboo baskets can be placed. He stands with feet planted firmly on the water-slick floor of the City Hall Chinese Restaurant kitchen. The lunch rush won't begin for half an hour, but cooks, chefs and choppers are busy. At the wok range, a cook nudges the heat lever with his knee and the flames rise

Dim sum chefs hand-make millions of dumplings and pastries each day to satisfy Hong Kong's passion for yàm cháh

while he drops a tangle of thin yellow vermicelli into a massive wok. In one corner lies a heap of gutted and skinned pigs, their foreheads stamped purple with government approval; a plastic bin of geese is carried into the roasting room, where ducks already hang on hooks inside the barrel-shaped oven. A stack of baskets of *chà sìu bâau*, the delectable barbecued pork buns, is loaded on a trolley. 'The way to tell good *chà sìu bâau*, is to look at the top of the bun,' says Tang. 'It must be open and smiling!' He has been with Maxim's for 20 years and he knows full well the prestige value of dim sum. 'Food costs are very high, but if people like your dim sum they will come back for dinner.' In the old days, he says, new dim sum restaurants in Guangzhou would try to entice repeat business by offering huge steamed chicken buns (*gâi bâau*)for the usual price during their first week of operation.

Beautifully presented sìu máai *from Spring Moon*

In the dim sum section of the kitchen (there are also roasting, cooking and chopping areas), a cook takes a square of wrapper dough made from rice and potato flours, smooths it paper-thin with his cleaver and places it on the palm of his left hand. With his right, he daubs a bit of duck egg yolk on the centre of the wrapper, then places on it a mixture of chopped shrimp and pork. Turning it again and again in his fingers, he fashions the round, slightly elongated body of a goldfish, then pulls fins from the sides, snipping away the excess dough with heavy black scissors. Finally, he takes an icing cone filled with duck egg yolk and carefully dots the 'head' with tiny bright eyes. Goldfish dumplings are a recent addition to the menu. Such variations on the dumpling (or steamed bun or tofu-wrapped) theme are continually introduced at the better restaurants. Dim sum staples like *hà gáau*, *sìu máai*, and *chà sìu bâau* may be altered with—for instance, extra vegetables or a spot of abalone in the *hà gáau*—but they never disappear.

The City Hall restaurant is a large open space, with a prime harbour vista from its second-floor windows. Renovation has stripped away the former gaudiness, replacing it with gentle tans and pinks; a huge rosy-coloured peony glows from one wall. The hubbub of friends and colleagues chatting and calling out to the trolley ladies builds. Every so often, a dim sum chef in white togs and tall white chef's hat winds through the room proudly holding high a tray of delicacies prepared by his own hands, fresh from the steamer or oven. Where there is prestige, there is pride.

———

A YOUNG couple open the door cautiously and ease into the small, crowded waiting area. After giving their name to the hostess who quickly inscribes the characters at the bottom of a discouragingly long list, they peer around the divider of etched glass and wood, scanning the room with practised eyes. Aha! That table is playing tug-of-war with the bill; now the father has snatched it from his son-in-law and pressed it and his credit card into the hands of the genial manager. Forget lusting after the booths filled with Westerners—they linger too long, chatting endlessly over their tea and beer. Didn't their mothers ever tell them, 'Eat, don't talk; sleep, don't murmur'? Obviously not. The hostess estimates they have a 25-minute wait, so the couple venture out into Happy Valley to wander through the new wine shop, the bakery, the florists, confident that when they return, their name won't have been scratched off or moved lower down the list. Some places still operate with cut-throat disregard for customer comfort, but not Dim Sum Restaurant.

'I remember fighting it out at dim sum restaurants,' laughs restaurateur Paul Hsu. 'Kids would be swarming everywhere, standing behind the chairs of people eating, so that they'd get the table next.' Pierre Tang remembers a long-gone riverside restaurant where the cost of the meal was totted up according to the number of plates on the table. When the owner realised that his cooks had prepared around 1,000 dishes, but he had charged for only 600, he found his sunken plates—and profits—in the river. Rules of elaborate courtesy surrounded rituals of seating arrangements and especially paying the bill. But that was *after* sitting down; no such *politesse* governed actually landing the table. Recently, a local newspaper described in lurid detail the tale of two rival groups jockeying for a table: one of the families dispatched a child to stand behind the chair of a customer who was on the verge of leaving. Bent on the same manoeuvre, a woman from the second group rushed to cut the child off and a loud argument broke out between her and the child's mother. Snatching up a cup of tea, one putative diner threw it at the other, only to see it land on a couple sitting at another table. Hong Kong's dubious claim of being the site of some of the most densely populated land on earth notwithstanding, public disputes are rare. Given the seating arrangements at some dim sum restaurants, however, what's surprising is that fisticuffs don't break out more often.

Dim sum is a leisurely meal, an extremely popular way for families to while away a couple of hours, and it is notorious for generating queues, especially on weekends. Most restaurants don't take reservations and some have arcane codes concerning the saving of places. One well-known venue drove patrons to splutter angrily because they would allow one person to take over an entire table. They would sit calmly drinking tea and reading the

The sheer variety of dim sum begs indulgence

newspaper as they waited for the rest of their group to arrive, while hungry hordes at the door looked on in frustration. Another huge restaurant, sacrificed to redevelopment some years ago, put its large waiting area to good use with the rule that no one got a table until their entire group was present and accounted for.

Dim Sum has drawn fans since it opened in 1992, one of the city's first retro venues. Those in the know either arrive before noon on a Saturday or Sunday, or they pop in to add their name to the list and then run a few errands before returning for lunch. Despite the steady stream of custom, the ambience is tranquil. Mahogany fans swirl in the recesses of an unusually high ceiling, and at the corner of each high-backed booth a spray of small lamps throws gentle pools of light on to the high polish of the tables. A measure of relaxation is built into the meal, with the provision of a choice of two boxes beside each selection on the tick-it-yourself menu: tick the first box, and those dishes will be served first; the second wave will be brought after a comfortable interval.

En route to Happy Valley, where Dim Sum restaurant serves dumplings day and night

There is neither trolley nor tray, yet Dim Sum philosophy is founded on adherence to tradition—even in its practice of serving dim sum from late morning into the evening, shocking though that was when it opened. Fifty years ago, it was not uncommon for tea houses to serve dim sum for dinner, but it has become primarily a lunchtime meal. When Dim Sum manager Herbie Eow found that night-time business was slow to take off, he made some additions to the menu. His customers often mix dim sum choices with several of a range of dishes, from steamed vegetable with bamboo shoots and conpoy to deep-fried boneless chicken to steamed squid in spicy shrimp sauce. Since then, dim sum after dark has caught on—in Happy Valley and elsewhere. The Broadway Seafood Restaurant in Wan Chai introduced midnight *yám chàh* in early 1996. It is a talking point, but few customers get around to actually placing an order for any of the ten dim sum dishes on offer, especially in winter when Broadway clients apparently have only one thing on their minds: hot pot. Super Star Seafood restaurants recently introduced evening dim sum from 5pm. Their menu is small, but well-rounded, with selections like steamed vegetarian dumplings (*sou choi gáau*), steamed fish ball, pan-fried Chinese sausage (*jìn laahp chéung*), and milk cream cake (*náaih yàuh dáan gòu*). The Furama hotel's much-praised Island Chinese Restaurant is stretching the dim sum habit the other way, with morning *yám chàh*, offering traditional, not trendy or East-West dishes. Super Star Seafood restaurants' Tsim Sha Tsui venue opens at 7am for a crowd that is usually an even mix of locals and tourists. But Super Star's Wan Chai and Central locations don't open until mid-morning.

'We want people to be able to enjoy traditional Emperor's dim sum,' says Eow. One story about the origins of dim sum traces it to interminable imperial banquets, where most of the dishes were grandiose and inedible, meant to impress not feed. Small savouries were served to placate the emperor's hunger, and these eventually gained their own culinary identity. Another tangent of the dim sum tale credits the 14th-century tea houses of Suzhou and Hangzhou with creating light delicacies to serve continuously to the noblemen who spent long hours there, gossiping, drinking tea and enjoying the entertainment of 'sing-song girls'. The Happy Valley restaurant has earned kudos for exceptional quality and creativity, so it is appropriate that Eow looks to the emperors for inspiration. Nine cooks begin wrapping and stuffing at 7am each day: everything is handmade on the premises. Eow works closely with his chefs to compose vivid new melodies for this very old song: roasted duck is added to the rich, sweet filling in *chà sìu bâau*, the steamed barbecued pork bun; the ever-popular steamed shrimp dumpling (*hà gáau*), includes bird's nest, while *lùhng hà gáau* is made with shrimp and lobster. Unwrap the smoky covering of lotus leaf for glutinous rice studded with hearty pieces of chicken, dried scallops and abalone. There are new combinations, such as *yùh chi gáau*, a shark's fin dumpling with shrimps and glass noodle topping, and a variety of northern specialities, such as *chùng yàuh beng*, Peking-style onion cake.

Decades ago, the Chinese tea house, *chàh gêui*, literally 'small tea hut', was very much like a neighbourhood pub in Britain. Each had its regular customers; mostly older men who brought along their prized bird, they would carefully hang their cage on a rail built especially for the purpose, then spend the morning sipping cup after cup of *bóu léi*, (*pu-er* in Mandarin) a dark fermented tea (though Westerners call it black tea) from lidded tea cups, reading the newspapers and studying the racing form. With their tea, they would have a few plates of dim sum, or maybe a bowl of plain congee into which they would dip a puffy stick of deep-fried dough (*yàuh ja gwái*).

One of the best-known *chàh gêui* is Luk Yu on Stanley Street in Central. With its well-aged redwood furniture, brass spittoons, stoic staff and imposing Sikh doorman, Luk Yu has carved out a distinctive reputation, due as much to its food and high-level clientele as to the generally disdainful attitude. 'You should have made a reservation,' unsympathetic friends tell a wealthy Chinese stockbroker on a visit to his hometown, when he complains of being snubbed by Luk Yu waiters. 'When?' he asks. 'Oh, 20 years ago,' his friends reply wickedly. 'That way you would be a regular customer and they would have served you properly the other day.'

Luk Yu is a 'Tea House, Eating House & Restaurant', according to the toothpick wrapper. 'Eating house' indicates that simple, small dishes are available, while 'restaurant' advises customers that more formal meals, including banquets, may be enjoyed. Mr Ma, of Guangzhou, opened the first venue in a small lane further south and west from its present Central site, to which it moved after World War II. The Ma family chose to rent instead of buy the premises

Rich and filling:
chà sìu so
(barbecued pork puff)

and several years ago skyrocketing costs nearly forced them to close down. The prospect of losing a favourite restaurant galvanised some of its wealthier customers to help the restaurateurs purchase the building and Luk Yu survived to serve many thousands more baskets of dim sum.

Luk Yu's notoriety tends to obscure the fact that, whether out of stubbornness or a belief that old equals best, its dim sum dishes are made to high standards and often incorporate elements that have been tossed aside by modern cooks. The steamed chicken buns are so immense they bring to mind the Canton restaurateur's marketing ploy. Inside is a mouthwatering mixture studded with large chunks of chicken and salted duck egg. Steamed glutinous rice wrapped in two layers of fragrant, papery lotus leaf is steamed, not fried as some establishments do to its detriment. Pan-fried meat dumpling, *jìn fán gwó*, is a mixture of fresh, never canned, bamboo shoots, pork and shrimp in rice-flour pastry. So far, so familiar. But beside the plate the waiter sets down a bowl of high-quality chicken stock in which the dumplings are meant to be dipped—a very traditional serving style rarely seen nowadays.

'THE FIRST thing you do is smell the aroma, then take a small sip.' Helen Chung lifts the delicate cup of tea first to her nose, then to her mouth. 'Take another sip and hold it in your mouth before swallowing. Let it slide down the throat slowly, so that you taste the tea from the tip of your tongue through the mouth, to the throat.' With one hand, the teacher of Chinese culture and language at a local international school traces a graceful line from her lips to the base of her throat, drawing the curve of taste along which tea should be savoured, properly and with respect.

Helen's gently impassioned discourse is taking place at Luk Yu Tea House, which the owners named for Lu Yu (Luk Yu is the Cantonese pronunciation), a scholar and politician in the Tang dynasty who wrote the most comprehensive and authoritative book on tea, *Chajing*, or *Classic of Tea*, communicating his vast knowledge about the planting, processing, tasting and brewing of tea. Having ordered three different teas—aromatic *bóu léi*, the lighter but slightly bitter jasmine, and sturdy oolong—Helen keeps a weather eye on her companions' tea cups, pouring from the lidded brewing cup (the only one of the eight at table to do so without spilling the tea), and topping up frequently with hot water.

Although tea has been drunk in China for thousands of years, it was first considered a medicinal beverage. Tea leaves were boiled with ginger, leek and

得通元府骨都灵

不到名山心未快

A predilection for tea is depicted by an unknown artist of the Anglo-Chinese school

other vegetables in a pot, in the manner of a soup. It wasn't until the Tang dynasty that its popularity as a stimulant, digestive and thirst-quenching drink spread throughout the country. Much of the ceremony surrounding the brewing and serving of tea was developed during this period. Tea leaves were steamed, dried and then pounded to produce a fine powder which was either stirred directly into boiling water or placed in a bowl into which boiling water was poured. A bamboo whisk was used to whip the mixture into a frothy brew. Steeping didn't come into fashion until the Ming dynasty. Because the tea leaves used at this time were finer, it took longer to coax from them their delicate flavour. The ensuing revolutionary steeping method gave rise to a new invention: the tea pot. The classic covered tea bowl, such as is used at Luk Yu and countless other Chinese restaurants, was created and refined during the Qing dynasty (1644–1912). It was during the Ming and Qing dynasties that the six principal categories of Chinese tea were developed: green, scented, compressed, white, oolong and black.

Britain's celebrated passion for tea is well known; what is less understood is the manner in which the coffee bean was supplanted by the tea leaf. During the 17th century, the brewing of dark, rich Arabian coffee had not only become *de rigueur* in the salons of noble houses and at court, where it was sipped from porcelain made for the purpose, its use had spread throughout all levels of society. Coffee was welcomed as the 'great soberer', writes Wolfgang Schivelbusch, in *Tastes of Paradise*, 'in contrast to previously known drinks, all of which were alcoholic.' The new wonder beverage was believed to fortify the liver, purify the blood, whet the appetite, or decrease it, stimulate wakefulness or induce sleep. Considering the lofty position of the coffee bean, Schivelbusch scoffs at theories suggesting that Britain's transformation to a nation of tea drinkers was prompted by either 'a mysterious transformation in English taste' or 'some purely economic reason'. Between 1700 and 1750, British tea imports increased more than 200-fold. Mystery boils around Britain's addiction to a 'cuppa' and Schivelbusch gives a meaningful nod in the direction of the powerful East India Company, which held the tea trade monopoly and so was in a position to dominate and eventually put out of business the independent merchants who traded in coffee.

However it happened, the introduction of tea to Britain was fateful for both importer and exporter. The English fast developed a national thirst for the stuff: according to *A History of Hong Kong*, 2lb 2oz of tea was imported into England in 1664. By 1738, over 2,600 tons were sold to the English public—and that's only the legal amount recorded: smuggling accounted for up to three times as much of the tea pouring from British tea pots. Eventually, of course, the East India Company and, once its monopoly was dissolved, other traders, facing China's disinterest in those items they proposed to trade for tea, resorted to peddling opium, the protection of which trade, in turn, provided the British government with a handy *cause célèbre* with which to force its occupation of a small slice of the mainland.

One might wonder whether a shared passion for tea brought Chinese and English gourmands together, breaching in some small way the gap of mutual disinterest that seems to have pervaded Hong Kong. If the maudlin Lt Orlando Bridgeman is anything to go by, one would be disappointed. In 1842, the unhappy soldier wrote in a letter to his sister: 'Your description of one [rat] being found drowned in the milk is certainly very nasty, but even there you are better off than us, for we have not even the luxury of milk for them to drown themselves in. Although in China, I have not tasted one cup of tea half as good as I have in England.'

He was not alone in his negative estimation of Chinese tea. Novelist, playwright and entertainer Albert Smith, who in 1858 performed a programme entitled 'The Travelling English and Their Autumnal Peculiarities on the Continent' in the Drawing Room of the Hong Kong Club, endeared himself to the Chinese community with his genuine interest in their traditions and lifestyle. But even he baulked at tea, writing: 'The tea was put into the cups, and water poured on it. Then they covered the

Fook Ming Tong seeks to re-aquaint people with the art of drinking tea

cup with the saucer, which fitted into it; and thus you strained the leaves back from the tea, when you drank. I thought our London tea much better—but everything in London is the best...'

IF THE *dai pai dong* invented milk tea, the Chinese café popularised the brew. *chàh châan têng* are perhaps the first East-West hybrid. Menus offer standard Chinese fare along with local interpretations of Western food. Some incorporate bakeries and produce daily batches of coconut-filled cocktail buns and pineapple buns. (The name refers only to the dimpling on the pastry; inside lurks red bean paste.) Before the debut of the self-service bakery, people ordered birthday cakes and bought their daily bread here. *Chàh châan têng* literally means 'a salon for tea and Western food'. 'Salon' tends to imply a certain upper-crustiness; but the ambience of the *chàh châan têng* is austere at best, with hard chairs and booths, formica tables and the occasional chipped cup or saucer. But diners attend to their midafternoon snack with great enthusiasm, choosing from the fresh buns and pastries displayed at cafés with their own baker and ovens. Milk tea, lemon tea, coffee, Ovaltine, Horlicks and *náaih séui,* a mixture of condensed milk and hot water, are served. When the weather heats up, sales of iced tea and coffee rise with the temperature.

Hong Kong has no shortage of tea salons. The Library at the Island Shangri-La, the Clipper Lounge at the Mandarin Oriental, The Lobby at the Conrad, the Lobby at the New World Harbour View—in fact, a trawl through the lobby restaurants of any 3- to 5-star hotel in Hong Kong will turn up numerous varieties of the traditional English afternoon tea. Ordering silver pots of English Breakfast and buttering raisin scones under the gaze of plump plaster cherubs and fierce gargoyles in the Peninsula Lobby has been *de rigueur* since, well, just since the mid-1980s. The Lobby of the Pen looks like it was designed with cream teas in mind, but the bells and whistles version was only launched a short 15 years ago. It was immediately successful and other hotels followed suit.

A Menu of Tea

Pu-erh (*bóu leí*)
Also known as *pu li,* the fully-fermented black tea is made with large tea leaves from southwestern China. Just like good wine, its mellowness increases with

age, so the older it is the better the quality. This tea is savoured for its subtle flavour of dates, and mild yet full-bodied character. Folk wisdom has it that *pu-erh* can remove grease from the stomach and ease hangovers. For many Cantonese, the tea is a must after a feast of greasy food and excessive drinking.

White Peony (*bai mu dan*)
White peony is made with very young leaves grown in Fujian province. In every picking, there is one bud and two leaves. Processing is kept to a minimum—comprising only sun-drying and light baking. When steeped in hot water, the tea leaves gently 'blossom' to resemble their namesake, a white peony. The tea is light in colour, but the fragrance is particularly pleasant and mild. Some connoisseurs like to mix it with silver needle pekoe for mellowness or dehydrated roses for added fragrance.

Lychee Red
Black tea leaves (called 'red' in Chinese) processed with lychee juice, hence the name lychee red. The tea's bitterness is subdued by the sweetness of the lychee juice, giving a palatable, mellow flavour.

Qimen Red
On a par with Darjeeling and Sri Lankan teas, Qimen tea, grown in the county of the same name, is one of the most sought-after from China. Considered the caviar of black tea, it has a fragrance all its own, often referred to as 'princely'. The tea is enjoyed for its strong, long-lasting, honey-like sweetness. Reddish brown in colour, the tea is rich with a long aftertaste.

Pearl Orchid
A combination of premium green tea leaves and flowers harvested from China's Yellow Mountain (Huangshan). In Cantonese, the flowers are referred to as orchids because of their special fragrance. When hot water is poured over this tea, the leaves are said to sink to the bottom of the pot like strings of pearls. It is refreshing, yet mild, and offers an elegant fragrance.

Rose
Dehydrated roses can be used to make rose 'tea', or combined with other teas for added fragrance. As the roses 'blossom' in the hot water, they send out an agreeable bouquet and pleasant pink colour.

Iron Kannon Buddha (*ti kuan yin*)

Made with the finest oolong tea, half-fermented and tightly rubbed, the tea leaves gain a heavy, hard character, hence the reference to iron. Long considered precious and elegant, this tea was named in honour of the Kannon Buddha—the goddess of mercy in Chinese Buddhism. The tea is golden in colour, full-bodied and gives an orchid-like bouquet. Its richness allows many servings with a long-lasting aftertaste and subtle sweetness.

Phoenix Shui Sin

The most renowned tea produced in Guangdong province. It features robust, yellowish-brown tea leaves, some with a metallic radiance. Heavily fermented, the bitterness is reduced to a minimum, producing a delightful sweetness. This rich tea is enjoyed for its special bouquet and is good for many servings.

A connoisseur's selection of tea

Dragon Well (lung ching)
This tea often occupies the top position amongst green tea lovers. The colour, shape, fragrance and taste are considered to be beyond comparison by dragon well loyalists. In one kilogram there are some 60,000 buds hand-picked according to strict specifications by skilful pickers in eastern China. When properly steeped in moderately hot water (70°C), the tea produces a delightful fragrance with a pleasant, yellowish-green colour. Rich in vitamin C and other vitamins and minerals, the tea has been proven effective in helping to reduce the level of cholesterol in blood.

Bi Lo Chun
Grown around the Dongting lake in eastern China, this green tea is one of the rarest. In one kilogram, there are close to 100,000 buds hand-picked in spring, and the buds are processed with great care. Literally translated, the name means 'green spiral spring', which is intended to indicate the colour, shape and feel of the tea. The delicate tea leaves should be steeped in hot water not exceeding 70°C. Rich in vitamin C and other vitamins and minerals, this tea is also said to be effective in reducing the level of cholesterol in blood.

Monkey Pick
Made from the choicest tea leaves rumoured to be picked by monkeys from inaccessible steep cliffs, hence the name monkey pick. Half-fermented and well-baked, the tea leaves are carefully rubbed into a spiral shape and are dark-green in colour. When served, the tea should turn reddish-brown and emit an unmistakable bouquet. Despite a little bitterness in the first serving, its full body and strong aftertaste has won over connoisseurs.

Oolong
Half-fermented selective tea from Fujian province, oolong has characteristics similar both to green tea and black tea. It has a pleasant fragrance and richness, and is best steeped in water at 95°C. It is yellowish-brown in colour and is renowned for its pleasing aftertaste.

Jasmine
Premium green tea leaves fermented with layers of jasmine flowers, this mellow tea is enjoyed particularly for its rich fragrance. It is pleasant and refreshing.

Silver Needle Pekoe
Made only with hand-picked buds in spring, this tea from Fujian province, often called 'flowery pekoe', ranks among the best and most expensive. Totally unfermented, the tea leaves are dried in the sun and very lightly oven-baked immediately prior to packing. Put about three grams of tea leaves into 200 ml of hot water, wait for around 10 minutes until the water turns yellow, then enjoy its mellowness, pleasant fragrance and richness.

DEEP AND MUSTY, the scent of Fook Ming Tong's 'unknown years [*pu-erh*]' (aged *bóu léi*) whooshes through the nostrils and down the chest to strike the belly with the resonance of a bass note. Jasmine needle, with its lighter white tea base, has more of a soprano effect, its sharp, thin fragrance flying from nose to forehead and just as quickly dissipating. It would be a mistake to choose tea while suffering from a head cold, for smell is all-important. With fermented *bóu léi* for instance, connoisseurs look for what they call the 'old' smell, a fustiness that evokes the thick odour of long-used wine barrels. The next step is a careful look at the product: tea that has been preserved in cake form is of better quality and correspondingly more expensive, so a mixture of leaves with what looks to be bits of bark, but is actually pieces of tea cake, is superior to just leaves. The last step is sampling the tea. Properly done, this also involves three stages: savouring the aroma, swirling the liquid so that the mouth and tongue are infused with the flavour, and finally, assessing the aftertaste, which might linger up to 30 minutes.

'Chinese tea in Hong Kong is like a lost culture,' says Lucy Yu, product manager for Fook Ming Tong, the upscale tea shop chain which opened in 1987. It is quite some years since the art of tea drinking, or *yám chàh*, was catered to. In the early part of the century, the district of Western boasted countless *chàh gêui*— the name given to a Chinese tea house catering to tea lovers. These establishments opened as early as 5am, closed at 10am and opened again between 11am and 3pm. They generally did no evening business. Later, in the 1950s and 1960s, tea houses stayed open from dawn through to 10pm. An article in the *Journal of the Royal Asiatic Society* described the ambience: 'The waiters used slang to report, usually in a loud voice, the consumption of patrons for making up their bills. The customers lolled about and took things at their ease, putting their legs on their own or another stool, often dressed only in a singlet and shorts in the summer months.'

Steamed shrimp and vegetable encased in paper-thin hand-made dough

Certain venues, like the long-gone Tim Nam Tea House, presented a special Cantonese musical entertainment called *nam yam*, or southern tunes. These revolved around historical epics and were often performed by blind musicians and singers. Boat people working on the cargo boats in the harbour flocked to Tim Nam to hear songs that had been passed down through generations. The singers were silenced by the tea house's demolition in 1968.

Prosperity and redevelopment, those twin enemies of tradition, gradually wiped out the *chàh gêui* and, in Hong Kong at least, *nam yam*. There remain only very few neighbourhood spots where old men and their caged songbirds can spend a few hours each day, downing innumerable cups of tea, reading the newspaper and chatting with friends. Fook Ming Tong attempted a small revival in the late 1980s, creating a tea-drinker's oasis in one of its first Central shops, where customers could sit at marble-topped tables and order a pot of impeccably brewed, intense-tasting *tit gùn yàm* (the most famous oolong tea, this is also called iron buddha) or *bóu leí* from Xishuangbanna in southern Yunnan. But customers proved reluctant to interrupt the hustle of their day for a spot of tea appreciation, and the service ended.

Compared to the studied grace of the Japanese tea ceremony, the Chinese carry out the process with relatively little ritual. Yet the emphasis on brewing the perfect cup is just as strict. One of the benefits of such a practical, direct method is that the uninitiated can learn the Chinese tea ceremony in as little as 30 minutes. When time permits, Fook Ming Tong staff teach customers how to bring out the aromatic flavour and colour of tea with the Kung Fu method. They begin by rinsing the small, empty pot with hot water. Tea leaves are placed in the pot and hot water is added again, this time to wash the leaves. This water is discarded, then more hot water is poured into the pot for brewing; any bubbles on the lid\of the pot are removed and the pot is covered. More hot water is poured over the surface of the pot to keep it warm while the tea brews. After one minute, the tea is poured into tiny delicate cups. These are filled only halfway, to avoid an imbalance of strength between the cups.

Antique-seekers who venture all the way down the steps of Cat Street in Central often stop on the second to last staircase, enticed into the Ngan Ki Heung Tea Company premises by the displays of tiny Xiying clay tea pots and glass jars of mysterious-looking leaves. The shop's kettle seems to be permanently on the boil. 'Rose tea?' asks the young saleswoman, proffering a tray of thimble-sized cups holding a pale yellow-pink liquid. Browsers accept with alacrity and soon the air is filled with murmurs of pleasure. Rose tea is not precisely tea; it is made by steeping tiny pink rosebuds from Taiwan in boiling water. Lock Cha Tea Shop, located on Queen's Road Central at the foot of the steep Cat Street steps, is similarly atmospheric, with shelves of large, antique pewter tins storing black, green and red teas. Lock Cha sells packages of the Taiwanese rosebuds alone or mixed with black tea. 'Drink it every day and it is good for the blood and the liver,' says the proprietor. 'And for women's skin!' she adds. A customer asks how long Lock Cha has been in business. 'Forty years,' says one of the staff. But she is hastily corrected by the owner: 'Seventy years,' he says with pride. 'A very long time.'

> 'Tea tempers the spirits, calms and harmonises the mind;
> it arouses thought and prevents drowsiness, enlightens and refreshes
> the body, and clears the perceptive faculties.'
> —Luk Yu

CHEF ROBERT TAM,
YEE TUNG HEEN RESTAURANT,
THE EXCELSIOR, HONG KONG
Glutinous Rice in Lotus Leaf

Glutinous rice*	280 g
Salt	3/4 tsp
Melted lard or oil	1 tbsp
Lotus leaves (20cm diameter)**	5 pieces
Filling:	
Lean pork, diced	120 g
Chicken (bite-sized pieces)	5
Yunnan ham	120 g
Shitake mushrooms	5 pieces
Carrot, diced	1 tbsp
Pork marinade:	
Cornflour	1/2 tsp
Sugar	1/2 tsp
Light soy sauce	1 tsp
Rice wine	1/4 tsp
Water	1 tbsp
Chicken marinade:	
Ground ginger	1 tsp
Cornflour	1 tsp
Rice wine	1/2 tsp
Light soy sauce	1/2 tsp
Water	1 tbsp
Gravy:	
Rice wine	1/2 tsp
Chicken stock	1/3 cup
Sugar	1 tsp
Oyster sauce, bottled	1 tsp
Light soy sauce	1 tsp
Cornflour	1 tsp (mixed with 1 tbsp water)

Boil enough water in which to soak the glutinous rice, add the rice immediately and soak for a few hours. Rinse and drain. Place a piece of muslin in a steamer. Pour in the glutinous rice and steam for 30 minutes. Remove from the steam, then add the salt and melted lard and mix well.

Add the marinade ingredients to the diced pork, mix well and leave for 20 minutes. Parboil the pork in a little hot oil until it is just cooked, drain and set aside, reserving the oil for future use. Add the chicken marinade ingredients to the chicken pieces and leave for 20 minutes. Parboil the chicken in hot oil until it is just cooked, drain and set aside. Dice the ham, boil or steam the mushrooms until just tender and blanch the carrot.

Heat a little oil in a wok, sizzle the wine, then add the remaining gravy ingredients and season to taste. Thicken the gravy with the cornflour and water mixture. Stir in the pork, chicken, ham, chopped mushrooms and carrot, mixing well and cook for about 1 minute. Turn off the heat and leave the mixture to cool.

Immerse the lotus leaves in boiling water and let soak for 30 minutes, then wash and dry. Divide the rice into ten equal parts. Place one lotus leaf on a preparation surface and place one portion of the rice in the centre of the leaf. Top the rice with 1/5 of the filling, then top with another portion of rice. Fold the leaf around the layered rice mixture as you would fold a small parcel, tucking in the edges so that it does not come apart. Repeat with the remaining lotus leaves, glutinous rice and filling. Arrange the packets in a steamer and cook over high heat for 15 minutes. Serve hot.

*   Glutinous rice (*noh máih*) is a different grain from the standard short-grain white rice (*baahk máih*); it is slightly longer and whiter in colour.

** Lotus leaves can be bought from wet markets or Chinese grocers.

CHEF FUNG HOI CHUN, REGAL CHIUCHOW RESTAURANT
Deep-fried Shrimp Rolls

Green shrimp (medium)	8 pieces
Waffle paper*	6 sheets
Sesame seeds	30–40 g
Egg white	1
Salt	1/4 tsp
Sesame oil	1/4 tsp
Rice wine	1/4 tsp
Pepper	1/4 tsp
Cornstarch	1/4 tsp (mixed with 1/4 tsp water)

Shell and de-vein the shrimp and place in a small mixing bowl. Season the shrimp with salt, sesame oil, rice wine, pepper and cornstarch-water and set aside. Cut 2 sheets of waffle paper in half to make 4 half sheets. Take one whole piece of waffle paper, lay it out flat and place one of the half sheets on top at its centre. Place 2 seasoned shrimp on the waffle paper and roll up, tucking the ends in to make a neat roll (approx. 8cm x 2–3cm). Brush the roll with 1/4 of the egg white, then roll it in a dish of sesame seeds, coating the roll. Repeat the process to make a total of 4 rolls. Heat peanut oil in a wok over medium heat to 65°C. Add the shrimp rolls and lower the heat. Fry the rolls for 1-1/2 minutes until golden brown. Drain and serve with mayonnaise.

* Waffle paper can be bought in ready-to-cook round-shaped sheets (about 20cm in diameter); it is white and slightly resembles confectioner's paper.

SPRING MOON,
THE PENINSULA, HONG KONG
Beef Balls

*Beef fillet**	*300 g*
Water	*200 ml*
Peanut oil	*1 tsp*
Water chestnuts, finely chopped	*1-1/2 tbsp*
Spring onion (white), finely chopped	*2 tsp*
Coriander	*1 tsp*
Salt	*1/2 tsp*
Sugar	*1/2 tbsp*
Cornstarch	*1/2 tbsp*
Oyster sauce	*2 tsp*
Pepper	*pinch*
Sesame oil	*2 tsp*

Mince the beef and blend into a purée by slowly adding the water. Once the beef and water are well combined, add all the remaining ingredients. Mix well and divide into 20 large walnut-sized meat balls. Steam for 8 minutes. (Makes approx. 20.)

* Use good quality beef for superior results.

6

Heaven In A Rice Bowl

'The Congee hawker has been up an hour or two before sunrise; now he sallies forth, two boxes hanging from the pole over his shoulder, each containing a large cooking pot and a small wood fire underneath. Each hawker cooks his own particular kind of Congee. ... You may have pigs' blood congee, fish congee, mulberry-root flavoured congee, or barley, or kidney or pork and a variety of other congees.' These comments about the thin rice porridge that is as malleable as Hong Kong's shoreline appeared in a *China Review* article entitled 'Chinese Street-Cries in Hong Kong' in 1873. Deciphering the words called out by sellers of food, earthen- and bamboo-ware, fans, pipes, oil, lanterns and repairers of clothing, umbrellas and clasps, writer J. Nacken painted a vivid picture of the open-air commerce that thronged the streets and pierced the air with up to half a million cries a day, he estimated. But he was intent on more than translation for entertainment's sake, for he regarded the street cries 'as one of the many outward signs by which we learn the *life* of the Chinese around us, their moral and domestic habits.' His observations bespeak a warm appreciation of the vociferous microcosm in which he lived.

As he unravelled the tangle of hawker life, Nacken couldn't help but shed a little light on colonial attitudes. As he tells it, the boisterous fanfare of everyday life brought about Ordinance No. 8 of 1872, requiring all hawkers to purchase a wooden ticket that was renewed every three months for 50 cents. On the back

'Travelling Cooked-food Stall', in pen, ink and watercolour, by Auguste Borget, c 1840s

Fresh food sellers remain a vivid part of Hong Kong's streetscape

of the ticket was a notice prohibiting crying out 'in Chung-wan [Central], on the great road [Queen's Road], and on the sea side [the Praya].' For all the muddle of sound and crowding that accompanied the activity, Nacken pointed out that the hawker's life was an ordered one. The vegetable sellers appeared like clockwork just before the two principal Chinese meal times of 9am and 5pm. 'In spring they sell celery, coarse greens, water cresses, salad, spinage [sic], and bean sprouts. In summer; pumpkins, squash, cucumbers, egg plant, popaga [sic], lotus root, bamboo sprouts, many kinds of beans, etc. In autumn: caraway plant, pepper, potatoes, taro, various cabbages etc; and in winter: mustard plants, white greens, colewort, parsley, onions, garlic, scallion, etc.' Other hawkers sold meat and fish; still others carried baskets of fowl, ducks and geese, either live or cured with oil. Some fruit hawkers sold a single variety of fruit; others carried a range of produce which they sliced into attractive portions.

In a nook off Lyndhurst Terrace, shaded by the Mid-Levels escalator that carries thousands of people down to Central each morning and back home each evening, a small group of office workers is gathered around a stall. It's more of a table, really, on which is propped a large stainless steel pot of sweet bean curd of a consistency somewhere between that of a custard and a jelly. The vendor wields her flattened scoop carefully, lifting section after wobbly section from the surface of the warm mixture. Some of the buyers take styrofoam containers of tofu flower (*dauh fuh fā*) back to the office; but most eat as they stand in the escalator's shadow. Hong Kong people don't like to eat while they're moving, all the better to concentrate on the food say some; others feel that walking while eating dirties the food. Whatever the reason, dipping into the sidewalk buffet of curried squid, pig skin, fish balls, deep-fried fragrant tofu and Western-style crêpes and waffles is a cheap, vertical experience. The preference for eating while stationary can be a boon for adventurous non-Cantonese speakers; joining the crowd and pointing at what is being eaten is an easy, non-confrontational way to experience a smorgasbord of taste.

A take-it-anywhere 'stall', is used by this hawker of sesame- and sugar-filled wafers

Street vendors follow schedules and routes as regular as a ferry timetable. Outside cinemas and entrances to schools and Mass Transit Railway stops, a gaggle of hawkers coincides with the prime time of movement. At 8:30am, oblivious to the bone-jangling din of jackhammers digging up the road between the nearby tram

Ambience is sidelined for choice barbecued duck in Shau Kei Wan

tracks, a small, serene-faced man props himself up in front of a main entrance to the large retail and commercial complex of the Landmark. On the glassed-in shelves of his perambulating shop are small bowls of a sweet gelatin pudding made with red or white beans. A man in a three-piece suit stops and points to one of the red puddings. The vendor skewers the mass with a small bamboo stick and lifts it free of the bowl. It looks for all the world like a round pudding popsicle. In the early afternoon, the same man can be found selling his unassuming, inexpensive desserts to the post-lunch crowd on Wellington Street, just a heartbeat from the chic of Lan Kwai Fong restaurants.

Usually only seen in older residential neighbourhoods, especially those where low-rise housing units predominate, olive sellers still cruise the streets and alleys in the afternoon, selling pickled olives, dried dates and sweet prunes. Calling out, song-like, they describe the wonderful qualities of their olives: they soothe the throat, stop a cough, restore the body's essence. Customers lean from windows or balconies to toss coins, and receive their orders by air mail. For the olive men package the order and then toss the bag to its destination with the deadly accuracy of a dart master, since a misdirected delivery would mean a loss—of revenue and of face. For obvious reasons, their wares are nicknamed 'airplane olives'.

They may appear out of step with the determinedly modern city around them, but these vendors are no anachronism. In the years since the streets literally rang with hawkers' cries, the selling of food—raw and cooked—has evolved into an orderly assortment of sub-cultures. From the itinerant fruit seller to the manager of a retro *dai pai dong* restaurant, each member of this multi-layered food chain is a major player in the Hong Konger's continual quest for nourishment. When it comes to food, concerns about class distinction vanish as quickly as the steam rising from a bowl of soup. Budding tycoons or—every restaurateur's wet dream—one of the ultra-visible cliques of Cantonese film stars are as likely to make a cult of a dreary hole-in-the-wall eatery as they are a venue where the prices are as haute as the cuisine. What matters is the food. Always.

> '*In the evening all the stalls and hawking tables are illuminated*
> *by paper lanterns, which, indeed, make the streets look lively and*
> *interesting.*'
> —J. Nacken, *The China Review*, 1873

DESCRIBING FOOD in Hong Kong as 'everything under the sun' is distinctly inaccurate. Here, food is everything under the sun, the moon and the stars. From the open-air food stalls in Temple Street Market to the hustle of the seafood strip at Lei Yue Mun, where customers choose their dinner from a row of bubbling fish tanks and take it to an adjacent restaurant to be cooked, great dining is not bounded by the petty restrictions of four walls or the hands of a clock. Food goes where people go, and in this city of cramped apartments, a considerable number of them spend much of their days and evenings outdoors.

This was particularly so in the late 1940s, when the city was again besieged by refugees fleeing the war between the Communists and the Guomindang. Open border aside, there was precious little welcome for the mainly poverty-stricken hordes. Rude squatter towns sprouted on almost every available patch of hillside, and tenements were filled to the rafters and beyond, thanks to inventive rooftop additions. After the horror of a Christmas Day fire in 1953 in a squatter town above Shek Kip Mei, a government resettlement programme was initiated and conditions were eventually eased. But while the crowding lasted, streetside grazing was as much a necessity as a choice, designed to cater to the masses of people whose living quarters allowed them space for sleeping, but not for cooking. This was the era when the *dai pai dong* reigned supreme.

Basic, rough, down-to-earth, the *dai pai dong*, or cooked food stall, was the crucible of Hong Kong's culinary scene. Cramped and often unhygienic, the outdoor food stall was nevertheless subject to the demands of a critical, fickle population for whom superior quality of food far outweighed any interest in ambience or style. People wrangle over the origin of the term *dai pai dong*. Some claim that '*dai pai*' refers to the licence that a food establishment must obtain; a *dai pai dong* is therefore a stall (*dong*) with a licence to sell food. Others say that since the word '*pai*' is Cantonese for 'a row of', *dai pai dong* is a row of food stalls and, indeed, in earlier times, the stalls were built in dutifully straight lines. There is, however, agreement that *dai pai dong* now means, simply, 'cooked food stall'.

The origins of the *dai pai dong* lie in the latterday portable lunch stands described by Nacken: tables shaded by large umbrellas, where the cook 'cries out his delicacies and the price of them, which varies from 2 to 8 cash a bowl. … There are beef, mutton, fish, and shrimp-congee, macaroni, vermicelli, sago soup, etc.' Over time, these temporary spots transmogrified into permanent stalls, surrounded by a clutch of stools and tables protected from the elements with a crude layering of tarpaulin and red, white and blue plastic sheeting. The stalls themselves are alarming, with walls leaning at crazy angles, overburdened electrical outlets sprouting cables, and shelves precariously stacked with tins of flour, sugar, salt, MSG and bottles of seasoning sauces. It's practically a given that the man presiding over the pots and woks looks as if he is unable to cook without a long-ashed cigarette hanging from his lips.

The lack of overheads (literal and figurative) means the stalls offer bargain basement prices. A filling breakfast of *ngàuh yuhk jùk* (beef congee), *yàuh ja gwái* (fried dough stick) and *chéung fán* (rice noodle roll) for about HK$17 is common— and there's no tipping. Like all-night diners in the West, many *dai pai dong* open early and serve past midnight, long after regular restaurants have closed their doors. Speed adds to their popularity; the stalls are renowned for placing a customer's order on the table within minutes of ordering. The menu is smaller than that of a conventional restaurant, but what they offer, they usually deliver well, using fresh and seasonal ingredients.

In their heyday, some *dai pai dong* specialised in elaborate dishes of seafood, glazed duck or claypot. But as Hong Kong's Chinese restaurant scene unfolded into one of ever-increasing diversity and experimentation, people sought simpler pleasures—congee and rice noodles—at the *dai pai dong*.

A dai pai dong, c 1950s

'CHEAP? That's not cheap!' The plump, fiftyish woman grins, remembering. 'When I was a little girl, a whole one cost 40 cents. Now, just one piece is six dollars!' She's come to visit her friend, a hawker who has parked her mobile stall at the mouth of the market in anticipation of a late-afternoon rush. Her speciality is 'folded cake', which she produces on a cart with built-in cooking pot, gas container and plastic tubs of batter. 'She goes out from noon to 2:30pm, then again from around 4pm to

Traditional fast food—griddle-cooked pancakes (bohk béng) are awaited with anticipation

8pm,' says the first woman. There's a burst of Cantonese and the friends laugh loudly. 'And she has to hide from the police; if they catch her, she has to pay HK$4,000!' The life of an unlicensed hawker is fraught, but even though the amount of the fine has been exaggerated, apparently it is worth the trouble. Customers too young to recall the glories of the 40-cent cake wait for the creamy batter poured into the black pan to set. The woman lifts the lid; the edges and bottom of the cake are brown and crispy and the top is still moist, and she lifts it from the pan. Quickly, she folds the cake in half, sprinkles on a mixture of sugar and crushed nuts, slices the half-moon into four triangles and slips each into a small plastic bag for the waiting customers. They down it immediately, for the snack is only worthwhile hot. When it cools, the cake turns from fluffy to chewy and tasteless, more of a trial to eat than a pleasure. But fresh off the griddle, it's rich and filling.

As in 1873, all purveyors of street food are supposed to be licensed. The 'folded cake' woman should have in her possession an 'itinerant hawker licence'. Those selling fruits and/or vegetables apply for a 'fixed pitch hawker licence', which restricts them to selling specified wares in a specified location. Hawker sales of fish, meat and fruit juices are illegal, as the portable stalls are not equipped with bacteria-preventing refrigeration. When it comes to the *dai pai dong*, however, strict rules of succession apply—rules aimed at the eradication of this Hong Kong institution.

The *dai pai dong* is on its way to becoming a memory. In the late 1970s, when Hong Kong was beginning to put on the contemporary face it wears now, they came under fresh scrutiny from the Urban Council, which decided that having these terminally scruffy restaurants in the heart of Central district (and, presumably, elsewhere) was 'not commensurate with the image of a modern city', as Mr Lo, chief health inspector for the Urban Services Department's Hong Kong Markets Division, so delicately puts it. There were problems of cleanliness and obstruction. Noise and cooking fumes disturbed people living around and above the stalls, often late into the night. So, since about 1980, no *dai pai dong* licence has been granted, and those in existence may be inherited only by the spouse of the original licensee. In addition, holders of current licences are encouraged to surrender their licence in return for a hefty cash payment.

'There are around four streetside cooked food stalls in Wan Chai, another twelve or thirteen in Central and two or three in Western, but these will be demolished soon.' To the passionate *dai pai dong* fan (just about every Hong Kong Chinese qualifies), Mr Lo's list makes depressing reading. The Urban Council's aim is to do away with the on-street *dai pai dong*, but not at the expense of this traditionally cheap and plentiful fare. Stall owners are invited to take up premises in the Council's purpose-built markets which accommodate produce, seafood and meat stalls on the lower floors, and the unappetisingly named 'Cooked Food Centre', usually on the top floor. The construction of one of these buildings signals the beginning of the end for all manner of food stalls in the neighbourhood: owners can either become a market tenant, with all the regulation-adherence that that implies, or shut down. Some *dai pai dong* owners choose the latter option; the hawker temperament isn't naturally drawn to a controlled environment. However, those who enter into a commercial relationship with the Urban Council can ensure their restaurant's

A hawker positions his stove-on-wheels to tempt passers-by with his fish balls and other fast-food snacks

future—their business can be willed to the person of their choice. And though the rules require that the tenant personally oversee his or her stall, the tenant may formally authorise a manager who is recognised by the council as responsible for daily operations.

IN EVERY dirge about disappearing *dai pai dong*, the Poor Man's Nightclub is sure to occupy several verses. This stretch of harbourfront between Central and Sheung Wan was for decades the focal point of outdoor night life for the working class. At its prime, it was home to over 200 stalls, completely eclipsing its Kowloon counterpart, Temple Street. A deserted site during the day, at twilight a mobile army of street vendors swarmed over the 40,000-square-foot site. As darkness descended, hundreds of kerosene lanterns brightened the moist night sky like mechanised fireflies. There were demonstrations of martial arts (side shows to pitch traditional Chinese herbal patches and pills), Chinese opera, acrobats, and countless fortune tellers who practised the ancient art of *tai sheung*, predicting a punter's fate by studying the bumps and planes of his head. And, of course, there were *dai pai dong*.

Fortunately, Temple Street Night Market in Kowloon lives on. Tourists go for the fake designer clothes and novelty calculators and watches; locals go to eat. During the day, Temple Street is an innocuous narrow road clogged with delivery vans and lined with small shops selling every household item in existence. Come late afternoon, the street begins to clear and stalls suddenly materialise. Racks of *faux* designer jeans are wheeled in, as are trays of compact discs, dubious Rolexes, digital clocks and Mont Blanc pen lookalikes. As the sky darkens to a navy blue, the aroma of beef tripe wafts along the evening breeze. As a tailor arranges his sample book of fabric swatches on the stool which comprises his made-to-measure shop, a nearby stallholder unfolds chairs and lays out canisters of bright orange plastic chopsticks on tiny wooden tables. Down the way, another man is firing up his portable stoves and stirring a couple of large cauldrons. A block away, a man parks his wheeled stove in a strategic spot: tonight's dish is glutinous rice flavoured with steamed pork sausage, pressed duck and preserved meat. The steam rises from the rice and he tends to it with slow, deliberate motions, as if he were serving dinner guests at home.

Dining in Temple Street tends to be a moving experience. A plate of pan-fried, silky-smooth tofu makes a pleasant starter. The brilliantly-lit snack shop at the corner of Parke and Nanking roads does brisk business, selling as many takeaway boxes of sweet or fried tofu to people standing in the mini-bus queue that snakes along both sides of the store front as it does to the ones who sit down for a quick bite. Down a glass of refreshing soya milk and it's time to join the crowds sauntering through Yau Ma Tei and consider the next course. Seafood restaurants seem to be Woosung Street's *raison d'être*. Menus alone aren't sufficient attraction; outside each venue is a tidy display of seafood—always fresh, much of it live. Crayfish lurch from their plates, clambering over prawns, snails and conch before the restaurant manager returns them to their rightful spot. A congee speciality is advertised with an amazing still life: an array of raw seafood and fish heads laid on a large bowl of shaved ice, above which is a flattened space for shredded meat. The endless food scenes stimulate a craving for the second course of the night: snails in black bean sauce, perhaps, or clams stir-fried with chilli.

Temple Street draws late-night diners

Temple Street's covered market shields a number of ancient *dai pai dong* from the night sky. The high peaked roof is just visible, but glancing through the dank and musty air, one feels those areas shrouded in darkness are probably best left unseen. At one table, a man applies equal attention to a horseracing form and a huge Pyrex pie plate heaped with tiny fried fish. When he gets up to go, he leaves behind screwed-up bits of newspaper and an excavation of fish skeletons. It's only tourists who look around to see if anyone's watching before they spit out prawn shells or fish bones. 'You see the heat and you think, oh well, no bacteria could survive that!' The elderly Australian woman points to the flames dancing fiercely beneath the woks and turns back to her plate of garlic prawns. Her husband has dined on a platter of chicken with cashews. They've eaten Western-style; no sharing. They've managed the chopsticks, though. If the aged stall owners see anything unusual in this approach, they're beyond showing it.

Poor Man's Nightclub was wiped out by government ordinances, but not far away, another relic of *dai pai dong* tradition soldiers on. At the turn of the century, Sheung Wan was dotted with loading docks, where thousands of coolies and stevedores laboured each day. Most of these people were of Chiu Chow origin. To serve this community, dozens of Chiu Chow *dai pai dong* emerged, offering meals of peanuts, pickled vegetables, salted egg, rice and congee—all for 30 cents. In the old days, splurging on a fish would set you back 40 cents; a plate of shrimp cost 50 cents. The stalls clustered around a small, twisting alley, which the local residents nicknamed 'Chiu Chow Alley', framed by Queen's Road West and Bonham Strand. This tiny clutch of seemingly ancient (in Hong Kong, anything over 50 years old qualifies) stalls still offers regional favourites like sliced goose marinated in master sauce. The owner of Chen Kun Kee claims that his 'bouillon', which is ritually boiled and carefully covered each day, has been ageing in the same cauldron for 50 years. Interested diners will have to keep a weather eye on these *dai pai dong* if they want to taste the veracity of this tale. An Urban Council market is planned for the area and the stalls will relocate to Mui Fong Street while it is being built. Then it will be decision time: to join the establishment or clean out that cauldron once and for all.

—·—

'BUSY? We're not so busy—look, there's an empty table over there.' Looking out at the sea of diners, Robbie Cheung's face eases into a smile as a family of six is seated, filling up the offending empty spot among the 55 variously sized tables.

Clad in Wellingtons, shorts, T-shirt and apron, Cheung works the room—in this case, the Cooked Food Centre atop the Urban Council Java Road Market in North Point—with incredible energy. He's at the seafood tanks (above them is a large sign declaring 'Don't worry! Foreigners pay the same price as Chinese!'), describing dishes that can be prepared with the shrimp, fish, eel and shellfish therein, then he's at the wok range laughingly harassing the cooks tossing mustard greens, noodles or crab in their gigantic woks, then he's darting amongst the diners with a large platter heaped with carefully arranged raw seafood and placing it beside a hot pot.

Seafood forms an integral and favoured part of the Hong Kong diet

Tung Po Seafood Restaurant is a *dai pai dong* that came in out of the cold and transformed into something more determinedly upmarket. Cheung, who has 14 years' experience managing restaurants in Hong Kong and Britain, took over what had been his father-in-law's *dai pai dong* four years ago. The extensive menu and superior quality of the food are evidence of Tung Po's upscale claims, but in ambience and style the experience is diehard *dai pai dong*. Folding tables and plastic stools are hauled into various contortions, depending on the size of the group. Tableware and cutlery are placed on the table in a shallow tin pan full of cold tea and then doused with another blast of tea from the pot, so that diners can follow tradition and rinse their bowls, chopsticks and spoons before ordering. 'Hong Kong people are used to doing this,' says Cheung, 'so even though our dishes are already clean, we make it easy for them.' Order a beer and the tall bottle is thunked down on the table, uncapped and poured into small soup bowls which have been cooling in the refrigerator alongside the rows of Heineken and Carlsberg.

There's no English menu, but Cheung and his young staff are capably fluent. Besides, much of what's on offer depends on what's swimming in the tanks as well as what's been trucked in from fields north of the border. Deep-fried bamboo fish, served whole with a sprinkling of shredded spring onion and coriander leaves, is a popular choice, the crispy coating surrounding impossibly tender fish. The English newspaper and Internet reviews pasted on the walls of the restaurant wax lyrical about the *fung sa* chicken (*fung sâ gai*). Dipping the thick chunks of moist meat topped with thin, crackly skin in a sauce of soy, vinegar and chopped garlic, it's easy to see how the writers were transported to such creative heights. Razor clams (ask for 'long shellfish') have the unsettling look of an old lady's fingers, all knuckle and thin bone, but are tasty when cooked with crunchy onion and peppers in a generous mix of rice wine and soy and sweet and sour sauces. Squid is boiled to just-done perfection, laced with a thick sauce made from the black ink and topped with parsley. The delicacy of taste is a luscious contrast to the messiness of eating the dish.

Many traditional dai pai dong, which have relocated to Urban Council cooked food centres, retain a loyal following

BUSINESS WAS always brisk at Ying Kee, especially on cool nights. And especially late on cool nights. Tram drivers, bus conductors and all-night taxi hustlers, kindred spirits, huddled in groups of two or three, blue-grey smoke rising from unfiltered cigarettes, a glass of Ying Kee's famous milk tea on the rickety wooden tables in front of them. It was time to catch up on who was doing what and to whom, maybe to marvel at the luck of the punter who hit the daily double at Happy Valley that week. There were other *dai pai dong*, but there was no better place for a late-night chinwag, and certainly there was no better place for *náaih chàh*—the strong brew of milk tea that was pioneered by *dai pai dong*. The huge tea urns at Ying Kee worked non-stop, making gallons of strong brew into which was poured huge dollops of sweetened condensed milk. The customers liked their tea strong and sweet, and they stirred in extra spoonfuls of sugar when the tea was served in a clear heat-resistant glass. A nocturnal visit to this legendary open-air food stall in Wan Chai was called a *gâ dihn*, or a charge-up, a reference to the establishment's caffeine-laden concoction. Those who had no time to sit and chat came with their own takeaway containers. In pre-styrofoam days, these were often large enamel mugs to be filled with *náaih chàh*; the next morning, many of those mugs would be put to another use, holding water as their owner brushed his teeth.

Fast forward 30 years. Ying Kee is still in business, although no longer in under-the-stars mode. Since Hong Kong's Urban Council curtailed the operations of open-air *dai pai dong* and brought most of them indoors, Ying Kee has operated from the top floor of the Wan Chai Urban Council Food Market on Lockhart Road. The business hasn't skipped a beat. The original owner handed the reins to his daughter and she keeps a vigilant eye on the ever-busy tea urns. 'Except for the move, we haven't closed a single day in 60 years!' she says with pride.

———

PROBABLY NO food defines Hong Kong's outdoor dining scene like won ton noodle. A simple dish at its best, yet elegant in that simplicity. The classic bowl of won ton noodle consists of four delicate fluffy dumplings filled with minced pork and freshwater shrimp. They are boiled in a savoury broth, and poured in a bowl with a small coil of egg noodle and chives. Red vinegar adds flavour to the won ton. Perfect dumplings resemble puffs of floating clouds.

In Cantonese, won ton means 'to swallow the cloud'. Although won ton noodle is sold in many noodle shops and restaurants, purists insist that the *dai pai dong* serves the best. During a late-night stroll through parts of old Kowloon, one follows the enticing aroma of the broth, and the sound of a bubbling cauldron and hissing butane flame. The tables are small and the stools rickety. Rinsing the chopsticks with hot tea (known as 'disinfection') is prudent. But when the steaming bowl is delivered, it's time to swallow the clouds and touch heaven.

Won ton noodle became a popular street food in turn-of-the-century Guangzhou. The Mak family had been noodle makers for generations before Mak Chee perfected the art of mixing whole eggs into the noodle dough. He

Carrying on a family tradition at Mak Aun Kee

sold his won ton noodle on the streets of Guangzhou from a portable noodle stand which he named 'Chee Kee'. He started business at 8pm daily, and when his stock sold out, he would call it a night. Legend has it that the fame of his noodles grew until word reached the ear of the wife of Guangzhou's governing general. The First Lady of Guangzhou supposedly started visiting the noodle stand in her chauffeured limousine. Her private bodyguards would stop traffic as her ladyship savoured a bowl of curbside noodles. Later, legend continues, Mak Chee was asked to feed the general's guests with noodles cooked in the general's kitchen. Mak Chee insisted on using his own stoves, so the general would send two vehicles—a staff car for the noodle maker and a truck for his stove.

By the end of World War II, Chee Kee had seven shops in Canton and one in Macau. After 1949, the family emigrated to Hong Kong and at the age of 82, Mak Chee started a noodle *dai pai dong* with his three sons. Today, his tradition is carried on by his sons and son-in-law. The family's best-known location is Mak Aun Kee, a noodle shop on Wellington Street in Central. '*Aun*' is Cantonese for small—meaning that the won ton noodle is served the traditional way, in small bowls. The dumplings themselves are also small, with a delicacy of flavour. In preserving tradition, the Mak family chooses to ignore the recent trend to serve dumplings the size of golf balls. 'Small bowl that costs twice as much,' sniff detractors, and it's true that across the street from Mak Aun Kee you can have half-again as much won ton for around 30 per cent less. Tell that to the gourmands who stream into the cosy old noodle shop for snacks of won ton noodle or beef tendon, with a side order of oyster sauce vegetables—taste counts to this crowd, and many of them follow up a serving of pork and shrimp dumpling with an order of beef with rice noodles. There's a high ratio of mobile phones and well-cut suits, and some diners go cross-eyed trying to keep one eye on their bowl and the other on their illegally parked Mercedes or BMW.

With the number of *dai pai dong* diminishing, won ton noodle is enjoyed in noodle shops, easily identifiable by the stoves and pots simmering at the front of the restaurant. Years ago, when the broth was cooked on wood-burning stoves, the Health Department passed regulations requiring that the smoky stoves be moved back to the kitchen. Reluctantly, many restaurants complied. It was a disaster. Customers wouldn't eat won ton noodle without seeing the fresh ingredients displayed and cooked in the aromatic, steamy mini-kitchen. They stayed away in droves, business dropped off and some restaurants were forced to close. The Health Department gave in and allowed the stoves to be returned to their original position, but only if they were gas-fuelled.

THE GRADUAL disappearance of the *dai pai dong* is a cause of great lamentation, especially amongst the post-war and babyboomer generations. They look upon Hong Kong as their home, unlike their parents and grandparents, who tended to view it as a temporary haven no matter how entrenched their lives became. It's no coincidence that the current retro trend in restaurants—characterised by decor heavy in wood panelling, etched glass, high-backed booths and menus emphasising authentic, traditional food—took off when the babyboomers and their elder siblings reached an age when nostalgia pangs began to make themselves felt. Some of those hankering for a taste of

Retro Dai Pai Dong feeds a hunger for nostalgia

their past became restaurateurs, re-creating tangible snapshots from a mental photo album of childhood memories and serving dim sum and congee in authentic, if gussied-up, fashion.

The originators of the Dai Pai Dong chain of restaurants, subtitled 'Passion of Old Hong Kong', timed brilliantly the launch of their old-style, basic restaurants serving food-stall favourites. The first outlet opened in late 1993; the fifth location in 1997, in Tai Po. Simon Wong Ka-Wo, chairman of Kamperi Co., which manages Coffee Chateau and BYOC (Brew Your Own Coffee), devised the concept. 'I'm middle-aged,' he explains. 'I was born here and I like Hong Kong. I have friends who share these feelings, and we figured that since we are in the food business, we should do something to capture the spirit of Hong Kong.'

Dai Pai Dong restaurants evoke the tastier aspects of the old-style food stall experience. The rosewood tables are highly polished; the roughed-up walls are clean and dotted with a few period calendars and posters. The ambience is appreciated by the older clientele but, as ever, the food's the thing. The cooks manning grill and wok are all former *dai pai dong* cooks completely at home cooking up fried rice, noodles, duck's gizzard, satay squid balls and pork knuckle with ginger. The *dai pai dong* treatment of Western basics can be tasted in toast served with condensed milk, fried egg, butter and jam. House special french toast is a tall (two slices of bread have been slapped together and dipped in the egg-milk batter before frying) golden slab, topped with a large pat of butter.

Dai pai dong coffee is a top seller. Into every glass goes a huge dollop of condensed milk and, no matter what one's feelings on the subject of this viscous substance in coffee, it's a little painful to imagine what the brew tastes like in its unadulterated form. With the milk, it's oddly palatable. *Yuân yâng* is more of an acquired taste. Described as half coffee/half tea, the blend is actually around three-quarters tea. Otherwise, says the waiter, the coffee would overwhelm. As it is, the milk does the domineering and *yuân yâng* tastes like strong, milky tea with a chicory aftertaste.

Wong has a passionate, almost visceral connection to the food stalls of his childhood, for it was his father, a supplier of coffee beans, tea and *yuân yâng* to restaurants and street hawkers, who conceived the method of brewing coffee, tea and *yuân yâng* that is uniquely *dai pai dong*. 'This was 50 or 60 years ago,' says Wong. 'They make a bag out of cloth and put either tea leaves or ground coffee inside. Boiled water is poured over the bag

A neon sign summons diners to try Ah Yee Leng Tong's hearty, traditional soups

and the coffee or tea drips into a pot. The coffee or tea is poured through the bag again—up to four times.' Crushed eggshell is sometimes added to the contents of the bag, for a smoothing quality. The origins of *yuân yâng* are a mystery, but Wong claims the caffeine-rich drink was popular with labourers seeking to boost their energy.

———··———

THE 1990s will be remembered for the period of intense competition that dominated the middle of the decade, and the flourishing of retro venues. Several years ago, Italian food was all the rage, until a pasta-sated public finally cried 'basta!' Nouvelle Chinese cuisine had a brief fling at the start of the decade. Lately, congee, soup, noodles, dim sum and desserts have all undergone a lavish retro-style sprucing up. Venues like Ah Yee Leng Tong (soups), Sweet Dynasty (desserts), the gone-but-not-forgotten Super Bowl (congee) and Dim Sum restaurant in Happy Valley reflect a community seeking its own identity. Having rejoined the mainland, Hong Kong people are examining their history and society for clues about what constitutes their identity. In culinary terms, there is much to celebrate.

DAI PAI DONG RESTAURANT
Yèuhng Jàu Fried Rice

Cooked rice	250 g
Barbecued pork*	75 g
Cooked small shrimp	60 g
Beaten egg	1
Lettuce, shredded	60 g
Spring onion	1 tbsp
Salt	1/4 tsp
Peanut oil	2 tbsp

Cook short-grain white rice the day before preparing the dish. If buying fresh shrimp, peel, wash, de-vein and poach the shrimp for a few minutes until tender, then set aside. Heat the oil in a wok and pour in the beaten egg. As the egg begins to coat the bottom of the wok, add the rice and stir-fry until the rice grains are coated with egg. Add the barbecued pork, shrimp and salt. Stir-fry until all the ingredients are well mixed. Stir in the shredded lettuce and sprinkle with the spring onion. Serve immediately. (Makes enough for 1 plate of rice.)

* Ready-cooked barbecued pork can be bought from selected supermarkets and barbecue restaurants.

Red Bean Sweet Soup

Chinese red beans	120 g
White lotus seeds	60 g
Sugar*	6 tbsp

Place the red beans and white lotus seeds in 8 cups of water in a saucepan and bring to the boil. Once the water is boiling, reduce the heat to low, cover the saucepan and simmer very slowly for 2 hours or until the red beans are tender. Add the sugar and stir until dissolved. Ladle the soup into small bowls and serve as a dessert.

* Dai Pai Dong uses rock sugar, an unrefined brown sugar sold in solid form in Hong Kong supermarkets. The rock sugar gives a less sweet result than refined white sugar.

CHEF ROBERT TAM,
YEE TUNG HEEN RESTAURANT,
THE EXCELSIOR, HONG KONG
Stuffed Crystal Prawns

Green prawns (medium)	8 pieces (250 g)
Chinese cabbage (choi sum), leaves only	100 g
Yunnan ham, thinly sliced	50 g
Salt	pinch
Chicken stock powder	3 tbsp
Sesame oil	3 drops
Egg white	1
Cornstarch	1 tsp (mixed with 1 tbsp water)

Peel prawns, leaving the tail intact, devein and wash. Make a deep 2–3cm-long incision in the middle of the back of each prawn. Take one prawn and stuff 1 small leaf of *choi sum* together with a small piece of Yunnan ham (5–6cm) into the prawn. Repeat with remaining prawns. In a bowl, mix together the chicken stock powder, sesame oil, egg white and cornstarch-water mix. Add the stuffed prawns and mix well. Heat about 5–6 tablespoons of peanut oil in a wok and add the prawns and egg white mixture to the wok and stir-fry for approximately 2 minutes or until the prawns are cooked through. Serve immediately.

FOOK YUEN SEAFOOD RESTAURANT
Double Boiled Papaya With Almond Milk

Papaya (small, just ripe)	2
Rock sugar	10-cm piece
Milk	1-1/4 cup
Blanched almonds	20

Cut off the top of the papaya and carefully scoop out the seeds and pith and discard. Replace the top and secure with toothpicks and set aside. Put water into the bottom of a double boiler and place the papaya into the top section, secure the lid then boil for 15 to 20 minutes, or until the papaya has softened. While the papaya is cooking, in another pan, heat the almond milk and rock sugar on medium heat until just boiling, stirring constantly to dissolve the sugar and taking care the milk does not scorch. Cook until the sugar is dissolved then set aside. Remove the papayas from the double boiler and scoop out the fruit into two serving bowls. Pour the warm almond milk over the hot papaya dividing it equally between the two bowls. Serve immediately.

Almond milk: finely crush the blanched almonds and put into a blender with the milk. Blend until combined. Alternatively, use 5–6 drops of almond essence, or to taste, if a completely smooth milk texture is preferred.

7

The No-so-wild West

'It used to be an incredibly leisurely existence. You had leisure, and more leisure.' Like most remembrances of things past, it takes some imagination to reconcile history with contemporary reality. Picturing 1930s' Hong Kong as a city of languid lifestyle, against the impatient energy that sets today's cracking pace, is a challenge. The propensity for demolishing buildings that, with their drawing rooms, their gracefully columned verandahs, their gardens and even the occasional ballroom, might remind one of a more gracious time adds to the wholesale conviction that Hong Kong was always thrustingly modern, always accelerating at full tilt. But, as a long-time resident recollected for Nigel Cameron's *Hong Kong: The Cultured Pearl*, colonial life was once unhurried and alcohol-sodden. 'Drink was so cheap that when you asked for a gin and lime in a bar—they served them then in flat champagne-type glasses, it was the cocktail era—the barman just went on pouring gin until you told him to stop. ... People drank themselves stupid in those days. ... You drank gin before dinner, whisky with the food and brandy after.'

The climate has to be a mitigating factor: there was precious little relief from the oppressive humidity and heat in those pre-airconditioning days. Fans did little more than stir the torpid air in teasing imitation of a breeze, and expatriates inexplicably overdressed in thick suits and fussy dresses that were uncomfortable at the least, and caused heat rashes and blisters at the worst. Then, too, time for

The opening of M at the Fringe ushered in a new era of superior, independent Western restaurants

Hong Kong's early social calendar was filled with tea dances, soirees and balls

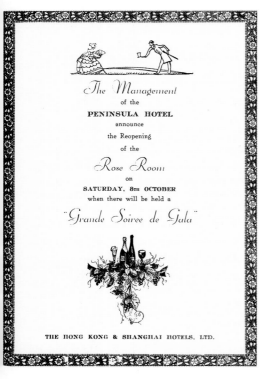

The *Management* of the
PENINSULA HOTEL
announce
the Reopening
of the
Rose Room
on
SATURDAY, 8TH OCTOBER
when there will be held a
"*Grande Soiree de Gala*"

THE HONG KONG & SHANGHAI HOTELS, LTD.

socialising didn't have to be snatched from a schedule filled with power breakfasts, multi-meeting days and business travel. That heavy-drinking colony was still a backwater, a dull little thing compared to Shanghai and its rip-roaring decadence and upper echelons of the massively rich and powerful.

Despite the Americans and other assorted nationalities who called Hong Kong home, British domination of the expatriate circle bred a social life which was decidedly British in personality. Picnics, dinner parties, regattas, balls, tea dances and amateur theatricals threatened to ruin a perfectly leisurely existence. For a time in the early 1930s, eccentricity literally ran riot in the New Territories as hunters rode to hounds trained to chase civet, paper or aniseed trails. The Fanling Hunt Ball joined a luminous list of formal functions like the St Andrew's Ball and the St George's Ball.

'I put it down to the British background, that people here generally don't like to talk about food.' Michelle Garnaut raps the table with mock severity. 'It's not stoic, it's not Protestant!' There was a lot of talk, though, when in 1989 the Australian opened M at the Fringe, known simply as Michelle's. Then, Western dining options were limited to the hotels, Chinese-run restaurants serving local versions of Western dishes and those stalwarts of Lan Kwai Fong, Post 1997 and California. With its rose- and mustard-painted walls, treble clef-shaped chairbacks, silver candelabras, old bone cutlery and funky tableware, Michelle's had confidence and style— oodles of both were needed to get this first independent upmarket restaurant to stake out Western territory off the ground.

'It was very difficult to get staff at first,' Garnaut recalls. 'People thought it was risky, that we were a fly-by-night operation.' It didn't help that she went against accepted practice by refusing to install the usual captain and junior captain combo to run the wait staff. 'I had been to too many restaurants where every table was served by nine waiters and you never knew who was responsible for you.' It must have seemed that her customers needed as much retraining as the waiters and cooks who finally joined the radical team. Nobody would touch the salad made with strawberries and strawberry vinaigrette from menu 1 or 2, for instance. Since then, tastes have changed enormously. There are no quibbles with menu 18, as Garnaut hears for herself on the long walk through her restaurant: diners call her over to introduce their friend, their parents, their spouse; they praise the Moroccan platter and chargrilled calves liver; one gentleman waxes lyrical about the tart-themed comestibles table ('Oh, the red pepper tart!'), smacking his fingertips with a *moue* of pure pleasure. Tellingly, he is not a Brit who has conquered a legacy of stoic behaviour through the therapy of great food; he is Chinese and completely comfortable showing his appreciation for culinary virtuosity.

FOR A TIME, squeezed into a cramped space on Staunton Street, there used to be unwitting evidence of the fragmentation that has occurred in Hong Kong's expatriate world over the last decade. Even five years ago, a takeaway based on the combination of Austrian, Finnish and Greek food would have been unthinkable. But an unlikely *ménage à trois* opened in early 1996 and O'Wien survived long enough to convince its owners that there was room for a Scandinavian restaurant, to which they eventually devoted their efforts. O'Wien's menu offered souvlaki with tzatziki, bratwurst with sauerkraut and grilled salmon steak. The split personality initially made for great newspaper copy, but the tiny hole-in-the-wall takeaway and sometime café outlasted the honeymoon period granted by bemused food writers.

Contemporary expatriate society has a personality even more splintered than that of O'Wien. At the beginning of the 1990s, Americans and Canadians outnumbered the British, but by 1996 the three groups each comprised around 30,000 people. (These figures include native passport holders and those who have fulfilled residency requirements and returned to Hong Kong.) Filipino residents outnumber all three. There are sizeable communities of Japanese, Australians, Indians, Thais and Malaysians, and smatterings of Scandinavians,

Heavy-traffic locations, especially shopping centres, generally house Western restaurants

Germans, Italians, Spaniards and French. But even as a combined group, they are not enough: Western restaurants must play to a wider audience than could ever be provided by the sum total of expatriates (who account for just five per cent of the population). They cannot flourish, let alone pay the astronomical rent (depending on the location, monthly costs of HK$500,000 are not unheard of), without appealing to a sizeable proportion of the Chinese population.

In the mid-1980s, Hong Kong's high-octane economy and internationalisation meant that, whether for business or pleasure, affluent Hong Kong Chinese went exploring Europe and North America as never before. Business was the prime motive, but the sampling of different cuisines had a gradual knock-on effect at home. Meanwhile, the brain drain of 1997-related immigration saw large numbers of the middle class go to Canada, the United States and Australia; not long after, the pull of Hong Kong's full-employment economy drew many of the recent migrants back. They returned with an appetite for the foods they had grown to love during their residency-seeking sojourns. The walls came tumbling down, figuratively and literally, as some restaurateurs chose to break free of the formality that had dominated since, well, forever, and went about installing California-style open kitchens and putting pizza ovens in full view of the clientele. Many of the grill rooms that had been considered an absolute necessity by every fine hotel were pulled from their decaying pedestals and in their place came a bevy of lighter, fanciful bistros, trattorias and American west coast-inspired venues. For better or for worse, 'concept' entered the vocabulary of chef and diner.

Where there had been all-purpose Italian restaurants, now there is Tutto Meglio and its Florentine menu, Va Bene's northern Italian food, Nicholini's upmarket trattoria, Grappa's olive oil-laced hunks of fresh bread and Toscana's Tuscan dishes at the Ritz-Carlton, among a raft of others. One of the most heartening developments is that fewer restaurateurs are altering their cuisine to

Luxury supermarkets, lavishly stocked with all manner of Asian and Western foods, are a new trend

suit the Cantonese palate, presumably because that palate no longer requires such coddling.

America was rediscovered in the salads, burgers and sky-high carrot cake of The American Pie, Dan Ryan's buffalo chicken wings and slabs of ribs, Gripps' surf 'n turf and 16-ounce steaks, and Caesar salad in a parmesan basket, mussels baked in saffron and desserts of Californian finesse at Napa. French cuisine came down off its high horse, and bistros like Le Fauchon, W's Entrecote and La Cité opened, along with The Pavilion's petite, luminous nod to the excesses of 18th-century France. Above Hollywood Road, narrow side streets whose only claim to fame had been that they survived the three-year building of the Mid-Levels escalator suddenly sprouted intimate Italian, French, Portuguese, Scandinavian and Nepalese restaurants, even a Himalayan coffee shop. The restaurateurs coined a name for the area and it stuck: Soho (South of Hollywood Road). The Ferrari-sleek espresso machines (and better, people who knew how to use them) of Café Central, Uncle Russ, Coffee Chateau and Pacific Cup turned a dire java situation into a coffee bean-worshipper's convention.

This is not to say, however, that the slate was simply wiped clean to make way for new ventures. Fine dining has been dealt a heavy blow, but Hong Kong is too fond of conspicuous consumption for it to completely disappear. The prominence of fussy French restaurants has diminished, but Petrus, perched on the 56th floor of the Island Shangri-La hotel, faces no such decline, or chances are they would not have enticed chef Verzeroli, formerly executive sous chef at Paris's Michelin-starred Restaurant Joel Robuchon, to take over the kitchen. Michael Hendler, in charge of the hotel's food and beverage, himself came to Hong Kong in 1979 as a chef in the Mandarin Oriental's French restaurant, Pierrot. 'There's still a market for Petrus,' he says. 'I'm amazed at how much vintage wine we've sold. Last month, one table bought almost HK$250,000 worth of wine—they drank some with their dinner and took some bottles home.'

Some old stalwarts have disappeared, but the Western dining environment expanded to sandwich the new amongst the existing strata. Sammy's Kitchen, in Sheung Wan, still features the complicated French and Continental dishes (escargots bourguignon, veal marsala, cherries jubilee) that the restaurant's eponymous owner, Sammy Yip, learned in the kitchens of the Peninsula, Miramar and Hilton hotels a few decades ago. Sammy presides over the Grill Room, a separately enclosed space that is decorated a little more smartly than the rest of the place, recommending wines from a surprisingly decent list to the courting couples and small groups of friends and family who make up his clientele. A

dapper, soft-spoken man, the restaurateur is gentle and hospitable; it was probably he who taught his non-English-speaking waitress to precede her delivery of dishes with a friendly 'Hello!', though he probably didn't intend her to speak with such gusto. True to the formal cuisine which dominated upper-crust dining when Sammy was learning his craft, the menu is a fiery one. Sammy himself slips periodically into the kitchen to flambé a slice of fish, a slab of meat, a dessert or one of 'Sammy's Special Coffees'. Dinner just wouldn't be quite right without at least one flambéed course.

People cling to their favourites, as the keepers of Hugo's at the Hyatt Regency know. When, some ten years ago, word got out that the hotel's restaurants were to be renovated, so many regular customers threatened to take their business elsewhere if an interior designer laid so

As recently as the late 1980s, cheese and speciality meats were difficult to find

much as a finger on their beloved Hugo's, that management decided to leave the baronial crossed swords and heavy black grills, as well as the menu with its broiled steaks and tableside preparation of salads, crêpes suzette and Spanish coffee, exactly as they had always been.

IT WAS a textbook case of 'Chinese whispers'. The story goes that when Westerners first tasted the chicken wings at Tai Ping Koon Restaurant they exclaimed, 'Sweet! Sweet!' To the restaurant staff, this sounded like 'Swiss! Swiss!' Thinking that the chef had somehow happened on an Alpine speciality, they dubbed the baked chicken wings doused in heavily sweetened soy sauce, 'Swiss sauce chicken wings'. It has remained so for almost 50 years, even though (or more likely because) the customers are all familiar with the malapropism.

Given the average Hong Konger's intimate knowledge of the multitude of cuisines within the area's small borders,

Local fast food chains offer a mixed grill of Chinese and Western dishes, with lunch specials like cream of chicken soup with pork chops and e-fu noodles with straw mushrooms

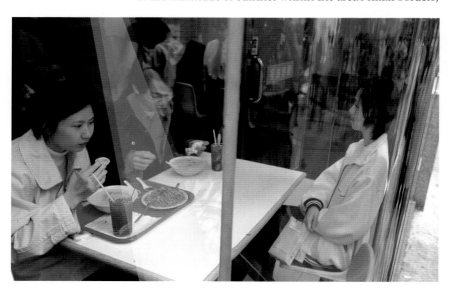

it's no surprise that *sih yàuh sâu châan*, literally 'soy sauce Western meals', are familiar to virtually every Chinese resident old enough to be trusted with a chicken wing. It is a little startling, however, to see the multi-generational queue forming outside Tai Ping Koon's Yau Ma Tei venue (there are locations in Tsim Sha Tsui and Causeway Bay as well) on a Saturday night. This is history preserved, but not in aspic. Within this era-specific environment of dark panelled walls, purple-jacketed, bow-tied waiters and kitschy geometric murals is relaxed, nostalgic immersion in the past for local diners and a curious, what-year-is-this-anyway experience for everyone else.

'This is Western food at the height of its bastardisation,' says food critic Stephen Wong cheerfully, as he tucks into a bowl of bird's nest cream of chicken soup. The thick, cornstarch-laced liquid is typical of the genre. (In the 1950s, similar restaurants popularised compradore soup: a sort of cream of shark's fin soup. Compradores were entrepreneurs who liaised between early Western businesses and the Chinese community, and in the process became fabulously wealthy; thus the dish linked expensive ingredients of East and West.) The menus of Tai Ping Koon, Boston, Czarina, Wellington and restaurants of their ilk have long offered a tentative exploration of Western cuisine. Heavy cream soup bases and hearty servings of meat, often presented on a sizzling platter, give a 'foreign' touch, while familiar Chinese ingredients—there are 38 rice dishes alone on the Tai Ping Koon menu—provide a comfort factor. The food is plentiful and, while not exactly cheap, the hefty portions make for good value. But it is more likely to thrill the sentimental than the gourmand.

Chinese interpretations of Western cuisine began in the restaurants and kitchens of the foreign factories of Guangzhou (Canton) and in the Portuguese enclave of Macau. The founder of Tai Ping Koon, Chui Lo-Ko, cooked Western food for the expatriate staff of a trading company. He opened his first restaurant in 1858 and, according to the menu notes, became renowned for his roast pigeon, smoked pomfret and Portuguese baked chicken. In Hong Kong, Western restaurants run by Chinese owners have been around since the beginning of the 20th century, when the Chinese population was moving eastward beyond the boundaries of Chinatown in Western, and merging with the former domain of the expatriate residents (primarily Central and Wan Chai). Chinese society was more complex by then, with a hierarchy encompassing more, and higher, levels than the fisherfolk, labourer and small merchant classes which had first settled in the area. While researching distinctions in Hong Kong's food culture, anthropology student Cheng Sea-Ling found: 'Merchants and others of the middle

Hotels dominated Hong Kong's culinary scene for more than a century

class, while not admitted to places of European exclusivity, started going to both Western-style restaurants like the Wellington and to grand Chinese restaurants like Ying King Grand Restaurant in Wan Chai. Those who aspired to Britishness felt that being able to eat the foreigners' food would bring them closer to the Westerners.'

Post-World War II Hong Kong was characterised by a fierce energy to rebuild the city, and a profound shift in the balance of power. The fall of Hong Kong and the Japanese occupation had dealt a stronger blow to colonial arrogance than any law could ever have done. By the end of the 1940s, money, not race, determined who would live where, and clubs and institutions had multiracial memberships. The prominence of Chinese-run restaurants serving soy sauce Western meals can, on a superficial level, be attributed to a desire to emulate the former, now fading, power class. The culinary adventurousness of the Chinese certainly played an important role. But the development of the trend is also symbolic of a generation's heightened self-awareness; showing an ability to incorporate a colonial legacy, but on its own terms.

PAUL HSU runs ten restaurants: four Italian, one Vietnamese, one American, two French, one Japanese and one Portuguese (in Macau). Today, however, the man has bagels on his mind. 'I love bagels,' he says wistfully. 'I was just in the States and I brought a dozen back from Berkeley, frozen, in my hand luggage.' The American bagel boom ('even in Oklahoma!') has a certain poignancy for him; a Hong Kong bagel venture he was involved in several years ago faded away when its American department store landlord closed down.

Hong Kong-born Hsu worked in hotel food and beverage for years, in the United States with Hyatt, then Hilton in Shanghai, before returning to his home town in 1991 to form Elite Concepts with Allan Zeman, a Canadian garment manufacturer who branched out into property and food and who is referred to as the landlord of Lan Kwai Fong, a two-street pocket of Central crammed with multi-storey buildings of bars and restaurants. Elite was Hong Kong's first concept restaurant business—a concept itself that throws up questions about the importance of form versus function. Some of its best achievements are natural, as in Tutto Bene's generous al fresco patio on Knutsford Terrace in Tsim Sha Tsui; others have been carefully shaped, as in the moody, evocative Indochine and discreetly chic Tutto Meglio in Lan Kwai

'Concept' entered Hong Kong's food lexicon in the early 1990s

Fong. The danger of over-dedication to environment is that the outcome might not sit well within its own skin; that too much is contrived. Hsu has a disconcerting habit of referring to food as 'product', but he insists that the cuisine comes first. 'We always go product first, but we look for atmosphere to bind it together,' he says. 'We try to blend our theme, atmosphere, service and food. We want it to be like a story: the service and atmosphere is the build-up, the food is the killer. Some places hit you right off, but it's much better to have it build to a climax.'

When the managing director of the 1997 Group, Nichole Garnaut (sister of M at the Fringe proprietor Michelle), first saw a proposed new warehouse space that one of her staff thought might be suitable for storage, she knew she had stumbled on one of the best entrances in Hong Kong. 'I walked down the lane into this rat-infested place and I could see it.' Tun Wo Lane, a slender alley between Lyndhurst Terrace and Hollywood Road, then bustled with activity during daylight hours with workmen cleaning and packing Chinese flowering cabbage (*choi sum*) and Chinese white cabbage (*baahk choi*) into large wicker baskets, and customers picking their way through the detritus of green vegetable to a vegetarian Chinese restaurant. A little further along were a few apartment buildings and the prize: an empty three-storey house. Over the next months, Garnaut and her 1997 Group colleagues evicted the resident rodents and created a petite, whimsical bar-cum-restaurant: Petticoat Lane. Featuring tall, plump scarlet banquettes, an undulating marble bar, blowsy fringed lamps and Modigliani-like portraits on the wall, comparisons to an upmarket bordello are inevitable. (A description employing at least a hint of the sexual is irresistible by virtue of its reputation as a gay-friendly venue.) The tiny kitchen dictated a necessarily tiny menu—soup, salads and a hot dish—but soon besuited professionals and members of the trendy classes were tripping down formerly unremarkable Tun Wo Lane, to the great amusement of the vegetable scrubbers and packers. A year or so later, Garnaut obtained the next-door site and opened The Pavilion, a small but sumptuous tribute to 18th-century French courtesan and mistress of King Louis XV, Madame Pompadour.

Ask an expatriate how they landed in Hong Kong and usually one of two stories emerges: the two- or three-year contract or the interrupted backpacking trip. Nichole Garnaut belongs to the latter contingent. 'I was on my way to Greece—I still haven't got there,' she laughs. She found work at Post 1997 and a future business partner in owner Christian Rhomberg. She has launched some of Hong Kong's most winsome restaurants, places steeped in personality without screaming 'concept!'.

'I have a passion for this business,' she says simply. 'I never really consider what the market needs or wants.' Her decision, for example, to replace the Middle-Eastern restaurant, Mecca 97, with an Italian antipasto and coffee bar was the stuff of inspiration, not marketing surveys. 'I'd just come back from Italy and I'd loved the roadside bars there and thought, why not? We sketched it out in one afternoon.' Dolce Vita's open-air conviviality packs them in. A more recent venture into far-flung Quarry Bay, Q Bar, is proving a harder sell, but the group has the sturdy profit base required to weather a slow start.

'I actually think the restaurant business is easier here than in Australia or the UK,' says Garnaut. 'If you have a bit of confidence about you, and if you're a bit pushy, you can get it done.' The drawbacks are in relation to food; specifically, to produce. Garnaut talks longingly of simple, pure salads, composed of fresh greens and juicy tomatoes, lightly drizzled with olive oil. But most European produce is imported, much of it arrives frozen and menus must be written accordingly. When simplicity is not available as an ingredient, strength comes with creative, informed melding of tastes and textures. At The Pavilion they make a glorious salad with wilted spinach leaves atop chargrilled leeks and topped with curls of fresh Parmesan—it's not the apex of simplicity to which Garnaut wishes her restaurants could aspire, but it's simply delicious.

EVERY YEAR, on an October morning, cooks clear the tables in the kitchen and set out masses of raisins, sultanas, candied peel and demerara sugar. Neil Mackenzie, kitted out in an apron, his shirt sleeves rolled up, steps forward, raises the brandy bottle in his right hand and the bottle of stout in his left and begins to pour. The alcoholic fragrances meet and mingle in the air, and smiling broadly as the smell stirs memories of years past, the staff and managers of Jimmy's Kitchen flex their arm muscles, and share jokes and reminiscences. When the ingredients are drenched, everyone takes a turn mixing the heavy batter. 'People look to Jimmy's Kitchen to uphold traditions,' says Mackenzie, managing director of Jimmy's Kitchen Ltd, a seven-restaurant group, including two branches of the original restaurant and Landau's. It's a legacy he takes seriously; in performing the pudding ritual he follows in the footsteps of his uncle, Emil Landau, and his grandfather, Aaron Landau, who started the business.

Inspired by a restaurant he'd worked at in Shanghai, Middle-European adventurer Aaron Landau opened Jimmy's Kitchen in 1928. The first independent eatery run by a Westerner, it was a rough, scrub-top place serving heaping plates of home-cooked food only to men, mainly sailors and old China hands. Jimmy's was aimed at the non-club member and people not comfortable in the Gloucester, Hong Kong and Peninsula hotels, the other sources of traditional English food and drink at the time. During World War II, Aaron's son, Emil, joined the Hong Kong Volunteers, and when the territory fell to the Japanese, he was interned in Stanley and Sham Shui Po prison camps. After liberation, he discovered that the Japanese had sold the family business to local Chinese, who had run it during the war. Rather than waste time and money sorting out the ownership issue, Landau simply bought the restaurant back. He needed all his energy to track down produce during post-war rationing, buying food off merchant ships and sourcing local fish and vegetables.

Perched atop Victoria Peak, Peak Café-goers enjoy superb views and a menu of diverse Asian and Western specialities

Landau got Jimmy's Kitchen back on its feet and set about upgrading its image and standards. He hired a French-Vietnamese chef who scandalised everyone by

cooking with butter—pounds and pounds of it—when everyone else was still using lard. He then opened the Parisian Grill, a European restaurant lavishly draped in red velvet, offering a decent Italian and French wine list, live band and dance floor. The White Russians who had fled Shanghai in 1949 had entered the scene, serving borscht and chicken Kiev in restaurants like Cherikoff, Chanteclerc, Tkachenko and Queen's Café. Gingle's on Nathan Road specialised in American steaks, and Victor's cooked up grills, curries and barbecues. The Peninsula opened Gaddi's, a fine French restaurant, in 1953, followed several years later by the Marco Polo Restaurant.

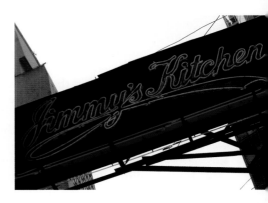

With its steak and kidney pie, garoupa shashlik and fish and chips, Jimmy's Kitchen is a Hong Kong institution

'Ask one of our regular customers what changes Jimmy's Kitchen has made over the years, and he'd say "None!" But look at us through a time warp and good heavens, what changes you'd see! Change happens all the time, in incremental ways,' says Mackenzie. Parquet floors and white tablecloths date from the mid-1960s, candles began to adorn the tables some years later, and uniforms have been redesigned more than once. And, yes, there *have* been changes to the menu, though chefs and management adopt a softly, softly approach. Julie Hume, the group's former marketing and public relations manager, is not kidding when she says customers would riot if they took lamb Madras, baked pig's knuckle, prawns Kiev or beef Wellington off the menu at Jimmy's; and when Landau's menu was revised recently, the designer was instructed to place in a prominent position a heavily bordered box informing customers that if they did not see their favourites, not to worry, as the chef would be happy to prepare their requests.

Mackenzie lived in Hong Kong between the ages of two and twelve; he was passing through in the mid-1960s when his uncle offered him a job. In 1985, he bought the company. The changes in his customers have not been nearly as incremental as the alterations in cutlery and cuisine. 'Ten years ago, if you ordered a Perrier at lunch your companions would be shocked,' he says. 'Even five years ago, we got the money market people at Jimmy's and they'd order a bottle of Champagne each, followed by port. And ten years ago, the place was still half-full at 2:30; now there will be just two or three tables.'

'It's fish and chips day,' grins a thirtysomething Chinese woman as she opens the massive menu. It's not only tourists and homesick expats who lust after beef stroganoff, pepper steak, macaroni and cheese and apple crumble with custard. For older diners, memories of long-ago tiffin luncheons are conjured up by the curries, the chutneys, the pickled onions. The heavy black chairs, panelled walls and unobtrusive lighting encourage the feeling that one has encountered something of a culinary dinosaur, but the copious pages of the menu also include vegetarian dishes, gazpacho, crunchy salads and grilled fish. The dishes are done well, and a light hand with sauces and gravies is evident—just another one of those incremental changes.

———··———

IN HIS 1849 memoirs, American Osmond Tiffany, Jr described local hotelkeepers as 'ravening wolves. ... They go upon the Grahamite principle of buttering bread, they put as little as they can on, and scrape as much as they can off.' Almost 30 years later, Lady Anne Brassey, who with her family was sailing around the world, was unimpressed with the 'scrambly sort of meal' served at the Hong Kong hotel. But in the 1930s the colony was a port of call for luxury ocean liners, and the local hotel spruced up its image to attract the titled and the wealthy who filled the passenger lists. In the 1960s, the dawn of mass travel made affordable by the jumbo jet sparked a frenzy of hotel building: Hilton, Mandarin Oriental, Hyatt and other international logos topped grand new structures.

Even now, when the choice of venue has greatly expanded, the hotels play a vital role in the territory's social life. For much of Hong Kong's first century, expatriates not only socialised at hotels, they lived there, too. Residential accommodation was overburdened, as were commercial premises. The Peninsula Lobby was the travel centre of Kowloon in the 1950s and 1960s: there were airline counters and a Cable & Wireless office; flight departures and arrivals were announced; and the airport bus picked up Kai Tak-bound passengers. The hotels capitalised on a captive audience by offering much more than the usual

coffeeshop. Fine dining, supper clubs, weekend buffets, tea dances and reception rooms for weddings, birthdays and corporate celebrations were standard fare. Stamping its own distinctive imprint on Western cuisine was the Swiss chef contingent.

Dining and dancing at supper clubs was de rigueur in the 1950s and 1960s

'I think they played into the role of extravagant food,' muses Michelle Garnaut. 'Up until five years ago, if you wanted caviar or truffles or just a good salad, you pretty much had to go to a hotel. But now those chefs have started emulating restaurants like this.' Swiss general managers ran the hotels and they tended to hire executive chefs from their homeland. Swiss nationality appeared to be a requirement for the position, and the term 'Swiss chef mafia' was coined. Neil Mackenzie remembers the trend gathering steam in the 1960s; he feels the Europeans brought 'a sophistication and an appreciation of quality'. The clique—as cliques will—has its detractors; some of them point an accusing finger in its direction when the touchy subject of 'East meets West' cuisine comes up.

Nothing riles Hong Kong's generally amiable restaurateurs like the mention of East meets West. 'People just throwing ingredients together,' says Bonnie Gokson, of Joyce Café, dismissively. Gokson was for many years a buyer and director of visual merchandising for the eponymous emporia of her sister, Joyce Ma, Hong Kong's long-reigning doyenne of fashion. Since a small cappuccino and sandwich bar in the Galleria Joyce boutique metamorphosed into a restaurant that is *tres à la mode* with the fashionable set (people whose Armani, Gucci and YSL shopping bags actually contain newly purchased designer clothing), she has employed her artistry in creating and refining dishes, menus and image. The first Joyce Café, in the Galleria on Queen's Road, has a new younger sibling, a 200-seat venue in the Forum at Exchange Square.

Joyce Café is based on a philosophy of wholesomeness, balance, purity. Joyce Ma is a strict vegetarian; Gokson took the decision to put chicken on the menu. The sisters' ashram retreats provide inspiration for dishes like 'swami's plate'. 'It's made of blended and sieved sweet peas with pickles like my mother used to make and sesame oil,' describes Gokson. 'We use a lot of complex grains and a lot of vegetables. I make a risotto without cheese and puréed soups with no cream. But our desserts are sinful.' There is, naturally, a pleasant balance of East (claypot rice in broth with seafood, Shanghainese won ton) and West (spinach salad, penne alla ricotta), but each keeps to its own corner.

'East Meets West is one of my least favourite things,' says Michelle Garnaut. Her view, which is shared by many restaurateurs of all nationalities, is that only a very deep understanding of both cultures can result in a happy marriage of ingredients. 'The most ridiculous experience I ever had with it was in Melbourne,' she laughs. 'I was served *chà sìu* lamb cutlets which I was supposed to eat with Japanese chopsticks!'

AT FIRST glance, the prospect that there could be anything linking the North Point eatery Sun Yun Kee with Felix, the Philippe Starck-designed brasserie looming over Kowloon from high atop the Peninsula hotel, is ludicrous. At second and even third glance, conjecture about a supposed relationship seems to melt in the face of the former's formica-tabled, hard-seated interior, with steaming pots of congee and won ton broth (*wàhn tàn tong*) sequestered in an open kitchen at the front and woks roaring in the back, and the latter's studied avant-garde chic, all mahogany and aluminium and nary a glimpse of cooking activity. Ah, but that would be the supposition of someone who has lost sight of the main event. As a born-and-fed-in-Hong Kong Shakespeare would have written, 'The food's the thing'.

The link is tenuous, but the clues are in the laminated pages of Sun Yun Kee's menu, where fried eggs and toast cosy up to fish ball and beef congee under the 'Breakfast' heading, and beef curry is a close neighbour of the daily soup: preserved vegetable with beef lung. Nurtured in the frenetic 1950s, at a time when Hong Kong Chinese were furthering their explorations of just what it was that the foreigners (*gweilos*) put on their plates, the Chinese café trod probably the first, tottering steps on the road to fusion food. The institution's Cantonese name, *chàh châan têng*, means tea and Western food salon, though these are all-day operations. Its distinction lies in an exceedingly lengthy and diverse menu, combining Chinese offerings with local interpretations of Western food, representing an East–West hybrid that far preceded the 'East Meets West' cliché that dogged hotel restaurants in the 1980s. The 'fusion' aspect comes into play with dishes like pork chops, which are served with a huge mound of steamed

Joyce Café in the Galleria encompasses the stylistic and culinary preferences of couture doyenne, Joyce Ma, and her sister, Bonnie Gokson

rice. It's also evident in the number of dishes and styles of food served: the *chàh châan têng* has gradually broadened its scope, embracing roast pork, goose and duck specialities, *dai pai dong* coffee and tea, congee and won ton noodle, and a breathtaking range of stir-fried, braised and claypot dishes.

The *chàh châan têng* was Hong Kong's original drive-through window. Before fast food and express counters, this was where bus and tram drivers would pick up a quick lunch. A bus would pause at the stop nearest the café of choice and the conductor would rush inside, shouting out his and the driver's order, then race back to the vehicle. On the return trip, the conductor would run into the café to fetch the order and quickly transfer the contents of the plates into his and the driver's personal food containers. The plates were left by the curb for the restaurant staff to retrieve, together with the money if the order had not been prepaid. For regulars, the owner of the café might run a tab.

No one knows how many *chàh châan têng* there are in Hong Kong. Their numbers ebb and flow in tandem with economic conditions. In tough times, *chàh châan têng* multiply, for like the *dai pai dong*, they serve good food at reasonable prices, and tipping is not required.

Felix is the other side of the fusion coin. In his eyrie at the Peninsula hotel, Hawaiian-born chef Bryan Nagao, who trained in his home state and in San Francisco, espouses Pacific Rim cuisine, which he describes as food using 'ingredients and a style of cooking from areas that touch the Pacific'. Which gives him free rein to use Thai eggplant, Japanese wasabi, Hawaiian guava, Chinese stir-frying

At Felix, the culinary fusion of East and West competes with highly stylised decor

and Californian techniques of presentation and sauces. It is a broad palette Nagao is working with, and while the results clearly appeal to a plentiful number of Hong Kong's young, trend-minded diners, Felix also comes in for its share of fusion-bashing—another popular trend. But those who aren't enamoured of the brasserie's creations are perhaps missing the point. Felix is theatre, pure and simple. Nagao talks of sculpting dishes, of building in height to compete with the showmanship of the surroundings. Where Felix deviates from its *chàh châan têng* forebear is that ambience and service are as integral to the experience as the food. The clash of form over function, of content over style, is classic, and it's waged every night in restaurants like Felix.

PAVILION, 1997
Avocado, Fetta and Hazelnut Salad

Fetta cheese, cubed	200 g
Avocado	2 pieces
Artichoke hearts (jar or tinned), chargrilled	8 pieces
Hazelnuts, chopped and roasted	100 g
Homemade semi-dried tomatoes*	2 pieces
Mesclun salad	100 g
Basil leaf, deep-fried	1
Dressing for leaves:	
Olive oil	50ml
White wine vinegar	10–15 ml
Mint, chopped	small bunch
Lemon juice	1 tbsp
Salt and pepper	to taste
Garlic, puréed	1/4 tsp
Cherry tomato vinaigrette:	
Cherry tomatoes	1/2 punnet
Sherry vinegar	10–15 ml
Lemon juice	1/2 tbsp
Extra virgin olive oil	50 ml
Garlic, puréed	1/4 tsp
Black pepper, milled	to taste

Place the artichokes in a shallow bowl. In another bowl, combine the salad leaves, hazelnuts and dressing. Place the salad on top of the artichokes. Slice the avocados and arrange over the salad. Add fetta. Top with semi-dried tomatoes and garnish with basil. Place all the vinaigrette ingredients in a blender, blend until well combined and drizzle around the plate.

* Semi-dried tomatoes: place two cored tomatoes into boiling water for 5–10 seconds. Remove and place in iced water, then peel and slice. Top with one or two slices of shaved garlic and with a little dry basil and place on a tray. Leave overnight in a warm oven (switched off). Store in a jar with olive oil and use as needed.

M AT THE FRINGE
Boned Roasted Pigeon With Middle Eastern Flavours

Pigeons, boned	4
Filling:	
Cooked rice	2 cups
Garlic, chopped	1 clove
Mint, chopped	1/2 tbsp
Parsley, chopped	1 tbsp
Coriander, chopped	1 tbsp
Preserved lemon, washed and diced*	
(or fresh lemon zest)	1/2 lemon
Rehydrated raisins (soaked in hot water	
for 15 minutes)	1/4 cup
Spring onions, chopped	4
Cumin, ground	1/2 tsp
Toasted pinenuts	1/4 cup
Butter	1 tbsp
Salt	1 tsp

Bone each pigeon, starting from the neck with the breast facing down. Slowly cut away the flesh, working your way around the carcass and removing all of the bones. To make the filling, mix the rice with all the other ingredients and set aside. Lay each bird skin facing down and season with salt and pepper. Place a large spoonful of stuffing in the middle of the bird and fasten with a bamboo stick or skewer.

Place the pigeons in a roasting dish, breast facing up, and brush with olive oil and a little melted butter. Roast in a very hot oven for 15 to 20 minutes. Remove and let rest for 10 minutes before slicing. Dress with fresh lemon juice, salt and freshly ground black pepper.

* Take 10 well-scrubbed lemons and 1.5kg coarse sea salt. Cut the lemons into quarters, leaving the base intact. Pack them into a sterilised jar with lots of coarse salt stuffed inside and around them and seal tightly. Keep at least 2 weeks in a cool, dry place. To use, remove from the jar with tongs, wash well and dice.

FELIX, THE PENINSULA, HONG KONG
Grilled Angus Sirloin With Shrimps and Sundried Tomato Sauce

Shrimps, peeled and de-veined	120 g
Butter	30 g
Garlic, finely chopped	10 g
Shallots, finely chopped	30 g
Basil leaves, chopped	30 g
Shitake mushrooms, sliced	110 g
Asparagus (stems removed), diced (leaving tips intact)	150 g
Green garden peas	180 g
Angus sirloin, trimmed	4 x 180 g steaks
Congee:	
Long grain rice	60 g
Garlic, finely chopped	10 g
Shallots, finely chopped	10 g
Ginger, grated	30 g
Water	2 dl
Sundried tomatoes	30 g

Put all the congee ingredients in a large pot and boil for 30 minutes. Purée, strain and set aside. In a pot, melt the butter and sauté the prawns with the garlic, shallots, basil, shitake mushrooms, asparagus and peas, until tender. Add 240 ml of the congee to the shrimp sauté and season to taste. If the sauce is too thick, add a little stock to give it the consistency of a usual steak sauce. Set aside and keep the sauce warm.

Season the sirloin steaks with salt and pepper and pan-fry in a little oil or grill as desired. To serve, spoon a generous amount of the congee sauce on a warmed plate and place a steak on top. Repeat with remaining steaks and serve immediately. (Serves 4.)

GADDI'S RESTAURANT,
THE PENINSULA, HONG KONG
Cherry Clafoutis

Eggs	2
Sugar	40 g
Milk	80 ml
Salt	pinch
Vanilla bean	1/5 piece
Cake flour	30 g
Almond powder	pinch
Butter, melted	35 g
Cherries, pitted	400 g
Icing sugar (for dusting)	

In a bowl, beat the eggs, sugar, vanilla and the salt until foamy. Add the sifted flour and mix together. Pour the milk into the mixture little by little. (If the mixture seems too thin, add a little more flour.) Brush 4 ramekins of 10cm diameter with a quarter of the melted butter and dust the dishes with the almond powder. Place the cherries evenly in the dishes and pour the batter over them. Bake in a pre-heated oven for 20 minutes at 180°C. Allow to cool slightly, dust with icing sugar and serve in the ramekin.

8

Dishing It Out

⌒

'Good fortune of the mouth is not shallow—to have good food to eat is important.'

The Chinese Cookbook (unattributed)

Introduction

Along with the myth about kung fu fights breaking out with breathless regularity in the densely packed streets, another of the popular misconceptions about Hong Kong is that its citizens talk about little else but money. Not so: where and what to eat are conversation topics that rival the fascinations of Mammon, though it must be said that assigning points on the value-for-money scale is integral to most food discussions.

Even with all this culinary chat, there nevertheless exists a huge gulf in communication which poses the greatest challenge to non-Chinese residents and visitors who wish to explore the depth of culinary experience that has made Hong Kong famous. Language is the least of the problems—the real task lies in convincing people of one's genuine interest in having something other than the usual *gweilo* (foreigner) set menu. It's not surprising that the typical restaurateur needs convincing: his or her awareness of the foreign palate has been honed by years of catering to less-than-intrepid expatriates whose knowledge of Chinese food extended to chop suey and deep-fried chicken covered in sweet and sour

Central at twilight

sauce and whose obvious distaste at such things as fish maw and deep-fried stuffed large intestine kept those dishes strictly on the 'if you can read it, then you're likely to order it' Chinese-language menu.

This communication gap was beautifully illustrated by a chef who kindly supplied a recipe for this book. When the recipe tester admitted bewildered defeat and the chef was consulted, he responded that of course it was authentic, except that a few ingredients had been left out, or altered, since he was sure Westerners couldn't come to grips with them. Armed with the genuine recipe, the tester returned to her kitchen, added the supposedly difficult items—fish sauce, soy sauce, chicken stock and peppercorns—and created a successful dish. It would be easy to attribute the episode to the secrecy that is an accepted feature of the Chinese kitchen (another chef

A congee restaurant dishes up the ultimate comfort food

said cheerfully and with no sense of compunction that he had left 'a few things out' when demonstrating a sauce recipe for an American television crew). But protectionist secrecy was not an issue here, and the incident speaks volumes about the insularity of a supposedly international restaurant scene. In recent years, Asian ingredients and cooking styles have had a major impact on both home cooking and eating-out patterns worldwide, and Hong Kong's restaurateurs would do well to recognise the potential of leading customers who are, at the least, semi-versed in Chinese cuisine to a greater appreciation of their art. At the same time, diners who evince keen interest in a broader eating experience will help to improve communication skills all round.

Most larger restaurants display both Chinese and English signs, and some helpfully cut across language barriers by incorporating neon geese, leaping fish or even giant cows into the design. But many smaller venues are identified by Chinese characters only and the list of dishes is often unilingual. Still, there are some ways to distinguish what is on offer. Noodle and congee restaurants, for instance, have a small open kitchen in the front window—the presence of two or more tall cauldrons into which a cook may be seen dipping coils of noodles and/or dumplings indicates that won ton noodle (*wàhn tàn mihn*), among other dishes, is available. If there is a vat of congee (a thin, white gruel made from rice) and a selection of plastic tubs piled with slices of raw beef, raw fish, liver and minced beef mixed with deep-fried rice vermicelli on the cook's countertop, one can request *jùk* (congee) and simply point to the ingredients to be added. Restaurants which display rows of *yàuh ja gwái* (fried dough sticks) are *jùk* specialists, since these addictive wok-fried treats are meant to be dipped in congee. Later in the day, when the rice porridge is not so sought-after, some proprietors roll leftover *yàuh ja gwái* in glutinous rice and plastic-wrap, this surprisingly tasty combination of starch and oil to be sold as a cheap, extremely filling snack.

There are literally hundreds of noodle shops in Hong Kong, most of them offering a choice of prawn dumplings, fish balls or sliced beef with noodles. It is impossible to predict quality before tasting. The number of customers is no indication—even fickle Hong Kongers are willing to sacrifice a little flavour to save a few dollars, particularly when they are after 'filling up the stomach' fare, something to down in mere minutes. Taste is the only test: good won ton dumplings are made with fresh, plump shrimp—if the seafood has a mealy texture, it is past its prime; and if bits of shell intrude, the cleaning process has been perfunctory.

The windows of barbecue and roast meat restaurants are helpfully decorated with strips of barbecued pork (*chà sìu*), whole roasted duck (*sìu ngaap*) and

chicken, hanging on hooks within easy reach of the cook. Here, one can order *chà sìu faahn* (barbecued pork with rice), or a range of noodle soup dishes topped with slices of *sìu yuhk* (pork tenderloin that has been marinated in soy sauce, sugar and spices, then oven roasted), chicken or duck, with a few sprigs of boiled green vegetable. Rice noodles (*hó fán*) are flat and soft, less chewy than egg noodles. They are boiled for only one or two minutes, and are usually served in small bowls, as the noodles tend to disintegrate if left too long in a hot liquid. The more robust round rice noodles, *laaih fán*, are amazingly slippery and they require great dexterity with chopsticks.

English menus may not be prominent, but even hole-in-the-wall shops will often have one tucked behind the cashier's counter. If a non-Chinese menu doesn't exist, there is usually a quick discussion and the staff member who is judged to be most fluent in English appears to take the foreigner's order. (Restaurants displaying the Hong Kong Tourist Association membership symbol undertake to provide an English menu and have at least one English-speaking staffer.) If neither of these options presents itself, pointing at a fellow diner's dish is foolproof and no one, not even the pointee, will be offended by what would be considered intrusive elsewhere. Every cook likes to see his or her efforts savoured and Hong Kong's restaurateurs, whether they are serving a humble bowl of sliced beef with noodles or an impeccably steamed fish laid out on a silver platter, tend to welcome foreigners with quiet pleasure.

Barbeque specialities are boldly displayed

Ordering

Sous chef Chan Yan Tak of Lai Ching Heen, the Regent hotel's famed Cantonese restaurant, advises: 'A well-balanced Chinese meal is comprised of the five basic tastes of Cantonese cuisine: sour, hot, bitter, sweet and salty.' Balance is always the goal when ordering any of the regional cuisines and can generally be achieved by choosing a combination of braised, stir-fried, baked and steamed dishes. Textures should vary; choose both dry dishes and those which have a sauce; dishes which are crisp and those which are tender.

Steamed whole fresh fish is not essential to a Cantonese meal—the sheer breadth of the typical Cantonese menu offers such an overwhelming choice as to make a mockery of this so-called rule. For one thing, cost is increasingly prohibitive: one small garoupa, suitable for two, can add upwards of HK$400 to the bill. In addition, ordering fresh seafood has some pitfalls for the unwary. 'There is a great difference, in taste and price, between farmed and sea

Won ton noodle (wàhn tàn mihn), comprised of pork and shrimp dumplings in soup, is savoured in hundreds of outlets throughout the city

*Rice in lotus leaf (*hòh yihp faahn) *is steamed to perfection*

fish,' says teacher Helen Chung. The former is considered inferior and rather mealy, lacking the firm-fleshed texture of the latter. 'In Sai Kung, Lamma and Lei Yue Mun, make sure you ask for sea fish,' stresses Helen, 'and take care that an unscrupulous restaurateur doesn't exchange it for a farmed fish.' Seeing 'market price' on a menu strikes fear into many a diner's heart: always ask the price before the fish, crab, lobster, geoduck clam, etc, is taken from tank to kitchen, and get it written down to prevent any post-meal confusion. Diners are usually given a price per catty (one catty is equivalent to 625 grams or 1-1/4 lb). Health concerns have caused many diners to avoid local seafood. Annabel Graham, a Hong Kong-born food consultant and writer who is researching a book on local seafood, has reluctantly given up eating local shellfish, but quite happily tucks into fish caught in nearby waters. Consider your own tolerance levels and order accordingly.

'Hà gáau (steamed shrimp dumpling), sìu maái (steamed dumpling filled with pork and shrimp), chà sìu bâau (barbecued pork bun).' Nancy rhymes off the list of dim sum she knows her Western lunch companions will order. Spring rolls (chêun gyún), barbecued pork puff (chà sìu so) and glutinous rice wrapped in lotus leaf (hòh yihp faahn) round out the typical foreigner's sedate dim sum meal. Straying off this well-trodden path has its rewards. Most restaurateurs are clearly not convinced of the foreigner's willingness to venture into fuhng jáau (chicken's feet) and gai jaat (bean curd wrapped around strips of chicken, ham and fish stomach) territory, since most of the English do-it-yourself menus, where customers tick the box next to their choice, usually list only a fraction of the dishes available. There are ways of overcoming this myopia. Chinese restaurants in the better hotels are scrupulous about offering bilingual menus; elsewhere, ask the advice of an English-speaking manager. The best solution is to seek out restaurants where trolleys are wheeled from table to table and the trolley ladies let you have a peek before deciding whether the dish appeals.

Waiters at Hong Kong's Sichuan, Thai and Malay restaurants often take it upon themselves to ask the kitchen to cool it on the chilli front for foreign customers. If you like your *dân dân mihn* and *tom yam koon* the way they're supposed to be—fiery hot—emphasise your love of hot food to the waiter or you may suffer a well-meaning but taste-depriving gesture.

Fook Ming Tong's Lucy Yu suggests drinking jasmine tea with a Chinese meal: 'It's not too strong, and it has fragrance and that helps to build your appetite.' Hong Kong people tend to ask for pots of *bóu leí* (*pu-er*) during *yám chàh* and after heavy meals, says Yu. '*Pu-er* is soothing; it helps digestion and helps get rid of grease.' Better restaurants will stock *yât kâp wu lùng chàh*—the first grade of oolong—for their connoisseur customers. Oolong acts on the body in much the same way as *bóu leí*, but the taste is more refined.

Most Chinese dining tables will have small dishes or bottles of condiments. Soy sauce, made by fermenting steamed soya beans, is the most common flavouring, along with chilli sauce, made from mashed chilli peppers, vinegar and seasonings. XO sauce, a pungent blend of chilli, conpoy, shrimp and seasonings, is popular in Hong Kong, and chefs at finer restaurants often create their own distinctive version. Oyster sauce, used to marinate beef and poured liberally over steamed *gai laan* (Chinese kale) served in most noodle shops, is produced only in the Pearl River delta and is made from oysters, salt, soy sauce and seasonings. Hoi sin sauce is a thick, sweet, brown paste which is served with barbecued meats and roast suckling pig. Tables at Chiu Chow restaurants are awash in a medley of dipping sauces (such as *sâ chàh jeung*, made with fish, dried shrimps and rice flour), each particular to one dish.

Restaurants

No one knows exactly how many restaurants there are in Hong Kong. Estimates hover around the 8,000 mark; some boldly go as high as 9,000, which means that if one were to have three meals in three different restaurants every day, it would take over seven years to try them all. 'It's a monster,' says one exasperated food writer, who echoes many restaurateurs and critics when he describes the Chinese restaurant scene as still undergoing a much-needed 'correction', following the overheated late 1980s, when trend and ostentation superseded

A view of Victoria Harbour from the Peak

quality. Navigating this maze in search of a great meal can be daunting—and rewarding. Here, with a little help from a disparate group of Hong Kongers—friends, friends of friends, strangers, restaurateurs, shopkeepers and a taxi driver or two, all of whom share an abiding love of food—is a mixed grill of suggestions. Restaurants which are discussed elsewhere in the text are marked with an asterisk; use the index to gain further detail. This is by no means intended as a comprehensive guide; rather, it should be seen as a source of signs illuminating a very crowded highway.

HONG KONG ISLAND
Central and Environs

Just 15 years ago, the area surrounding Lan Kwai Fong was known as 'fringe Central'. The raising of new commercial buildings in the Central business district was mainly focused on the waterfront; up the hill past Queen's

Road Central were streets that rose at an uncomfortable incline, with markets and small tradesman's shops at ground level. Lan Kwai Fong was a quiet, rather grubby road, mostly lined with warehouses stacked high with embroidered linen from Shantou, in China. The opening of Disco Disco, followed by California restaurant and disco in the mid-1980s, was the thin edge of the gentrification wedge. Central was becoming a place to work and play, and budding club owners and restaurateurs began eyeing, then buying or renting, the spaces formerly occupied by metal workers, tofu makers and flower sellers.

Lan Kwai Fong has since transformed into a smorgasbord of restaurants, spiced with a few art galleries, fashion ateliers and clubs featuring live music. There is Venetian food at the terribly elegant **Va Bene**; Florentine at chic little **Tutto Meglio**; Vietnamese at the graciously colonial-era **Indochine**; antipasti at **La Dolce Vita**; Australian-flavoured continental at **Oscar's**; sushi, teriyaki

Lan Kwai Fong, c 1930s

Streetside flower sellers prevail amid a smorgasbord of trendy restaurants and bars in today's Lan Kwai Fong

and tempura at **Tokio Joe**; lobster dumplings at **The Noodle Bar**; all-day breakfast, hummus and salads at **Post 97**; crab cakes and burgers at **California**. And that is just a sampling. More a focal point than the centre of Hong Kong's entertainment universe, if such a thing exists, Lan Kwai Fong is conspicuous for choice and a generally high quality of food and ambience.

'I always take visitors to **Ying Kee** [32–40 Wellington St] for roast goose and I order the left leg, because there's a saying that geese and ducks use their right leg more so it is tougher,' says Wilson Kwok, restaurateur and holder of a Master's in Oenology from the University of Bordeaux. In around 1942, Ying Kee was a food stall; the restaurant now occupies three floors, and customers are hustled into an elevator by a walkie-talkie-toting hostess who alerts her colleagues on high about the party headed their way. The 87-year-old founder, Mr Kam, still watches over the operation. The menu is lengthy, but plates of delectable roast goose are seen on just about every table. Double-boiled winter melon soup, served in the scooped-out melon, is popular, as are steamed chicken, braised eggplant and shrimp paste in green pepper. A takeaway section, on the ground floor, offers more than 100 reasonably priced lunch boxes (slices of roasted, barbecued or steamed meat on rice) and noodle, wok-fried and congee dishes.

Directly across the street is **Tai Woo Restaurant** (17–19 Wellington St), a solid choice for dim sum. There is no room for trolleys; instead, waiters holding trays of food weave around the tables. The *gai jaat* (bean curd wrapped around strips of ham, chicken and fish stomach) is particularly good, as are *hà gáau, chà sìu bâau* (barbecued pork buns) and fried noodle dishes (ordered from the menu). Next door, at 15C Wellington Street, is **Lok Heung Yuen**, a scruffy bakery/coffee shop over 40 years old. It is also called 'snake café', because lazy people are known to skip out of work for an afternoon cuppa of Horlicks or milk tea (*náaih chàh*) and some hot buttered toast or a chicken bun. Coffee is served with lashings of condensed milk unless you order *jàai fè* (*jàai* means singular or simple, hence 'black' coffee). 'They have the best "pineapple" buns (*bò lòh bâau*) in town,' says accountant Kuen Leung. Customers receive no bill; as they get up to go, waiters simply yell out what they owe and no matter how many people converge on the cashier, he never confuses the amounts. Further along is **Mak's Noodle*** (77 Wellington St), famous as much for its superb won ton dumplings and beef brisket as for the fact that customers flock there to pay 'twice as much for servings half the size,' remarks Kuen. Another historic restaurant can be found at 50 Lyndhurst Terrace. This outlet of **Law Fu Kee** is sister to the original branch at 140 Des Voeux Road; both are highly regarded for fine congee (with kidney, beef, fish ball, egg, etc) and noodle dishes.

Running parallel to Wellington Street is Stanley Street, home of **Luk Yu Tea House*** (24–26 Stanley St), with its imposing exterior and grandly uniformed Sikh doorman. 'The cooks here mince the meat by hand; they don't put it through a machine.' A longtime patron of Luk Yu, Helen Chung adores this attention to detail and tradition. Her recommendations include chicken buns stuffed with chicken and salted duck egg, pork dumplings with liver, pan-fried bean curd roll, pan-fried meat dumplings—the menu description does a disservice to this delicious mixture of fresh bamboo shoots, pork and shrimp in rice flour pastry, served with a bowl of chicken stock for dipping. ('Very unusual, very traditional,' says Helen.) **Lin Heung Bakery and Restaurant*** (160–164 Wellington St) offers a different sort of traditional dim sum. Ambience counts for little at this working-class restaurant and the dishes lack the subtlety one finds at Luk Yu, relying on heartiness of execution and flavour to keep the punters happy. Stanley Street ends in a cluster of ancient *dai pai dong*, some of the last remaining in Central. Save for breakfast and noodle dishes, many of the offerings are seasonal and a general lack of English means foreigners must resort to peering and pointing. Further into the back streets of Central, where Mee Lun Street meets Gough Street, is a *dai pai dong* renowned for the quality of its one dish: beef brisket with your choice of noodle (e-fu and vermicelli are recommended). 'They're snobby,' Kuen says of the owners. 'Sometimes they won't serve you—but the noodles are very good.'

Ning Po Resident's Association (4/F, Yip Fung Bldg, 2–18 D'Aguilar St) is regarded as one of the better Shanghainese restaurants. 'For a balanced meal, I'd order chicken with wine sauce [drunken chicken], mock goose, fried freshwater shrimps served with wine vinegar, seasonal vegetable with shredded hard bean curd, braised pork dumplings and red bean jam cake to finish,' says restaurateur Paul Hsu, who is a regular here. Also on D'Aguilar Street, at No. 18, is The Source of Health, offering takeaway fat-free bagels, salads and zucchini muffins on the ground floor, and a larger menu of salads, soups and vegetarian dishes upstairs. Towards the bottom of Wyndham Street is the stalwart Jimmy's Kitchen*, where the capacious menu ranges from steak and kidney pie, rock oysters and gazpacho to chop suey and garoupa shashlik. Super Star Seafood Restaurant* (Wilson House, 19–27 Wyndham St) packs them in for lunchtime dim sum and seafood dinners. Weekday dim sum ordering is

Dim sum (clockwise from top left): custard-filled náaih wóng bâau, sìu máai, deep-fried pork and vegetable dumplings, hàahm séui gók and custard-filled bò lòh bâau

done by ticking off boxes on a paper menu; trolleys roll through the crowded rooms on weekends. A limited English menu, with photo illustrations, lists mixed vegetable dumplings, glutinous rice wrapped in lotus leaf, shrimp rolls with sesame and barbecued pork shortbread. Specialities like custard-topped barbecued pork buns are only on the Chinese menu. Other specialities include braised superior shark's fin, steamed lobster with yellow wine, and pan-fried crab with chilli and black bean sauce. Take a left turn at the top of Wyndham Street on to Lower Albert Road and you'll find the **Fringe Club**, housed in the former Dairy Farm premises, where a vegetarian lunch buffet of soup, salads, bread and cheese can be had for less than HK$100 (Mon–Sat). Upstairs is **M at the Fringe***, also known as Michelle's. The food (loosely described as Mediterranean) is consistently inviting: grilled calves' liver, oven-steamed salmon, a Moroccan platter of aubergine bisteeya, pumpkin and black olive tajine and spiced almond couscous are samples of the creativity.

The assured service and delicious Italian dishes like seafood and saffron risotto and ricotta and pumpkin ravioli at **La Trattoria**, in the Landmark (15 Queen's Rd), are enough to make diners forget they're sitting in a shopping mall. **Peking Garden***, in the basement of Alexandra House (entrance on Chater St), belongs to the Maxim's chain of restaurants and is a favourite for beggar's chicken (dubbed 'fortune chicken', to dispel any superstitious concerns about the unsalubrious name) and Peking duck. Evenings, the noodle chef demonstrates his skill at tossing and turning large lumps of dough into long, perfectly formed noodles. Tucked into the Alexandra House lobby is Hong Kong's first gourmet coffee purveyor, **Café Central**. Grinding beans brought in from—where else?—Seattle, Judy Merton and her quick-brewing crew serve over 700 cups of espresso, *latte*, cappuccino and granita *latte* (flavoured iced drinks) a day, and they do it with a smile. A stone's throw from the Star Ferry is one of the most popular dim sum restaurants in Hong Kong: **City Hall Chinese Restaurant*** (2/F, Lower Block). The large room, with its unobstructed view of the harbour, is a trolley-lover's heaven. Each day, some 40 different dim sum dishes are prepared in the kitchen; 30 are traditional recipes, others, such as goldfish dumplings, are variations on the dim sum theme.

At the top of Wyndham Street, where oriental carpets and Asian antiques begin to dominate the shops, is a clutch of chic restaurants run by the same group: **La Bodega, Wyndham Street Deli** and **Wyndham Street Thai** (at 31, 36 and 38 Wyndham St, respectively). La Bodega presents upmarket Spanish food; Wyndham Street Thai uses the spices, herbs and ingredients of Thai cuisine as a

Fine Italian food at Vino & Olio in Lan Kwai Fong

creative springboard. At the Deli, food provides both sustenance and decor. Pitchers of passionfruit and strawberry juices adorn the countertop, and gorgeous salads, breads, cheeses and desserts are flaunted within; shame about the often imperious staff. Indian eatery, **The Village** (57 Wyndham St, down the steps), is friendly and reasonably priced. Further along, where Wyndham Street becomes Hollywood Road, the home-style lunch and dinner buffets at **Club Sri Lanka** (17 Hollywood Rd), with pots of dhal, eggplant and fish curries, sambal and coconut desserts, are great value for money.

Restaurants have sprouted like mushrooms along the Mid-Levels escalator route. It was 1992 when people daily began travelling the world's longest escalator path—a series of 20 escalators and three travelators— which begins on Des Voeux Road and ends some 800 metres later at Conduit Road. This unique addition to the infrastructure sparked a flurry of development, particularly on and around Staunton and Elgin streets, such that the area now has its own identity: Soho (for 'south of Hollywood Road'). Disappointingly, Soho prices match the high figures elsewhere, but the decidedly different character of the environment and the cosy style of the restaurants, which are mainly located in converted houses, has created something of a happening.

There is great ethnic variety of cuisines in Soho: **Cafe Au Lac** (20 Staunton St) serves Vietnamese specialities like pancake stuffed with prawns and meat, and fried soft-shell crabs; **Nepal** (14 Staunton St) introduces little-known Nepalese dishes; **Sherpa**, a Himalayan coffee bar, offers *sukati saduko*, Himalayan meat marinated in Nepalese herbs, and *jhir kabob*, minced lamb or chicken mixed with herbs and spices and roasted on a skewer; **Club Scandinavia** (16 Staunton St) has a small, interesting menu, with spring vegetable soup and smoked salmon steak cooked in a traditional 'wood-box' among the best items. At **Le Fauchon**, one of the first to venture into Staunton Street (at No. 6), the dishes change according to what meat, seafood and produce arrives that week from Paris, which is presumably why the menu consists of two messily handwritten scraps of paper. Put it down to eccentricity and enjoy sumptuous, if costly, wine, foie gras, goat's cheese salad, steak and complimentary *crème brulée*. **Desert Sky** (36 Elgin St) provides another choice for Middle Eastern dishes (dolma, kofta kebab, falafel) in Central; and **Club Casa Lisboa** (21 Elgin St) has a menu that, save for the prices, will be familiar to Macau-goers. **Café Gypsy** (29 Shelley St), a bar, restaurant and creperie, has a great wine list and an eclectic menu, including escargots, lamb tagine with dates, apricots and eggplant and grilled tuna with almond and caper sauce. The Sunday all-day breakfast packs them in.

The Dumpling House (24 Cochrane St) serves northern Chinese fast food: of note are the vegetarian dumplings in clear broth or hot and sour soup and steamed pork dumplings. **Petticoat Lane*** and **The Pavilion*** have transformed tiny Tun Wo Lane, located between Lyndhurst Terrace and Hollywood Road, into a rare oasis. Both are run by the 1997 Group; the former is a lively bar with a petite lunch menu, and the latter is a paean to Madame Pompadour, done out in gilt, crystal chandelier and silk banquettes. The menu is continental with Australian flair: salads of wilted spinach arranged on chargrilled leeks with shavings of fresh parmesan; and for Sunday brunch, French toast with a compote of apricots, and eggs Benedict on baguette.

The original **Joyce Café*** (1/F, The Galleria, 9 Queen's Rd Central) has a larger, younger sibling in Exchange Square (One Exchange Square, 8 Connaught Place). The brainchild of Hong Kong's doyenne of style, Joyce Ma, and her

Spoiled for choice in Staunton Street's restaurant and café scene

sister, Bonnie Gokson, Joyce Café exudes healthfulness—at a price. The 16-inch-long dhosas, megahorn-like crêpes made by a chef brought in from south India, filled with spinach and roasted garlic, masala potatoes or roasted vegetables with mozzarella and basil, are truly delightful, as are the beautifully arranged 'Hail Caesar' salad (built inexplicably around a waffle) and sampan plate of grilled salmon covered with roasted garlic. Joyce lays claim to the best vegetarian club sandwich in town; few would quibble.

Heading west towards Sheung Wan, hotel public relations manager Amy Yeung speaks highly of the baby oyster congee at **Leung Hing** (35 Des Voeux Rd West): 'It's unbeatable.' **The Original Health Café** (27/F, Wing Shan Tower, 173 Des Voeux Rd; look for Sincere department store, the elevators are to the left of the main store entrance) offers a healthy, cheap vegetarian buffet (brown rice, miso soup, vegetables and fruit salad), a great range of fresh fruit and vegetable juices and sandwiches stuffed with vegetables and bean sprouts. Half of the space is given over to shelves of health food snacks and remedies, aromatherapy oils and 'green' shampoos. You can't miss **Sammy's Kitchen***** (204–206 Queen's Rd West)—just look for the giant cow. Here, one steps back into the era of fussy French food, with dishes like *grand champignons à la French hors d'oeuvre* and piccata of veal marsala. West of Sheung Wan is Sai Ying Poon district, where the long-established Chinese dessert restaurant, **Yuen Kee** (32 Centre St), features fresh walnut or almond soup, fresh green bean soup with lotus seeds and egg custard cake.

Hotel restaurants should not be overlooked. Afternoon tea in the **Clipper Lounge** of the Mandarin Oriental hotel is a civilised, silver-service affair; the **Mandarin Grill** is the place for power breakfasts; and **Man Wah**, the hotel's Cantonese restaurant, is ranked among the very best in town. **The Chinnery** is infamous for having barred women until 1990; this snug, club-like former hold-out of macho solidarity stocks 75 single-malt whiskies and presents terribly British food, such as Stilton soup, mushroom pie and spotted dick. The elegant **Island Restaurant** in the Furama hotel (1 Connaught Rd Central) is deservedly popular for dim sum. Other specialities include marinated pigeon with jellyfish, and crispy chicken with Yunnan ham and walnuts. Next door, the Ritz-Carlton hotel (3 Connaught Rd Central) has **Toscana**, for hearty Italian food; and in the basement, **Shanghai Shanghai,** a beautifully decorated restaurant which evokes the spirit of 1930s' Shanghai.

Just below Hong Kong Park, with its aviary, fountains and the Flagstaff Tea Museum, is Pacific Place mall. There, one will find **Grappa's** (Shop 132, The Mall, 88 Queensway), serving luscious pastas, pizzas and salads. At the other end of the mall is **Zen** (LG/1), where a formerly overblown nouvelle menu has relaxed into one of solid, well-presented Cantonese dishes. Three hotels are attached to Pacific Place. **Petrus**, on the 56th floor of the Island Shangri-La, is one of the last bastions of fine French cuisine. The menu includes quail and sweetbread salad, shellfish crustacean soup flavoured with orange and vanilla, and pan-fried fillet of barramundi in sesame seed crust. **The Library** serves a genteel afternoon tea and **The Summer Palace** Cantonese restaurant is hushed and elegant. On the fifth floor of the Conrad hotel, **Golden Leaf's** renown for healthy, tasty cooking has made it terrifically popular. **Nicholini's** (on the 8th floor) serves northern Italian cuisine. ('The osso bucco is absolutely divine,'

Scallops and vegetables stir-fried to preserve individual flavours

says journalist Patricia Chew.) **JW's California** promotes the JW Marriott's American origins, with a menu that matches Eastern and Western flavours.

Wan Chai, Happy Valley, Causeway Bay

Classic Passion Restaurant* (188 Wanchai Rd; branches in Tsim Sha Tsui East and on the Peak) is a revelation. Bean curd with mushrooms and shrimp resembles a creamy smooth fritatta; the braised eggplant is topped with roasted, chopped garlic; steamed chicken melts in the mouth. **Harbour City Chiuchow Restaurant*** (2/F, Elizabeth House, 254 Gloucester Rd) has steamed cod, cold crab and tasty sweet and sour pork (a dish they insist is authentically Chinese, if not Chiu Chow), with tender chunks of boneless pork and a sauce thick with crunchy vegetables served on the side, and staff who are happy to explain the dipping sauces. Roti, prawn laksa and tea tarik ('pulled' tea) are a few of the very enjoyable Malaysian dishes available at **Coconut Curry House** (5/F, Kwan Chart Tower, 6 Tonnochy Rd). On the fourth floor is **Long Xing Lou***, serving high-quality Beijing cuisine. Lovers of Shanghainese food stream into **Lao Ching Hing*** in the basement of the Century hotel (238 Jaffe Rd).

Odd working hours and, one suspects, a natural fascination, have made restaurateur Wilson Kwok (of W's Entrecote, W's Paris 13th, Café Gypsy and others in the planning stages) a noodle shop aficionado. 'I'm in the office most of the day and then in the restaurants in the evening, so I often stop for a snack in the middle of the night,' he explains. One of his favourites is **Wah Nam** (5–11 Thomson Rd), an earthy *dai pai dong*-like venue that only gets going after 11pm and is usually jammed with taxi drivers. 'I've been going there for 10 years; I usually have beef tripe with rice noodles,' says Wilson. 'They serve brisket, but it's a little too lean for me. You can also have French toast, won ton or fish ball with noodles.' Wilson is particular about his won ton: 'You have to go to a specialist, where they have the right soup base made with dried shrimp.' His choices are **Wing Wah** (89 Hennessy Rd), and **Ho Hung Kee** (2 Sharp St, next to Lee Theatre Plaza). For the full array of Cantonese cuisine, Wilson recommends **Chui Wu Seafood Restaurant** (1/F & 2/F, 107 Hennessy Rd). 'The employees used to work at Orchid Garden a long time ago,' he says. 'When that closed, they set up Chui Wu and inherited the Orchid Garden recipes from the owners. I love their stir-fried milk, which is actually egg white, milk and nuts, sprinkled with Chinese ham. And they make the old-style pomelo dish, where the skin is first burned to remove the green coating, then scraped off and toasted, before it's simmered for hours in a fish base soup.'

The samovar-like polished brass and aluminium urns of **Quality Herb Tea House** (corner of Johnston and O'Brien roads) contain a variety of densely dark, cold medicinal drinks and teas. There is chrysanthemum tea, anti-cold herbal tea, medicinal turtle jelly and many more. Indicate which is your pleasure and a woman will fill a blue and white rice bowl to the brim. Also on O'Brien Road (at No. 13) is **Tai Hing Roast Shop**, where handy picture menus on the window, of roast pork and goose, or steamed chicken with rice or noodles, help circumvent the lack of English spoken inside.

'I'm not keen on drunken dishes, but my mother thought the drunken chicken and pigeon here were quite good.' John manages the family tea trading business; his Shanghainese mother's visits to Hong Kong from her home in the United States revolve around meals at restaurants specialising in her home town's cuisine. A fairly new entrant, **Lao Yuen** (1/F, CRE Bldg, 303 Hennessy Rd), recently won the family vote. 'The vegetarian dumplings were very good, slightly sweet,' John said. 'And the jellyfish is especially tasty, because they use the head, which is the best bit.' Amy Yeung seconds this recommendation: 'I ordered crab coated with duck egg; it was delicious, something I'd never eaten before.'

American Peking Restaurant (20 Lockhart Rd) is a stalwart which probably owes its steady business as much to longevity as to quality. 'If our group is larger than six people, we'll order Peking duck,' says Catherine. 'Also, the onion cake and a dish, I can never remember the name, it's "something" wearing a hat.' Ask the waiters about the 'hat' dish and they scribble something illegible on the order form and neglect to tell you the real name (the dish is not on the menu).

*A Chiu Chow venue
in Causeway Bay*

The mound of noodles, bamboo shoots and shredded beef is shaped into a cone and topped with long strands of fried egg that do manage to look like a hat. Shredded beef in 'spectacle cases', pockets made of flaky pastry and coated with sesame seeds, is popular; and sizzling hot prawns briefly counteract the arctic airconditioning.

Dominated by the massive Hong Kong Convention and Exhibition Centre, the area known as North Wan Chai is five-star hotel territory. The Grand Hyatt (1 Harbour Rd) has **Grissini**, for Italian fine dining, **Kaetsu** for an impeccable Japanese experience, and **One Harbour Road**, perhaps the most popular choice for a business meal conducted over Cantonese food. The next-door New World Harbour View's **Dynasty** is consistently rated Hong Kong's top dim sum spot. Amongst the convention centre's seven restaurants is **Dragon Court**, serving Sichuan cuisine, and **Congress Restaurant**, with its famous international buffet (1 Harbour Rd). **Victoria City Seafood Restaurant** (2/F, Sun Hung Kai Centre, 20 Harbour Rd) is highly regarded for its dim sum, not least because it's one of the few restaurants to take bookings on weekends.

'**Three Thousand Bowl** is my favourite restaurant,' enthuses David, a British publisher. Since discovering this casual, compact northern eatery (470 Lockhart Rd) earlier in the year, he has brought so many friends there that the staff know him. Bright and down-to-earth (expect to share a table) with service that borders on the brusque, Three Thousand Bowl has a bit of flash, with a noodlemaker performing in the front window at frequent intervals. 'Vegetarian goose is the best dish,' says David. 'Fried noodles with eel is great and the vegetarian dumplings are succulent, perfectly steamed.' **Fook Yuen Seafood Restaurant*** (9/F, Causeway Bay Plaza 2, 463 Lockhart Rd) 'never lets me down—even on race day!' Catherine's theory is that the horses tend to distract kitchen staff, which is why the consistency of this Cantonese restaurant, even on Wednesday nights and weekend afternoons, is impressive. 'I like the fish with vegetables, the steamed chicken and the double-boiled papaya with almond milk.'

The Excelsior hotel's Cantonese restaurant, **Yee Tung Heen***, is deservedly popular, while the hotel's mezzanine-level Coffee Shop meets even the most grandiose buffet expectations. (Hong Kong's love affair with the buffet makes for extravagantly-laid grazing tables.) There are mini-stalls where a chef waits to prepare noodles with fish balls; there is dim sum; there is sushi; there are pork chops and frothy desserts. **Tott's**, on the top floor of the Excelsior, serves fusion cuisine with great panache in eclectic surroundings (mirrored ceilings, faux leopard-skin carpets and stool covers, undulating walls). Next door, in the World Trade Centre, **Green Willow Village** (on the 4th floor) is gaining popularity for its light Shanghainese cuisine. 'I like the spicy steamed beef, layered with vegetables, which is served in a bamboo bowl,' says Catherine.

Kappo Katsura (1/F, Yeung Iu Chi Commercial Bldg, 460–462 Jaffe Rd), according to a Hong Kong-based Japanese news correspondent, is not only a closely kept secret among the Japanese community, but the only place he will eat his native food in Hong Kong. The extensive menu includes grilled fish, tempura and yakitori. Fine Lebanese cuisine at **Zahra** (409A Jaffe Rd) has won this small restaurant a devoted clientele. **Banana Leaf Curry House** (440

Lavish traditions: a 1960s buffet at Marco Polo, the Peninsula, Hong Kong

Jaffe Rd) is a large, rambunctious Malaysian/Indian eatery, where fronds from banana trees serve as plates for some of the dozens of curries. Specialities include Hainan chicken, satay, samosas and fried clams. In a row of bright, plastic noodle houses, Peking Shui Jiao Wong, or **Peking Dumpling King** (118 Jaffe Rd), stands out for a few reasons. The place is older, for one thing, and nondescript compared to its neighbours. Then there's the fact that most of the waiters don't speak Cantonese, responding to Hong Kongers and foreigners alike in *Putonghua*. Fortunately, the trusty English menu is quickly retrieved from beneath the cash register. 'These are the best dumplings in town,' declares a foreign correspondent, who has very firm ideas on how to get the best out of the Dumpling King: 'You should only order the boiled pork and cabbage dumplings. They come with a big plate of chilli and vinegar, for dipping.' Shanghai-style pork and vegetable dumplings, floating in a bowl of light, flavourful broth, are also very good; eggplant in garlic sauce has a robust heat.

Kung Tak Lam*, the vegetarian Shanghainese restaurant, faces Victoria Park from premises on the ground and first floors of Lok Sing Centre (31 Yee Wo St). Walk off the effects of a hearty meal in the park; or wander through in the morning when you can see people going through their *tai chi* motions and others ballroom dancing to music from a small tape player perched in the crook of a tree. Across Hennessy Road is the Regal Hongkong hotel, with the high-quality **Regal Chiuchow Restaurant** on the third floor (which serves excellent dim sum with a Chiu Chow spin) and the Mediterranean **Riviera Restaurant** on the 31st floor. Moving away from the harbour, behind Hennessy Road is Caroline Centre, with Cantonese (**The House of Canton**), Chiu Chow and Beijing (**Imperial Kitchen**) restaurants on the first, second and third floors, respectively. 'After noon, the Cantonese restaurant is always full; then I have Chiu Chow food,' says Helen Chung. 'If I get there after 1pm, I go straight to the Beijing restaurant: they'll still have room.' **Perfume River** (89 Percival St) is a friendly, low-key restaurant serving good-quality Vietnamese food and 333 beer. **Cheun Cheung Kui** (108–120 Percival St) is one of the few old-style (flashy marble entrance notwithstanding, customers still have to find a table for themselves) Hakka restaurants still operating on Hong Kong Island. Linda Lee, a journalist of Hakka extraction, recommends the salted chicken (the bird is encased in rock salt and steamed) and preserved salty vegetables layered with pork belly (*mui choi yuhk beng*). **Andy's Kitchen** (25 Tung Lo Wan Rd), a low-key Shanghainese restaurant started by a group of housewives, serves great drunken pigeon, braised pig's knuckle and claypot chicken.

The opening of the nearby shopping centre Times Square (1 Matheson St) spawned a flurry of culinary activity in the area. Russell Street, directly across from the sprawling edifice, is a foodie's row, with a **Dai Pai Dong*** (20 Russell St), **Times Noodle** (54 Russell St) for noodles and congee, and an outlet of the dessert chain **Hui Lau Shan** (No.28: no English sign; look for flashy red and gold signage) serves drinks and snacks, such as double-boiled egg with rock sugar, herb tea, watermelon with coconut milk and mixed fruits with sago. The four-floor Food Forum inside Times Square is fussily organised in categories like International Delights and Hometown Favourites. Similarly irritating are the elevator queues. These quibbles aside, the Forum has an inviting blend of

Eating out rivals shopping as a leisure-time pursuit in Causeway Bay, where some retailers enjoy brisk business until 11pm

cuisines. On the 13th floor is the Mexican **La Placita Bar and Restaurant**, and **W's Entrecote***, billed as 'le steak house Français'. 'We bake our own baguettes and serve Bayonne ham,' says owner Wilson Kwok, whose in-depth knowledge of wines is reflected in the monthly specials and extensive wine list. On the 12th floor is **Yunnan Kitchen**, **Wu Kong Shanghai Restaurant** and **Bistro Gold***; the last two take decidedly different approaches to Shanghainese food (traditional and nouvelle, respectively). Grouped under 'Spice Market', on the 11th floor, are the extravagantly decorated **Roy's at the New China Max**, the ultimate fusion food venue, much improved since renowned Hawaiian chef Roy Yamaguchi took hold of the reins. **Ke Du Seafood Restaurant** has an odd combination of Hakka specialities (deep-fried stuffed large intestine, braised bean curd with minced meat, fried shrimps with bamboo shoots and wine) along with Yunnan and other regional Chinese dishes.

Despite looming apartment buildings, Happy Valley still has a neighbourhood feel to it—except, of course, when the races are on and punters in their thousands stream to the track. When the betting windows are shut, football and hockey teams take over the lawn at the centre of the race course and joggers trot around the perimeter. Limited accessibility (proximity to a Cross-Harbour Tunnel entrance causes major back-ups) bestows a rare peace on this part of town. Weeknights, restaurants are unlikely to be busy. Weekends, however, **Dim Sum*** (63 Sing Woo Rd) attracts major crowds. This small restaurant makes 'The Art of Chinese Tit-bits' accessible to all with a well-translated, illustrated menu. 'I dream about the lobster bisque,' admits journalist Patricia Chew. 'And they make the best *hà gáau* in town.' **Taiwan Beef Noodle** (13 King Kwong St; other branches at 462 Lockhart Rd in Wan Chai, 78–80 Canton Rd and 77 Mody Rd in Kowloon) offers reasonably priced, good-quality dishes like Tianjin cabbage with dried shrimp, noodle with braised beef in clear soup and soup with shredded pork and spiced salt. **Kissho**, a Japanese restaurant at the corner of Blue Pool and Sing Woo roads, has sushi and good wine, says John, who lives in the area. 'It can be pricey, but the sushi is very fresh.' John also recommends **Chok Yuen**, a seafood restaurant located where the trams come to a halt on Wong Nai Chung Road. 'You can get good rice dishes, noodles and seafood up on the cooked food floor in the **Urban Council Building** on Sing Woo Road, and one or two of the staff speak English,' he adds. 'The best egg tarts in town are made in Happy Valley,' says Patricia Chew—a bold statement if ever there was one. **Cheung Hing** (9 Yik Yam St) is one of the few surviving old-style tea houses and serves the usual coffees and teas, a few noodle dishes and the delectable tarts (*daahn tâat*).

Further Afield

In the 1950s, Shanghainese moving to Hong Kong tended to settle in either North Point or Castle Peak on Kowloon. Not surprisingly, then, the area around North Point is known for its eastern Chinese cuisine. Long-time fans prefer the original **Snow Garden** (233 Electric Rd; newer branches at 2/F, Eight Plaza, Sunning Rd in Causeway Bay; 10/F, London Plaza, 219 Nathan Rd and 4/F, Park Lane Square, 132–134 Nathan Rd in Kowloon). 'I like the deep-fried eel appetiser,' says Wilson Kwok. 'It's caramelised, quite sweet. The steamed meat dumplings, drunken chicken, duck's tongue and mock goose are very good.' Accountant Kuen Leung seconds the braised eel and nominates Snow Garden's hot and sour soup as well. Another Shanghai favourite is **Hong Kong Old Restaurant*** (Basement, Newton hotel, 218 Electric Rd).

Were the owners being modest or clever? Whatever the motivation, **Quite Good Chinese Cuisine** (100 Electric Rd) has been irresistibly named. The menu is inspired by the famous Yunnan dish, 'Crossing Bridge Noodles' (the folk story, involving a hungry scholar and his dedicated wife, appears on the menu), with several styles available. The seafood dish has sea cucumber, elephant trunk (geoduck), salmon, scallops, seasonal vegetable, bean sprouts and preserved Sichuan vegetables; two other versions combine Yunnan ham with fish slices, chicken and/or pork. **East Lake Seafood Restaurant** (68 Hing Fat St), facing Causeway Bay from across Victoria Park, is a good dim sum choice, complete with all the noisy brouhaha that comes with the

Jumbo Seafood Restaurant in Aberdeen is one of the largest floating eateries in the world

midday meal. **Tung Po Seafood Restaurant*** (2/F, Cooked Food Centre, 99 Java Rd) is excellent value for fresh seafood, hot pot, delicious steamed chicken and shrimps fried with garlic. The English menu is limited, but the young waiters are fluent and helpful.

Hei Fung Terrace, in Repulse Bay (1/F, The Arcade), wins praise for its interior—complete with waterfall, red lanterns and staircase—which is modelled after a Chinese garden in Suzhou. The main menu changes monthly, offering mainly Cantonese dishes, rounded out with Peking and Sichuan specialities. 'I'm not a fan of dim sum, because of the MSG, the noise, the lining up, but the dim sum at Hei Fung Terrace is very delicate,' says Wilson Kwok. Travelling further south, **Stanley's French** (86–88 Stanley Main St, Stanley) offers respite from the hurly-burly of the Stanley Market stalls. The restaurant makes the most of its three-storey house-on-the-seaside location, with glassed-in terraces and open-air dining on the top floor. Down the road, **Stanley's Oriental** (90B Stanley Main St) takes all of Asia for inspiration, with Indian, Japanese, Chinese and Malay dishes. **Lucy's** (64 Stanley Main St), tucked away in a nook near the market, lacks the pleasure of a sea view but makes up for it with unpretentious, reasonably priced, good-quality food. Also on the south side of Hong Kong Island, the famous Jumbo Floating Restaurant in the formerly isolated fishing village of Aberdeen (take a sampan from Aberdeen Praya Rd) 'has excellent, reasonably priced dim sum,' says Helen Chung. She counsels foreign visitors to resist all attempts to herd them towards the 'tourist floor', a measure probably intended as much for the diners' comfort as the staffs', but one that dilutes the experience somewhat.

The Peak offers plenty of 'food with a view' options. '**Classic Passion*** [2/F, Block B, 100 Peak Rd] is a great place to take visitors for dim sum—along with good food, there's that wonderful view,' says Patricia Chew. In the old days (15 years ago), **The Peak Café** (121 Peak Rd) was a comfy, rather run-down place where curries and burgers were the order of the day. Its transformation into a large, stone chalet-type space, with outdoor patio, caused an uproar, but the restaurant has won over its nay-sayers. The menu has gone pan-Asian and Western, with duck curry, shrimp brochettes on noodles and salmon naan bread. **Café Deco** (Peak Galleria, 118 Peak Rd) is a bit of a barn, albeit a well-fitted barn. Given the location (think 'view!'), this is a good place to take visitors with a low threshold for Asian food. The menu is creative, yet comfortingly recognisable, with vegetarian samosas fashioned from won ton skins and Peking duck wrapped in thin naan bread.

KOWLOON

The eight hills that were the inspiration for the name 'Kowloon' (in the Sung dynasty, a boy emperor fleeing Mongol invaders died on the peninsula, but not before the child noted its eight hills and called them 'Eight Dragons'; a servant pointed out that his master was also a dragon, hence '*Gáu Lùhng*', or 'Nine Dragons') were levelled into fit-for-development submission long ago. The flatness, coupled with the lack of super-skyscrapers, gave this ten square kilometres a distinctly different atmosphere. (A recent change in height restrictions for buildings along the Kai Tak flight path has led to tall towers sprouting up, but it will be some years before the area is completely replanted.)

Until 1972, when the Cross-Harbour Tunnel opened, people could only cross the harbour aboard time-consuming, if pleasant ferries. Mass Transit Railway trains

Weekend café-goers travel to the Peak, Hong Kong Island's highest point, to enjoy some time away from crowded city streets

didn't bridge the gap until 1979. Perhaps this accounts for the pervading 'two sides–one city' attitude among residents. Hong Kong Island taxi drivers are not required or expected to know their way around Kowloon, and vice versa. People sigh heavily when they have to cross the harbour for a meeting, and Island- and Kowloon-dwellers are surprisingly unknowledgeable about the entertainment facilities 'on the other side'.

Kowloon's first claim to fame was as the location of the terminus for the Orient Express, which in the early decades of this century carried travellers to and from Europe and Britain. Its status as a tourist focal point has continued. Nathan Road, also called the Golden Mile, fairly bristles with hotels. Restaurants in the area accommodate their visitor trade; English menus and signs are helpfully prominent and many Chinese venues offer a mixed bag of ethnic cuisines (Shanghainese/Peking/Sichuan, for example).

Within the immediate radius of the tourist centre known as the Golden Mile in Tsim Sha Tsui hotel restaurants naturally abound—and, just as naturally, dominate. Just about every four- and five-star hotel operates several restaurants, from coffee shop to fine dining room, and in a range of cuisines, from Western to Swiss to Cantonese. They may be smack dab in the middle of the tourist-oriented 'shopper's paradise', but hotel venues (on Hong Kong Island as well as Kowloon) are patronised as much by Hong Kong residents as by visitors. Local custom is vital to the bottom line, and faced with a demanding market, hotels meet the challenge by providing superb quality and consistency of food, value for money and service.

Afternoon tea in the cinquecento gilt- and gargoyle-encrusted **Lobby** of the Peninsula hotel (Salisbury Rd) is considered a 'must'; best enjoyed on a weekday, unless you relish eating scones and cucumber sandwiches and sipping *lapsang soochong* under the gaze of hungry hordes waiting for a table. Upstairs, on the mezzanine floor, is **Chesa**, modelled after a cosy Swiss inn and offering raclette, fondues and hearty soups. **Gaddi's*** has held on to the reputation it carved out in the 1950s as a superior French restaurant. With its tycoon-heavy clientele, pricey menu and impeccably orchestrated service, Gaddi's belongs to the 'very special occasion' category. At the top of the tower added to the hotel in 1994, **Felix*** presents a dramatic take on the fusion theme, with Pacific Rim-inspired dishes served in an avant-garde vision designed by Philippe Starck. Kicking the night off with a drink in the American Bar, or winding it up with coffee and a liqueur at the Long Table, offer great views—inside and out. The aspect through massive windows is spectacular from every vantage point (including the infamous

toilets—everyone makes at least one trip), and the
Chuppies and the flush-with-cash crowd who frequent
Felix late in the evening make for great people-watching.
The Pen's Chinese restaurant, **Spring Moon***, is reputed
to be one of the most successful (that is, highest earning)
in Hong Kong. The mainly Cantonese menu is augmented
with Chiu Chow specialities—recipes picked up by Chef
Ho Pui Yuen, who learned on the job in a Chiu Chow
restaurant years before he joined The Pen). The dim sum,
in particular, receives high praise.

Across and along Salisbury Road, The Regent's **Lai
Ching Heen*** (18 Salisbury Rd) Cantonese restaurant is
consistently rated one of the best in the world. A superb
harbour view, through floor-to-ceiling windows, adds to
the pleasure of being cosseted in this quietly elegant space.
Specialities include deep-fried scallops with pears, minced

*Residents and tourists
alike fill the Peninsula,
Hong Kong Lobby for
high tea*

pork and eggplant with hot plum sauce, and minced beef with bamboo pith in soup. The hotel's haute cuisine **Plume** still gets rave reviews for its classy fusion style, but tellingly, one floor of the formerly two-level restaurant was transformed a few years ago into the hipper **Yü***. With its massive wall-embedded aquariums, Oyster Bar and tanks from which waiters pluck yabbies, garoupa, lobster and crab, there are no prizes for guessing that the place takes its name from *yú*, the Cantonese word for fish.

Who needs to travel to try the world's cuisines?

Dynasty at the New World hotel, next to the Regent, carries on its sister hotel's tradition of home-style Cantonese cooking, with an emphasis on quality of ingredients and service.

The Chinese Restaurant at the Hyatt Regency hotel (2/F, 67 Nathan Rd) is highly regarded. Chef Chow Chung is respected for his skill in marrying the art of Cantonese cooking with Western presentation. Across the road, Holiday Inn Golden Mile has revamped its above-ground restaurants, with **Café Vienna** looking particularly inviting. The afternoon tea buffet, from 3pm to 5pm, is a good deal. The basement **Delicatessen Corner** keeps on serving authentic German specialities, like homemade sausages and dark rye bread.

At the opposite end of the spectrum is the notorious Chungking Mansions (36–44 Nathan Rd), with its rabbit warren of curry houses and low-budget guest houses. The cheap and cheerful (once the dank and claustrophobic staircase has been negotiated) **Taj Majal** (4th floor) is recommended by Angela, an Australian journalist, who cautions diners to be prepared for a certain 'starkness' of decor in return for a tasty, inexpensive Indian meal. Steps up in the cleanliness stakes, but no less quirky, is the **Mexican Mess Association** (C4, 11/F, Hankow Centre, 1C Middle Rd). Some ten tables are crammed into this converted flat and from the small kitchen emanates Tex-Mex dishes such as nachos, enchiladas and fajitas. **Wild Poppies** (65A Kimberley Rd) celebrates an unusual combination of flowers and coffee—you can stop by for a cappuccino and a light meal and gather a bunch of blooms at the same time.

Another branch of **Super Star Seafood Restaurant*** (1/F, Tsim Sha Tsui Mansion, 83–97 Nathan Rd) begins serving 'pieces from the heart' at 7am. Their custom is pretty evenly split between tourists and residents, making this a lively place to experience *yàm chàh* as it was enjoyed a couple of decades ago—leisurely, that is. **Wu Kong** (Bsmt, Alpha House, 27–33 Nathan Rd) plays to its market, with a supposedly Shanghainese menu that actually owes much to northern and eastern Chinese cuisines. The *síu lùng bâau* (meat-filled dumplings) receive special mention. They also require careful eating if you don't want hot juice spurting out over your face and clothing: don't be delicate, either bite the top off first and suck out the liquid, or simply pop the whole thing in your mouth.

Canton Road is practically brimming over with restaurants. Bringing a whiff of New York chic is **DKNY Coffee Corner** (7 Canton Rd), with its bagels, salads, brownies, juices and cafés *latte*, espresso and *macchiato*. 'They make the best grilled ham and cheese sandwich in town,' says Ann, an illustrator. They also stock great magazines for diners to pore over while looking inexpressibly cool. **Happy Garden Noodles and Congee Kitchen** (76 Canton Rd) makes 28 kinds of congee (lettuce and mud carp balls; scallops and shrimp balls), and a similarly varied tangle of noodle dishes. With pretty rosewood furniture and good service, this is preferable to the fluorescent-lit, plastic-furnished chain noodle shops. **Taiwan Chicken Farm** (78 Canton Rd) is part of the Taiwan Beef Noodle chain (there's a branch right next door; see Happy Valley section for menu details). Along with chicken cooked many, many ways, the restaurant offers fried eel with XO sauce and steamed King Shan bean curd. **The Sweet Dynasty** (88 Canton Rd) follows in the tradition of retro ambience shared by others in this chain, and offers reasonably priced sweets like warm sago pudding, mango pudding and water chestnut in soup, as well as congee and noodle dishes. **Nanjing Kitchen** (98 Canton Rd) leaves no stone unturned in the pursuit of customers: there must be an entire photo album of dishes taped to the window, along with menus in English and Chinese. Eastern specialities include Nanjing spiced won ton, 'wined' (drunken) chicken and Nanjing beef.

Fortune Barbecue Chain Shop (according to the neon sign, that is—on the menu, the place is called Hung Wan Roasted Meat Shop; 28 Ashley Rd) is just the spot for a quick bowl of noodles. The English menu lists roast pork, barbecued pork, soy chicken and barbecued suckling pig with your choice of rice, rice noodles or vermicelli. 'For Hangzhou cuisine, I like **Tin Heung Lau** [18 Austin Rd],' says Wilson Kwok. 'I order shark's fin with crab roe, and in winter, stir-fried bamboo shoots.' Other specialities include frog's legs and cold duck.

Au Trou Normand (Bsmt, 6 Carnarvon Rd) has one of the best lunch deals in town, comprising an appetiser buffet, choice of a long list of vegetarian, fish or meat entrees (whole grilled trout is especially good), dessert and coffee. This bistro-like spot has been serving Chateaubriand, *escargots* and *mousse de foie d'oie d'armagnac* for over 30 years and has the regular clientele to prove it. Not far off is the second branch of **Kung Tak Lam*** (45–47 Carnarvon St), the vegetarian Shanghainese restaurant.

In Tsim Sha Tsui East (across Chatham Rd), Californian tastes, with a dash of Mexican and southwestern flavours, are found at **Napa** (21/F, Kowloon Shangri-La hotel, 64 Mody Rd). In the basement is a popular Japanese restaurant, **Nadaman**, which is tipped as a great lunch bet. **Sabatini Italian Ristorante** (3/F, Royal Garden hotel, 69 Mody Rd) is sister—in both cuisine and decor—to the original Sabatini in Rome. Hong Kong's decade-plus love affair with Italian food has been marred by a sad lack of authenticity; reports from Sabatini-goers indicate that this venue more than redresses the balance. **W's Paris 13th** (Shop 202, Toyo Mall, 94 Granville Rd) is the unwieldy name of a casual Vietnamese restaurant, so dubbed by owner Wilson Kwok in honour of the Paris arrondissement which is home to many Asians. **Woodlands** (5–6 Mirror Tower, 61 Mody Rd) is a gem. Best on this down-to-earth Indian vegetarian menu are the south or north Indian thalis, where a large platter with a heap of saffron rice draped with leavened bread is surrounded by small pots of individual dishes.

Moving northward, **Great Shanghai** (1/F, 26–36 Prat Ave) has reasonably priced home-style Shanghainese food. Mock goose and braised eel are good choices; the vegetarian dumplings are delicious. Man Man Kee (on Parkes St, near Jordan MTR) 'has the best *gai laan* [Chinese kale],' says Wilson. 'It's so crunchy! They also have flowering garlic chives [*gáu choi fa*], served with soy sauce, when it's in season. I like this place because you can tell them, "*jau hòuh yàuh*, literally oyster sauce go away".' According to Wilson, noodle shop waiters have their own 'argot', or vocabulary. 'For "five", they say "grab", because you use all your fingers to grab something; for "seven", they say "week". And won ton is often called "yong", or "pupa",' says the restaurateur.

House of Tang (Metropole hotel, 75 Waterloo Rd) is a little off the beaten path (take exit B at Yau Ma Tei MTR station and walk along Waterloo Rd for about 10 minutes), but worth the trip, as this is one of the few respected Sichuan restaurants. Elsewhere, spicy Sichuan noodles (*dân dân mihn*) are overloaded with peanut sauce and a grudging hint of chilli; House of Tang applies both in good measure, making for a spicy treat and a harbinger of tasty things to come.

When a seafood blow-out is called for, Patricia Chew shepherds her visitors and friends to **Lung Tang Restaurant** (1–2 Hoi Pong Rd Central) in Kowloon East's Lei Yue Mun. 'My regular taxi driver recommended it to me,' she explains. 'Meals out there aren't cheap, but it's reasonable if you go with a large group.' Customers first choose their dinner from the waterside tanks, then tell the cook at the restaurant of their choice how they want it cooked. 'Chinese like lobster stir-fried with ginger and onion, or with black pepper and garlic,' says Helen Chung. 'Europeans like it grilled with butter and garlic, but at Lei Yue Mun the cooks will partly deep-fry the lobster because Chinese kitchens don't have grills.' Helen suggests shrimp steamed with soy sauce, onion and chilli or medium-sized shrimp fried with pepper and salt. Whole fish should be steamed. Oysters can be deep-fried in batter or stir-fried very quickly with garlic and ginger; geoduck clam, which is called 'elephant tongue', is usually sliced and stir-fried. 'It doesn't have a lot of taste,' says Helen, 'but it feels good on the tongue.' She prefers scallops

Lei Yue Mun vendors cater to a passion for fresh seafood

steamed and topped with garlic and black pepper. Steamed fish head is a favourite, as is soup made from small fish, bean curd and vegetables.

Further north, Kowloon City is easily reached by taking any Kai Tak-bound airport bus. Disembark at the airport, follow the luggage-toting crowds into the terminal, then leave the pack behind and find the walkway to the Regal Airport hotel. Traverse this bridge, descend to street level and walk one short block to Kai Tak Road. There, you find a mini-Bangkok, streets lined with cosy *dai pai dong*-like venues selling a few noodle dishes, Thai supermarkets and a rich assortment of Thai restaurants. Most people think Thai food when they think of Kowloon City, but this intensely urban pocket, with aircraft flying low overhead, is also home to Chiu Chow, Islamic, Vietnamese, Indian and Shanghainese restaurants, among others. It's the perfect spot to take a big, unfussy (in terms of cuisine, not quality) appetite.

The first Thai restaurants in Kowloon City were supposedly opened by Thai airline staff who decided if they couldn't get the real thing, they'd provide it. The result is some of the most authentically Thai restaurants in Hong Kong—and probably the cheapest, too. 'One of the best dishes is the raw Thai prawns, seasoned with lime juice, chilli, coriander and other Thai spices—I think everyone should try this at least once in their lives,' declares Amy Yeung. **Friendship Thai Food** (38 Kai Tak Rd) serves up a great chicken curry with green paste and coconut, spicy and sour boneless chicken's feet salad, baked rice in hot pot, and seafood with lime juice and chilli. Seafood salad is a medley of mussels, squid and prawns, topped with sprigs of green onion and coriander. The menu is pretty much the same at **Heng Chun Chun Sau Thai Restaurant** (68 Kai Tak Rd). Outside **Tung Tai Thailand Food** (on Nga Tsin Wai Rd), spices and sauces are ground in a huge mortar and pestle, then poured into bowls (for customers at the few tables) or plastic bags (for takeaway). **Golden Orchid Thai Restaurant** (12 Lung Kong Rd) has developed a good reputation in a very competitive market, with a menu that strays from the traditional to offer dishes like pumpkin stuffed with curried seafood and chicken wings stuffed with glutinous rice. **Cheong Fat Co.** (25 South Wall Rd; 'Specialize in Thai Spices' says the sign) is a tiny grocery store brimming with the ingredients for Thai curries, noodle dishes, salads and desserts. 'We're open till 1am,' says the Cantonese-speaking Thai proprietor, surrounded by shelves of fresh rice noodles, Thai eggplant, lemongrass, and jars of fish sauce and pickled fish. **Chong Fat Chiu Chow Restaurant*** (62 South Wall Rd) is a rough-and-ready venue that has something of a cult following.

Jasmin waxes lyrical on the subject of **Islam Food** (1 Lung Kong Rd; also 35–37 Hau Wong Rd, both locations in Kowloon City): 'I drool at the thought of their "burger" dumpling—it consists of a large beef patty, which is steamed, then encased in pastry and deep-fried,' she says. Instead of rice, meals are accompanied by a thin crepe-like bread with scallions. The menu embraces Sichuan, Shanghai and Peking cuisines, as well as Western cooking, with dishes like veal goulash.

Sai Kung Village, on the Sai Kung Peninsula and surrounded by a protected country park, is a popular day-trip for tourists and visitors looking to shrug off Hong Kong's urban trappings. The picturesque town's main square is studded with restaurants. **Jaspa's** (13 Sha Tsui Path) does hearty, Australian-style roast meals, good soups and, with a nod to the fishing boats bobbing along the Praya, a variety of fish dishs. The **Chinese-Thai Restaurant**, on one corner of the square, has a voluminous menu; alternatively, customers can purchase fish from the waterfront tanks and present it to the Chinese-Thai staff to be cooked. **Ali-Oli Bakery** (G/F, 11 Sha Tsui Path) has a reputation well beyond its secluded, rural location. 'The salmon paté is the best I've tasted—they make it with caviar,' says Angela, a former Sai Kung resident. Ali-Oli also bakes a selection of pies, bread and quiches.

OUTLYING ISLANDS

'We call this place "4-1/2 Rice Bowls", but the name is actually **Hang Luk**,' says Cathie, an American musician who has lived on Cheung Chau Island for close to ten years. The nickname comes from a glowing review given the restaurant several years ago. 'But the writer was worried that if he gave Hang Luk the top rating—five rice bowls—the owners would relax their standards; so he gave it four-and-a-half.' Hang Luk (13 Pak She Praya Rd) is singled out for consistently good food (especially steamed fresh fish) from among the row of seafront restaurants that line the waterfront. **Fat Larry's** (9A, Pak She Praya Rd), near the Pak Tai Temple, is also recommended. In recent years, Cheung Chau's restaurant scene has expanded beyond stock Cantonese/seafood/Western snacks. People wending their way to the beach often find irresistible the smell of fresh-baked red bean cakes emanating from **Hometown Teahouse/Island Art Gallery** (12 Tung Wan Rd). It is run by an endearing Japanese couple, Mr and Mrs Yoshino, who brew up a range of healthful teas and, on weekends, make sushi and red bean cakes. **Sakura Japanese Restaurant** (96 Tai San St) gets a strong vote from Cheung Chau residents. **Lotus Thai Restaurant** (1 San Kai Shi Lane) is directly across from the unattractive market block, but good

Cheung Chau offers relaxed waterfront dining

decor and reasonable food means diners turn a blind eye to what's outside the door. **Coffee or Tea** (1–2 Kin Sun Lane) is ideally placed near the waterfront with tables in a tree-lined square. 'The drinks are good, but the food is just so-so,' says an islander.

What with near-identical menus, and decor that varies only in the colour of the plastic chairs and rainproof sheeting, there is not much to distinguish one seafood restaurant from another out of the bevy lining the Sok Kwu Wan waterfront on Lamma Island. Regular junk-trippers mention the **Hilton**, **Wan Kee** and **Fuk Kee** restaurants, where they enjoy the standard meal of steamed fish, stir-fried mussels and/or clams, deep-fried squid, salt and pepper prawns and seasonal vegetable. Helen Chung favours **Rainbow Seafood Restaurant** (16–19 First St).

Call **Hon Lok Yuen** (16 Hung Shing Yea, Yung Shue Wan, Lamma Island) for a booking (reservations are a must) and the voice on the telephone will bark, 'How many people? How many pigeons?' Known simply as the pigeon restaurant, this place offers a totally al fresco experience: it's about a 15-minute walk through town and fields from the Yung Shue Wan ferry pier and most of the tables are on a wide cement patio. The birds are served either halved, for eating with your fingers, or minced, for wrapping in a lettuce leaf with a daub of hoi sin sauce. Squid, steamed fish and the rest of the usual suspects are also on the menu.

Po Lin Monastery, with its massive sitting Buddha, is one of the major attractions of Lantau Island. Hiking is another, and, when the weather is clement and the currents running right, the beaches are still another. On **Lower Cheung Sha Beach**, near the village of Tong Fuk, are two Chinese restaurants with near-identical menus and ambience. 'I like the one closest to Babylon Villas,' says David, a former resident. 'The salt-and-pepper squid is superb.' In Mui Wo, there is not much to distinguish the restaurants in the row across from the pier, on the way to the beach. **Sang Lee Seafood Restaurant** (No. 1 Shung Hau Road) is friendly and consistent.

A Final Note

Restaurants in Hong Kong are continually under threat of massive rent increases and the perils of re-development. Every effort has been made to ensure that this information is correct, but it is worth noting that over the course of putting this chapter together, the information on various new and long-time venues had to be deleted or altered. Happily, there were plenty of newcomers to take their place, but the sands on which Hong Kong's restaurant scene are built are constantly shifting.

CHEF SATOSHI ITO, TOKIO JOE
Spinach Salad With Sesame Dressing

Spinach (large-leafed European variety)	300 g
White sesame seeds	30 g
Light soy sauce	5 tsp
Dashi stock*	4 tsp
White sugar	1-1/2 tsp
Toasted neri, shredded**	1 tsp

Trim the white stalks from the spinach leaves and discard. Wash the spinach leaves. Bring a large pan of water to the boil, add the spinach leaves and cook for approximately 3–5 minutes until the leaves soften and darken in colour. Pour the spinach into a sieve and cool under running water. Let all the water drain away from the spinach and use the back of a wooden spoon to press the extra water from it. Form the spinach roughly into a long sausage shape and place on one end of a 30cm x 24cm bamboo rolling mat and roll up tightly to shape the roll and squeeze out all the moisture. Leave the spinach tightly wrapped up in the mat for 20 to 30 seconds (it can be left longer while the rest of the ingredients are prepared).

Toast the sesame seeds in a dry pan until golden brown, then blend coarsely in an electric blender. Add the soy sauce, sugar and dashi stock to the blended sesame seeds to form a soft paste and set aside. Toast the shredded neri in a dry pan or under a grill until lightly browned but not scorched and set aside. To serve, unwrap the spinach roll, cut it across its width into 2cm-thick rounds, then divide the spinach amongst 4 small plates. Top each serving of spinach with a little of the sesame paste and sprinkle with the shredded neri.

* Dashi, a Japanese vegetable, can be bought fresh and cooked to make a vegetable stock, or it can be bought in powder form (often called Konbu stock) from most Japanese department stores or speciality Asian delicatessens.
** Neri is a seaweed, which can be found in Japanese department stores or Asian delicatessens.

TRATTORIA AT THE LANDMARK
Fennel Risotto With Peas, Mint and Proscuitto

Aborio rice (unwashed)	1-3/4 cups
Garlic cloves, finely chopped	2
Shallots, finely chopped	2
Peas (fresh or frozen)	2/3 cup
Fennel bulbs (small–med.)	2
Proscuitto, finely ribbon-sliced	50 g
Fresh mint, finely chopped	20 g
Olive oil	40 g
Butter	25 g
Fresh parmesan, finely grated	4-1/2 tbsp
Vegetable stock, hot	(2-1/2 times volume of rice)
Black pepper, milled	pinch
Fennel bulb leaf, chopped	2
Shaved parmesan for garnish	

Cut the tops off the fennel bulbs, chop the leaf finely and set aside. Halve the bulbs, leaving the base intact; chop 1-1/2 bulbs into 12 wedges and dice the remaining half. Place the wedges on a tray, brush with half the olive oil, season with salt and pepper and roast for 20 minutes at 210°C, turning once. Heat the remaining olive oil in a pan. Add the shallots, diced fennel and garlic and cook for 5–10 seconds, taking care not to brown. Add the rice and stir well, taking care the rice does not colour. When it begins to stick to the bottom of the pan, add about 1/4 cup of stock. Continue to stir, gradually adding all of the stock, 1/4 cup at a time.

After the rice has been cooking for 15 minutes, add the peas, mint, grated parmesan and the last of the stock. Cook for 1 to 2 minutes more or until the rice is of a creamy and slightly loose consistency. Remove from heat and add the butter and fennel leaf. Add a little more parmesan and pepper. Transfer the risotto to a serving bowl, garnish with the roast fennel, proscuitto ribbons and shaved parmesan.

THAI LEMONGRASS
Gaeng Pet Bet Yang—Roast Duck Curry

Coconut cream	1 cup
Curry paste (see below)	3 tbsp
Fish sauce (bottled)	2 tbsp
Palm sugar	1 tbsp
Coconut milk	1-1/2 cups
Duck (together with liquid from the duck's cavities, boned and neatly sliced)	1/2 bird
Long red chillies, halved and de-seeded	2 pieces
Kaffir lime leaves, torn	2 pieces
Apple eggplants (aubergine)	2 pieces
Pea eggplants	60 g
Thai basil leaves	

In a medium-sized pan, boil the coconut cream over medium heat for 3–5 minutes or until it has separated, stirring constantly to prevent scorching. Add the curry paste, stirring constantly. Cook for 5 minutes or until the colour of the paste deepens and it smells fragrant. Add the fish sauce and palm sugar and cook for a further 1–2 minutes. Add the coconut milk, chillies, lime leaves, eggplant, duck and basil. Simmer the curry until the duck is tender. The curry should be slightly salty, sweet and creamy.

Curry paste: *dried red chillies, de-seeded and chopped, 6–10 pieces; red shallots, chopped, 4 pieces; garlic cloves, chopped, 6 pieces; stalk of lemon grass, finely chopped, 1 piece; galangal, chopped, 1/2 tbsp; coriander (cilantro), 1 tbsp; kaffir lime zest, 1/2 tbsp; white peppercorns, 1 tsp; coriander seeds, roasted, 1 tsp; cloves, roasted, 3 pieces; mace, roasted, 3 blades; salt, 1 tsp; shrimp paste, 1 tsp.* Purée the chillies with the shallots, garlic, lemongrass, galangal, coriander and lime zest. Heat a little vegetable oil or ghee in a pan and fry the puréed mixture for a few minutes, add the shrimp paste and stir well. Remove to cool. Grind all the remaining spices and combine with the purée.

MAXIM'S PEKING GARDEN
Fried Prawns in Chilli Sauce

King prawns, green	4
Egg white	1 tbsp
Flour	2 tbsp
Peanut oil	1 tbsp
Garlic, mashed	1 tbsp
Rice wine (brewed with apple, and Shaoxing yellow wine)*	1 tbsp
Vinegar	1 tbsp
Chilli powder	1 tbsp
Chilli sauce, bottled	1 tbsp
Sugar	1 tbsp
Peanut oil, for frying	1/2 cup
Ginger, mashed	1 tbsp
Extra peanut oil	2 tbsp

Shell the prawns, de-vein and rinse, then cut each prawn into two pieces, place in a bowl and set aside. Mix together the egg white, 1 tablespoon of peanut oil and the flour and add to the prawns, ensuring they are thoroughly coated. Heat 1/2 cup of oil in a wok until very hot, add the prawns and deep-fry for 3–4 minutes, then remove, drain and set aside. In another wok or pan, heat 2 tablespoons of peanut oil, add the mashed ginger, mashed garlic, chilli sauce, chilli powder, rice wine and vinegar and stir-fry for 1–2 minutes. Add the prawns to the sauce and stir-fry until the sauce thickens. Serve immediately with steamed rice.

* The restaurant brews its own rice wine mixture, using fresh apple, in large quantities. To approximate the taste, mix together a little rice wine, apple juice and Shaoxing yellow wine.

PETRUS, ISLAND SHANGRI-LA
Warm Scallop and Leek Salad
With Coriander Vinaigrette

Scallops, large	4 pieces
Leek, large	200 g
Baby leek	6 pieces
Thai asparagus (6cm-long tips)	6 pieces
Red pepper, julienned	40 g
Mixed salad leaves	80 g
Vinaigrette	3 tbsp
Coriander dressing	6 tbsp
Coriander leaves	1/2 tbsp
Salt	to taste
Black pepper, freshly ground	to taste
Vinaigrette:	
Peanut oil	30 ml
Sherry vinegar	5 ml
Red wine vinegar	5 ml
Salt	pinch
Black pepper, milled	pinch
Coriander dressing:	
Fresh coriander	1/2 bunch
Olive oil	40 ml
Peanut oil	40 ml
Lemon juice, freshly squeezed	1/2 lemon
Salt	pinch
Black pepper, milled	pinch

Wash the large leek and discard any damaged outer leaves. Cook in boiling water for about 15 minutes. Remove, slice and brush it with half of the coriander dressing and set aside. Wash the baby leek and asparagus, drain and boil the vegetables separately (the leek for about 4 minutes and the asparagus for 2 minutes). Remove, slice the leek and set aside. In a bowl, toss the mixed salad leaves with the vinaigrette dressing, add to it the red pepper julienne, baby leek, asparagus and coriander leaves and season to taste. Place the salad in the middle of two serving plates and arrange the pieces of large leek around the salad.

Wash the scallops and cut them in half. Sear them quickly in a little olive oil and arrange on top of the salad. Drizzle with the remaining coriander dressing and serve immediately. (Serves 2 as an entrée.)

Vinaigrette: combine the peanut oil, sherry vinegar and red wine vinegar in a blender until the dressing is emulsified. Add the salt and pepper.

Coriander dressing: in a food processor, combine the olive oil, peanut oil and lemon juice. Add the salt and pepper and blend at high speed until the dressing is emulsified. Correct the seasoning if necessary.

Glossary

A desire to encourage the reader who cannot speak or read Chinese to explore Hong Kong's restaurants, *dai pai dongs* and markets is the principal objective of this glossary in English, Pin Yin and Chinese. Pin Yin is the transliteration of Cantonese words into the roman alphabet to allow the words to be read and pronounced by non-Chinese speakers.

Pin Yin Pronunciation Guide

The glossary follows a system favoured by Cantonese teachers in Hong Kong. Accents and the letter 'h' are used to indicate the seven tones in Cantonese: (à) high falling; (á) high rising; (a, at) middle level; (â, ât) high level; (àh) low falling; (áh) low rising; (ah, aht) low level. For example, in *'hà gáau'* (prawn dumplings), the *'hà'* is high falling, the *gáau* is high rising; the double vowel indicates a longer vowel sound. Note the use of the letter 'h' within or at the end of a word to indicate the low tones, as in *'hòh yihp faahn'* (glutinous steamed rice in lotus leaf); the first word is low falling and the second and third words are low level.

abalone w/ oyster sauce, sliced	hòuh yàuh sìn bàau	蠔油鮮鮑
'alcoholic' crab	jeui háaih	醉蟹
almonds	hahng yàhn	杏仁
baby abalone	bàau yuh jái	鮑魚仔
baked salt chicken	yìhm guhk gài	鹽焗雞
bamboo shoots, stir-fried (Hangzhou-style)	cháau dùng séun	炒冬筍
bananas	hèung jìu	香蕉
barbecued chicken (whole)	(yât zhi) sìu gài	(一隻) 燒雞
barbecued duck (whole)	(yât zhi) sìu ngaap	(一隻) 燒鴨
barbecued pork bun	chà sìu bâau	叉燒包
barbecued pork puff	chà sìu so	叉燒酥

barbecued pork rice	chà sìu faahn	叉燒飯
bean curd in black bean sauce	sih jàp jìng dauh fuh	豉汁蒸豆腐
bean curd pudding (tofu flower)	dauh fuh fâ	荳腐花
bean curd roll (dim sum)	fuh pèih gyún	腐皮卷
bean curd soup	dauh fu tông	豆腐湯
bean curd wrapped around chicken, ham and fish stomach	gài jaat	雞扎
bean sprouts	ngàh choi	芽菜
beans	dáu	豆
beef ball (dim sum)	ngàuh yuhk kàuh	牛肉球
beef congee	ngàuh yuhk jùk	牛肉粥
beef (dry-fried with chilli) w/ sesame pockets	gôn cháau ngàuh yuhk sî / jì màh siu béng	乾炒牛肉絲／芝麻燒餅
beer	bê jàu	啤酒
beets	tìhm choi	甜菜
beggar's chicken	hât yî gài	乞兒雞
bi lo chun tea	bîk luó chêun chàh	碧螺春茶
bird's nest	yin wò	燕窩
black sea moss	fat choi	髮菜
braised duck with spring onion	gêung chùng ngaap	薑葱鴨
braised eel (with garlic)	hùhng sìu sîhn wú	紅燒鱔鍋
braised superior shark's fin	hùhng pàh qún chi	紅扒羣翅
butter and jam	ngàuh yàuh gwó jim	牛油果占
cabbage (Western-style)	yèh choi	椰菜
candied peel	maht jian gwó pèih	蜜餞果皮
cane sugar	je tòhng	庶糖
carrot noodle	gàm sèun mihn	甘筍麵
chicken buns	gâi bâau	雞飽
chicken's feet	gâi geuk / fuhng jáau	雞腳／鳳爪
chicken in lemon sauce	nìhng mùng gài	檸檬雞
chicken shredded w/ bean vermicelli	pun gài sì lâai pèih	拌雞絲拉皮
chicken, steamed	baahk chit gài	白切雞
chicken wings	gâi yik	雞翼
chicken with Sichuan pepper	chin jiu gâi	川椒雞

Chinese cabbage, stir-fried	cháau baahk choi	炒白菜
Chinese celery	kàhn choi	芹菜
Chinese flowering cabbage	choi sum	菜心
Chinese ham	laahp yuhk	臘肉
Chinese pressed duck	laahp ngáap	臘鴨
Chinese sausage with rice	laahp chéung fan	臘腸飯
Chinese sausage, pan-fried	jìn laahp chéung	煎臘腸
Chinese white cabbage	baahk choi	白菜
Chiu Chow sauce made with fish, dried shrimps and rice flour	sâ chàh jeung	沙茶醬
Chiu Chow spring rolls with taro	chiu chow chêun gyún	潮州春卷
chive dumplings, deep-fried	jìn gáu choi gáau	煎韭菜餃
chive shoots	gáu choi	韭菜
cocktail bun	gâi méih bâau	雞尾飽
conch	hói loi	海螺
condensed milk	lín náaih	煉奶
condensed milk with hot water	náaih séui	奶水
congee	jùk	粥
coriander	yuán	蔦
corn	sûk máih	粟米
corn, tiny cobs	sùk méih zài	粟米仔
crab	háaih	蟹
crab, cold (Chiu Chow-style)	dung háaih	凍蟹
crab with chilli and black bean sauce, pan-fried	sih jìu cháau háaih	豉椒炒蟹
cucumber	chèng gwà	青瓜
curry squid	galêi yàuh yú	咖哩魷魚
custard-filled buns	náaih wóng bâau	奶黃包
deep frying	jaa	炸
dim sum	dím sàm	點心
dim sum lunch	yám chàh	飲茶
double-boiled papaya with almond milk	hahng jâp dahng muhk gwà	杏汁燉木瓜
double-boiled soup with Chinese ham, cabbage and fish maw	seuhng tòng dahng fâ gâou	上湯燉花膠

dragon well (*lung ching*) tea	lúhng jéng chàh	龍井茶
dried scallops	gòn yìuh chyúh	乾瑤柱
drunken chicken	jeui gài	醉雞
duck egg yolk	hàahm dáan wóng	咸蛋黃
eastern star garoupa	dung síng bahn	東星班
eel	síhn	鱔
eel (shredded), fried	cháau síhn wu	炒鱔糊
egg tarts	daahn tâat	蛋撻
eight treasure sweet pudding	baat bóu faahn	八寶飯
elephant clams	jiang búht pòng	象拔蚌
figs	mòuh fà gwó	無花果
fish	yú	魚
fish ball, steamed	yù dáan	魚旦
fish congee	yú jùk	魚粥
fish maw	fâ gâau	花膠
flowering garlic chives	gáu choi fa	韭菜花
folded cake	gahp béng	夾餅
food stall	dai pai dong	大排檔
fortune chicken	hahng wahn gài	幸運雞
French toast (*dai pai dong*-style)	sâi dô	西多
fresh crab meat	háaih yuhk	蟹肉
freshwater hairy crab	daaih jàp háaih	大閘蟹
freshwater shrimp, stir-fried	ching cháau hà yàhn	清炒蝦仁
fried dough stick	yàuh ja gwái	油炸鬼
fried egg	jìn dáan	煎蛋
fried fresh meat bun (Shanghai-style)	jìn síu lúng bâau	煎小籠飽
fried rice	cháau faahn	炒飯
fried sea perch	jìn lóuh yú	煎鱸魚
fried vermicelli	cháau máih fán	炒米粉
fung sa chicken	fung sâ gaí	風沙雞
garoupa	sehk bàan	石斑
garoupa, steamed	ching jìng sehk bâan	清蒸石斑

glutinous rice (uncooked)	noh máih	糯米
glutinous rice in lotus leaf	hòh yihp faahn	荷葉飯
glutinous rice with egg, pan-fried	jin bohk beng	煎薄餅
goose (sliced, Chiu Chow-style)	lóuh súi ngo pín	鹵水鵝片
goose web, stewed	màn ngó jéung	炆鵝掌
grandmother's tofu	màh po dauh fuh	麻婆豆腐
green crab	chìng séui háaih	清水蟹
green salad	choi sà léut	菜沙律
Hakka bean curd	hak ga dauh fuh	客家豆腐
Hakka steamed bean curd with minced shrimp paste	baak fâ jìng yeuhng dauh fuh	百花蒸釀豆腐
hot and sour soup	syùn laaht tong	酸辣湯
hot pot	fó wò	火鍋
iron buddha tea (*ti kuan yin*)	tit gùn yàm chàh	鐵觀音茶
jasmine tea	hèung pín chàh	香片茶
jellied blood	jyù hùhng	豬紅
jellyfish, cold (appetiser)	hói jit	海蜇
jumping shrimp	sín hâ	鮮蝦
Kale (Chinese)	gai laan	芥蘭
kumquat	gàm gwàt	金橘
leeks	syun	蒜
legumes	dauh	豆
lettuce	sâang choi	生菜
lobster	lùhng hà	龍蝦
lobster and shrimp dumplings	lùhng hà gáau	龍蝦餃
lobster, steamed w/ yellow wine	fâ diu jìng lùhng hà	花雕蒸龍蝦
longan	lùhng ngáahn	龍眼
lotus root	lìhnn gáuh	蓮藕
lychee	laih jì	荔枝
lychee 'red' tea	laih jì hùhng chàh	荔枝紅茶
macaroni	tùng sàm fán	通心粉

macaroni and cheese	jì si tùng sàm fán	芝士通心粉
mango	mòng gwó	芒果
marshmallow rabbit	mìhn fâ gâi	棉花雞
mashed taro	làih wuh	荔芋
milk cream cake	náaih yàuh dáan gòu	奶油蛋糕
milk tea	náaih chàh	奶茶
monkey pick tea	hàuh jí chói chàh	猴子採茶
monosodium glutamate	meih jìng	味精
mushrooms	sìn gú	鮮菇
mushrooms coated in seaweed, deep-fried	jí choi dùng gù gyún	紫菜冬菇卷
mussels	cheng háu	青口
mussels, fried	cháau cheng háu	炒青口
mustard greens	gaai choi	介菜
mustard	gaai laaht	介辣
mutton	yèuhng yuhk	羊肉
noodles	mihn	麵
octopus	baat jáau yùh	八爪魚
onion cake (fried)	chùng yàuh beng	葱油餅
oolong tea (first grade)	(yât kâp) wu lùhng chàh	（一級）烏龍茶
orange	cháang	橙
ostrich with spring onion, stir-fried	chùng baau tuó líu yuhk	葱爆鴕鳥肉
oyster	hòuh	蠔
oyster cake/omelette	hòuh béng	蠔餅
oyster sauce (go away)	(jau) hòuh yàuh	（走）蠔油
(a little) oyster sauce	(siu) hòuh yàuh	（小）蠔油
papaya	muhk gwà	木瓜
parsley	yùhn sài	芫茜
pea shoots	dauh mìuh	荳苗
peaches	tóu	桃
peanuts	fâ sâng	花生
pear	léi	梨

pearl leaves	jàn jyù yihp	珍珠葉
peas	chèng dáu	青豆
pearl orchid tea	jyú láahn fâ chàh	珠蘭花茶
pea paste cake	buut jái gòu	砵仔糕
pea shoots with crabmeat, sautéd	háaih yuhk pàh dauh mìuh	蟹肉扒荳苗
Peking duck	bâk gìng tin ngáap	北京填鴨
pepper steak	hâak jìu ngàuh pa	黑椒牛扒
phoenix *shui sin* tea	fuhng wòhng séui sín chàh	鳳凰水仙茶
pickled cabbage, spicy	syùn laaht choi	酸辣菜
pickled vegetables	syùn choi	酸菜
pig skin	jyû pèih	豬皮
pigeon	yúh gaap	乳鴿
pigeon boiled in soy sauce	sih yàuh wòhng yúh gaap	豉油皇乳鴿
pigs' blood congee	jyû hùhng jùk	豬紅粥
pineapple bun (custard-filled)	bò lòh bâau	菠蘿飽
pomelo	sà tìhn yáu	沙田柚
pomelo skin with shrimp sauce	hâ jí yàuh pèih	蝦子柚皮
pomfret	chòng yú	鯧魚
pork and shrimp dumplings, steamed	sìu máai	燒賣
pork, cold sliced w/ minced garlic sauce	syun yùhng yuhk sì	蒜蓉肉絲
pork dumplings (northern), pan-fried	jin gáau jí	煎餃子
pork dumplings, pan-fried (dim sum)	jìn fán gwó	煎粉果
pork dumplings, pan-fried (Shanghai-style)	wò tip	窩貼
pork dumplings, steamed (northern)	síu lùhng bâau	小籠飽
pork knuckle with ginger	jyû geuk gêung	豬腳薑
pork lung	jyù fai	豬肺
pork, shrimp and bamboo shoot dumpling, deep-fried	hàahm séui gók	咸水角
pork spare ribs, steamed	jìng pàaih gwàt	蒸排骨

pork, stewed	màn jyû yuhk	炆豬肉
pork tripe soup	jyû taó tóng	豬肚湯
pork with preserved cabbage	syut choi yuhk sí	雪菜肉絲
prawns (large)	daaih hà	大蝦
preserved salty vegetables layered with pork belly		
pu-erh tea	bóu leí chàh	普洱茶
pumpkin	nàahm gwà	南瓜
Qimen 'red' tea	kee mùhn hùhng chàh	祈門紅茶
raisins	tàih jí	提子
red peppers	hùhng laaht jìu	紅辣椒
rice (steamed)	baahk faahn	白飯
rice (uncooked)	baahk máih	白米
rice cake	maih beng	米餅
rice noodles (flat variety)	hó fán	河粉
rice noodles (round variety)	laaih fán	瀨粉
rice noodle rolls with shrimp, steamed	sìn hà chéung fán	鮮蝦腸粉
rice vermicelli	máih fán	米粉
rice vermicelli with beef	ngàuh yuhk máih fan	牛肉米粉
rice wine	máih jáu	米酒
roast chicken	sìu gài	燒雞
roast suckling pig	yúh jù	乳豬
roasted duck	sìu ngaap	燒鴨
roasting	sìu	燒
rose tea	mùih gwai chàh	玫瑰茶
sago soup	sài máih louh	西米露
salt and pepper shrimp, parboiled	jìu yìhm hà	椒鹽蝦
salted egg	hàahm dáan	咸蛋
sampan congee (raw fish congee)	yú pin jùk	魚片粥
satay squid ball	sa tai yauh yú kàuh	沙嗲魷魚球
scallops, steamed	ching jìng daai jì	清蒸帶子

seafood	hói sin	海鮮
sea moss	hói dài	海帶
sesame oil	màh yàuh	麻油
shallots	gòn chùng tàuh	乾蔥頭
Shanghai cold noodles	Seuhng hói láahng mihn	上海冷麵
shark's fin dumpling	yùh chi gáau	魚翅餃
shark's fin soup	yúh chi gàng	魚翅羹
shrimp	hâ	蝦
shrimp congee	hà máih jùk	蝦米粥
shrimp dumplings, steamed	hà gáau	蝦餃
shrimp sauce	há jeung	蝦醬
shrimp and bamboo shoot dumpling, steamed	fán gwó	粉果
Sichuan noodles	dân dân minh	担担麵
side dishes	sung	餸
silver cod	ngàhn syut yú	銀雪魚
silver needle pekoe tea (often called 'flowery pekoe')	ngàhn jâm baahk háo chàh	銀針白毫茶
smoked fish	fàn yú	燻魚
snacks	siu sihk	小食
snake soup	sèh gàng	蛇羹
snapper	hùhng sàam yù	紅衫魚
soy sauce	sih yàuh	豉油
soy sauce, dark	lóuh cháu	老抽
spare ribs	pàaih gwàt	排骨
spinach	bò choi	菠菜
spring onion	chùng	蔥
spring roll	chêun gyún	春卷
squid	yàuh yú	魷魚
squid, deep-fried	ja sìn yáu	炸鮮魷
squid with broccoli, sautéd	sìn yau cháau sài làahn fà	鮮魷炒西蘭花
steamed bread, Chinese-style	jìng aun sì gyún	蒸銀絲卷
steaming	jìng	蒸
stewed black chicken	màn wú gài	炆烏雞
stir-frying	cháau	炒

sugar cane	je	蔗
sugar snap peas	tóhng dauh	唐豆
sultanas	tàih jì gôn	提子乾
sweet-and-sour vegetarian pork	gù lòu so yuhk	咕嚕素肉
sweet potatoes	fàan syu	蕃薯
taro	wuh táu	芋頭
tea	chàh	茶
tea/Western food house	chàh châan têng	茶餐廳
tofu	dauh fuh	豆腐
tomatoes	fàan ké	蕃茄
treasures in a wooden bowl	pán choi	盤菜
turnip cakes	lòh baahk gòu	蘿蔔糕
turtle oil with herbs, crispy, deep-fried	cheui pèih gwai lìhng gòu	脆皮龜苓膏
two-sides yellow noodle	yuân yâng mihn	鴛鴦麵
vegetables, stir-fried	cháau choi	炒菜
vegetables w/ oyster sauce	yàuh choi	油菜
vegetarian dumpling, steamed	sou choi gáau	素菜餃
vegetarian goose	sou ngòh	素鵝
water chestnut	máh tái	馬碲
watercress	sài yèuhng choi	西洋菜
watermelon	sài gwà	西瓜
wheat-based bread	mahk bâau	麥飽
white peony (bai mu dan), high grade sauh mei tea	(sauh méi) baahk mauh daan chàh	(壽眉) 白牡丹茶
wine	jàu	酒
winter-melon soup	dùng gwà jûng	東瓜盅
won ton noodle (soup)	wàhn tàn mihn	雲吞麵
won ton soup	wàhn tàn tong	雲吞湯

Bibliography

Cameron, Nigel, *Hong Kong, The Cultured Pearl*, Oxford University Press, Hong Kong, 1978.

Cantonese Cooking, Hilit Publishing, Taiwan, 1993.

Chang, K.C. (ed.), *Food in Chinese Culture*, Yale University Press, London, 1977.

Cheng, Sea-Ling, *Food and Distinction in Hong Kong Families*, M.Phil Thesis, Hong Kong, 1996.

Cotterell, Yong Yap, *Wok Magic: Chinese Cooking for Pleasure*, Weidenfeld and Nicholson, London, 1987.

Cree, Dr Edward H, *Naval Surgeon*, E.P. Dutton, New York, 1982.

Bond, Michael Harris, *Beyond the Chinese Face*, Oxford University Press, Hong Kong, 1991.

Dahlen, Martha, *A Cook's Guide to Chinese Vegetables*, The Guidebook Company, Hong Kong, 1995.

Eu, Geoffrey (ed.), *Hong Kong*, APA Publications, 1995.

Hom, Ken, *The Taste of China*, Papermac, London, 1992.

Lai, T.C., *At the Chinese Table*, Oxford University Press, Hong Kong, 1984.

Lai, T.C. (ed.), *Hong Kong & China Gas Chinese Cookbook*, PPA Design, Hong Kong, 1991.

Lam, Chua (ed.), *Eating in Hong Kong 1997*, Stallion Publishing, Hong Kong, 1997.

Leeming, Margaret and Huang Man-hui May, *Chinese Regional Cookery*, Rider and Company, London, 1983.

McLachlan, Robin (ed.), *Oh For the Joys of England*, Journal of the Royal Asiatic Society, Vol. II, 1962.

Mark, William, *The Chinese Gourmet*, Weldon Russell, Sydney, 1994.

Mennell, S., Murcott, A., Van Otterloo, A.H., *The Sociology of Food*, 1992.

Morris, Jan, *Hong Kong: Epilogue to an Empire*, Penguin, London, 1993.

Pope-Hennessy, James, *Half-Crown Colony, A Hong Kong Handbook*, Jonathan Cape, London, 1969.

Schivelbusch, Wolfgang, *Tastes of Paradise: A Social History of Spices, Stimulants, and Intoxicants*, Vintage Books, New York, 1992.

Vernon, Ken, *George Duddell 1821–1887, A Hong Kong Pioneer and a Brighton Nobility*, 1990.

Welsh, Frank, *A History of Hong Kong*, HarperCollins, London, 1994.

White, Barbara-Sue, *Hong Kong: Somewhere Between Heaven and Earth*, Oxford University Press, Hong Kong, 1996

Wu Thompson, Yvonne, *From Market to Kitchen: A Chinese Culinary Experience*, Oriental Culinary Institute, Hong Kong, 1995.

Index